DICKENS AND SHAKESPEARE

DICKENS AND SHAKESPEARE

(A Study in Histrionic Contrasts)

by

Robert F. Fleissner, M. A., Ph. D.

HASKELL HOUSE
Publishers of Scholarly Books
NEW YORK
1965

published by

HASKELL HOUSE
Publishers of Scholarly Books
30 East 10th Street • New York, N. Y. 10003

Copyright © 1965
ROBERT F. FLEISSNER

Library of Congress Catalog Card Number: 65–28337

Preface

The purpose of this dissertation is to examine the indebtedness of Dickens
to Shakespeare as revealed in the novelist's life and work. Since the ground to
be covered is extensive, it is divided into six major sections: (1) A general
introductory survey of the relationship between the two authors; (2) a consideration
of the scope of the inspiration as well as of its import; (3) an analysis of the
Shakespearian element, primarily that from Hamlet, reorganized in David
Copperfield and in (4) Great Expectations; (5) an analysis of the inspiration
mainly of King Lear in Martin Chuzzlewit and in (6) The Old Curiosity Shop.
When mentioning a particular stage production, Dickens would refer to "the
Shakespeare." If he was not always directly under the influence of the wholeness,
structure, or uniqueness of any one play of the master dramatist, there was none
the less a definite influence of "the Shakespeare" throughout his work. It is
principally this Shakespearian genesis of Dickens's creativity that I am studying
here.

Whenever possible, I saw the original letter that Dickens wrote rather
than a transcript, a virtual necessity since the most complete edition of the
letters now available contains numerous inaccuracies and only one volume of the new
edition has come off the press. My purpose in presenting the authentic text of the
letters will be to help ascertain the original intent of the author, and not even
crossed-out words will be neglected, but inserted within the following marks: < >.
Likewise, the novelist's own punctuation and spelling will be retained. If an error
of Dickens's intrudes, I may suggest a plausible correction but shall not contaminate

i

the text itself by altering what has been written. Because Dickens did not underscore titles of books or plays, neither shall I when I directly quote him. If a major deviation is evident in Walter Dexter's edition of the letters, the Nonesuch Edition, I shall indicate as much in a footnote or within brackets. The MLA Style Sheet has been followed throughout except when bibliographical principles required greater caution: thus I have inserted quotation marks before and after long passages whenever interpolated material might be confused with the text proper.

My work on Dickens's letters has been made possible through the generous help of Professor William E. Buckler and Dr. John Frost, both of whom introduced me to Professor Egerer, Custodian of the Fales Collection at New York University. Aside from the Dickensiana in the Fales Collection, I have seen the Dickens letters in the Berg Collection of the New York Public Library and those available in the Pierpont Morgan Library. I have scrutinized original letters by Dickens in the Olin Research Library of Cornell University and in the Free Library of Philadelphia. My thanks are due to Mrs. Madeleine House, widow of the late editor of the forthcoming edition of the letters, the Pilgrim Edition, and to Mr. J. C. Thornton, indexer of the same edition. They have been very kind in answering queries. I have also to acknowledge my indebtedness to Sister Miriam Joseph Rauh of Saint Mary's College, Professor Fredson Bowers of the University of Virginia and editor of Studies in Bibliography, and Professor Peter Alexander of the University of Glasgow, Scotland, at the time of writing visiting professor at New York University; all three have guided me in understanding the proper hermeneutics of Shakespeare, particularly with regard to his punctuation in Hamlet.

In order to arrive at the most proficient results, I have narrowed my interests in this volume. Since the dissertation was formally accepted, Dr. J. C. Maxwell has pointed out to me a number of allusions to Macbeth in Dickens's writings not stressed in the study I completed. No doubt, in the course of years sufficient references to Shakespeare in other novels of Dickens's will come to light and demand further treatment than I have been able to provide here. I hope only that my work thus far will make up for the deficiency recently noted by Ada Nisbet in her monumental survey of Dickens scholarship in Victorian Fiction: A Guide to Research. She then wrote: "There has been no comprehensive study of the influence of Shakespeare upon Dickens or of the many fascinating parallels in their respective careers." There now is one.

The dissertation has been slightly revised for publication.

R. F. F.

New York City, 1965

"Dickens and Shakespeare were alike in many things. I am not
sure that a whole volume could not be written upon their
resemblances."   --W. Walter Crotch, The Soul of Dickens

Contents

Chapter   **Page**

   I.   SOME SHAKESPEARIAN ELEMENTS IN THE NOVELS OF DICKENS . 1

          A. Pneumatological Factors
          B. References to Magic
          C. General Observations

  II.   HOW SUBSTANTIAL WAS THE SHAKESPEARE INFLUENCE? 49

          A. Shakespearian Allusions in Dickens's Letters
          B. Articles Dealing with Shakespeare

 III.   THE INDEBTEDNESS TO SHAKESPEARE IN DAVID COPPERFIELD . 141

          A. Plot Structure
          B. Annotated List of Shakespearian References (45)
          C. Detailed Analysis
          D. Character Structure

  IV.   THE INDEBTEDNESS TO SHAKESPEARE IN GREAT EXPECTATIONS .185

          A. Annotated List of Shakespearian References (15)
          B. Character and Plot Structure
          C. The Derangement Theme
          D. The Religious Issue

   V.   THE INDEBTEDNESS TO SHAKESPEARE IN MARTIN CHUZZLEWIT . 219

          A. Annotated List of Shakespearian References (66)
          B. Linguistic Associations
          C. Nil-factor
          D. Detailed Comparison

  VI.   THE LEAR-CORDELIA MOTIF IN THE OLD CURIOSITY SHOP . . .258

 VII.   BIBLIOGRAPHY 274

Appendix I

        THE TRUE TEXT OF DICKENS'S REVIEW OF MACREADY'S
        PRODUCTION OF KING LEAR HITHERTO UNPUBLISHED:
        "HAYMARKET THEATRE" 289

CHAPTER ONE:

SOME SHAKESPEARIAN ELEMENTS IN THE

NOVELS OF DICKENS

I

In recent years a number of Dickens scholars have been reconsidering the
commonplace that their novelist took a literary interest in ghosts.[1] Some of their
scholarship is of special current interest because of recent work on ghost-lore
in Shakespearian drama, particularly that in Hamlet. Since, as will be seen, there
evidently was an influence of Shakespeare's apparitions--and especially of the
Hamlet specter--upon Dickens, the dramatist's own conception of the spirit world
as related to the pneumatology of Elizabethan times has a direct bearing upon
Dickens's ideas about the supernatural.

---

[1] Philip Collins, "Dickens on Ghosts: An Uncollected Article," The Dickensian,
LIX (1963), 5-14; Harry Stone, "Dickens's Artistry and The Haunted Man," The South
Atlantic Quarterly, LXI (1962), 492-505; Angus Wilson, "Charles Dickens: A
Haunting," The Critical Quarterly, II (1960), 101-108; Albert F. Ziegler, "The
Haunted Man: Sermon," The Dickensian, LVIII (1962), 145-148. The article reprinted
by Collins is in The Examiner, ed. Fonblanque (26 Feb. 1848), and is authenticated
in an unpublished letter to Emile de la Rue (29 Feb. 1848). Dickens's short story
alluded to is "The Haunted Man and the Ghost's Bargain: A Fancy for Christmas-time";
cf. "A Haunted House," Household Words, VII (23 Feb. 1853), 481-483.

1

Dickens's popular short tale "A Christmas Carol" contains what is probably the best-known of his apparitions. Thus Marley's Ghost, the dream image that finally materializes into a bedpost, may also have a special attraction for the Dickensian when interested in ghost-lore. It may serve as a kind of touchstone or point of departure. Those who excavate further are bound to encounter other apparitions, sometimes in the form of emaciated individuals who exhibit a type of male amenorrhea or "tired blood." Old Chuffey in Martin Chuzzlewit serves as a typical example. However, scholars are obligated to interpret the term ghost literally: the late Professor Elmer Edgar Stoll pertinently remarked, in his review of Richard Flatter's volume on Hamlet's Father, that Shakespearian ghosts retrace their earthly steps "in dead earnest"; he implied thereby that too clinical an interpretation, one that tries to explain away the supernatural by claiming that it is just a product of mental aberration, is on dangerous grounds because it is anachronistic. The Hamlet Ghost is such a "dead earnest" spirit. And the Honorable Albert S. G. Canning writes that "the ghost of Marley in deep grief deplores the hardened, selfish conduct he had always shown in life, and answering the terrified Scrooge, briefly describes his own condition in words somewhat like those of the ghost in 'Hamlet.'"[2] Indeed, of all the references to apparitions in Dickens, the

---

[2] The Philosophy of Charles Dickens (London, 1880), p. 194. In a footnote, Canning adds, "Marley's ghost answers Scrooge, 'Nor can I tell you what I would. A very little more is permitted to me; I cannot rest, I cannot stay, I cannot linger anywhere.' The ghost in Hamlet says, likewise, that he is 'doomed for a certain time to walk the night' and 'forbid to tell the secrets of his prison house.'"

allusions to the one in this most famous of revenge tragedies have, as one shall see, priority. The novelist also alludes to other spirits, such as the famous, even notorious, "Cock Lane Ghost,"[3] and the interests he professes in the occult outside of his novels are striking. Consider his review article of Catherine Crowe's The Night Side of Nature; or, Ghosts and Ghost Seers. He comments on her work as follows:

> Disclaiming all intention "of teaching, or enforcing opinions," and desiring only to induce people to inquire into such stories and reflect upon them, instead of laughing at them and dismissing them--and with the further object of making the English public acquainted with the sentiments of German writers of undoubted ability in reference to the probability of an occasional return of travellers from that solemn bourne to which all living things are always tending--Mrs. Crowe, without enforcing any particular theory or construction of her own, but apparently with an implicit belief in everything she narrates, and a purpose of communicating the same belief to her readers, shrinks neither from dreams, presentiments, warnings, wraiths, witches, doubles, apparitions, troubled spirits, haunted houses, spectral lights, apparitions attached to certain families, nor even from the tricksy spirit, Robin Goodfellow himself; but calls credible witnesses into court on behalf of each and all, and accumulates testimony on testimony until the Jury's hair stands on end, and going to bed becomes uncomfortable.[4]

One may recall a letter of Dickens's expressing the same feeling: "I am charmed to learn that you have had a freeze out of my Ghost story. It rather gave me a

---

[3] E.g., "The Ghost of the Cock Lane Ghost Wrong Again," Household Words, VI (15 Jan. 1953), 420. In A Tale of Two Cities, he says at the outset that "even the Cock Lane ghost had been laid only a round dozen of years" and comments on "chickens of the Cock Lane brood" (I, 2). (All Dickensian quotations in this dissertation are from the Cleartype Edition, which "contains all the copyright emendations made in the text as revised by the author in 1867 and 1868." Thus it corresponds to the standard Gadshill Edition. An occasional printer's error has been silently corrected.) Cf. Edith M. Davies, "The Cock Lane Ghost," The Dickensian, XXXV (1938 / 1939), 10-13.

[4] Collins, p. 6.

shiver up the back, in the writing" (6 January 1865, to Mary Boyle). The reference to Robin Goodfellow recalls Puck of A Midsummer Night's Dream, and significantly the reference to the "return of travellers from that solemn bourne to which all living things are always tending" is an allusion to Hamlet, III.i.79, "The undiscover'd country from whose bourne / No traveller returns."[5] Though one of the most remembered lines in the tragedy, such a reference to the other world seems to admit that ghosts have no real access to our world (unless the passage means only that no disembodied spirit comes back for permanent settlement,[6] or that it does not visit its previous earthly habitat in the same form). The words have to be properly understood within their immediate context first of all. For a thoroughly objective interpretation of what is entailed, Madeleine Doran's article "That Un-discovered Country"[7] is worthy of notice. That Dickens preserves the true meaning of the passage with all its complexity argues in favor of his ability to grasp the nature of the so-called "ghost problem." The very same reference to Hamlet recurs at the end of Chapter One of David Copperfield: "I lay in my basket, and my mother lay in her bed; but Betsey Trotwood Copperfield was for ever in the land of dreams and shadows, the tremendous region whence I had so lately travelled; and the light upon the windows of our room shone out upon

---

[5]
 Added as a footnote by Collins, p. 6. All Shakespearian quotations are from the old standard Globe (Cambridge) Edition as revised in 1861, except references to King Lear, for which I have had recourse to the New Cambridge Edition.

[6]
 The point is made by William J. Rolfe in his edition of Hamlet (New York, 1878), p. 218, n. 80. Rolfe's comment is especially pertinent since he was also an editor of Tennyson's poetry, which contains allusions to Hamlet including this passage.

[7]
 Philological Quarterly, XX (1941), 413-427.

the earthly bourne of all such travellers, and the mound above the ashes and the dust that once was he, without whom I had never been" (I, 12).[8] The phrases "the land of dreams and shadows" and "the earthly bourne of all such travellers" relate again to Hamlet, III.i.79. One might compare a similar allusion in Tennyson's "Ulysses":

> Yet all experience is an arch wherethro'
> Gleams that untravell'd world, whose margin fades
> For ever and for ever when I move.[9]

For the poem has been traced to a Hamlet influence by Douglas Bush.[10]

Dickens's interest in the Hamlet role of the French actor Charles Fechter also needs close attention, particularly because the novelist played a vital role of his own in helping to establish this performer's reputation. Leslie C. Staples, editor of The Dickensian, has an article pertaining to Dickens's involvement in a dispute over the role of the Ghost in a production of the play: "The Ghost of a French Hamlet."[11] He cites a letter by Dickens (21 May 1863, to Phelps) and quotes the novelist as saying, "Mr. Barnett has informed Fechter that you in so many words told him (Barnett) that you would

---

[8] It is worth speculating whether Dickens might have entertained some ideas on human knowledge as recollection (in the Wordsworthian sense). The phrase "whence I had so lately travelled" suggests the possibility. But that is beyond the scope of this dissertation.

[9] Valerie Pitt's commentary, in Tennyson Laureate (London, 1962), pp. 10-11, is outstanding.

[10] "Tennyson's 'Ulysses' and Hamlet," Modern Language Review, XXXVIII (1943), 38.

[11] The Dickensian, LII (1956), 70-76. Staples's work on Dickens and Shakespeare is notable. Cf. his "Dickens and Macready's Lear," The Dickensian, XLIV (1948), 78-80.

not play the ghost in Hamlet 'to a Blasted Frenchman.' Now assuming
these words to have been actually used they are both personally and nationally
so exceedingly discourteous and offensive. . . ."[12] Dickens supported the
actor in various ways, as Hesketh Pearson tells us: "He first saw Fechter act
in the fifties, and was so much struck by the performance that he made the
actor's acquaintance. Fechter came to England and played Hamlet in a manner
that was new to the stage. The soliloquies were rendered pensively, not spouted
in the usual manner, and Dickens thought his conception 'by far the most coherent,
consistent, and intelligible Hamlet I ever saw.' . . . Dickens backed him
financially, advised him about plays and players, sometimes rehearsed his company,
praised him in the press, started him off to America with a laudatory article
in the Atlantic Monthly,[13] and helped him in every possible way. The only person
who did not hear Dickens sing the Frenchman's praise was Macready. . . . Dickens
thought him a genius."[14] Thus the novelist most probably had seen Hamlet enough
times for it to have "influenced" him throughout his work. He certainly saw
Macready also in the title role and probably Kean. But what is especially
pertinent regarding Fechter's presentation is that he saw in the pseudo-
procrastinating Dane a philosophic motivation ("the soliloquies were rendered
pensively," one remembers, "not spouted in the usual manner"). Thus his

---

[12] Staples, p. 75.

[13] "On Mr. Fechter's Acting," The Atlantic Monthly, XXIV (1869), 242-244.

[14] Dickens: His Character, Comedy, and Career (New York, 1949), p. 290.
The pertinent quotation from Dickens on Hamlet is from a letter to W. F. De
Cerjat (16 March 1862).

impersonation was a sedate one, too much so for Macready but very convincing to Dickens.[15] One may be reminded here of Dickens's stoical orientation toward the play, a point of importance revealed also in his attachment to Julius Caesar, a drama about the stoic spirit, its ideals and limitations. Dickens refers to the Roman tragedy significantly in at least two novels: David Copperfield and Great Expectations. In the first, the hero witnesses a performance and encounters Steerforth again; in the second, there is a reference to the same play in connection with Wopsle, whose later Hamlet performance elicits a reaction from Pip on what he thinks is his own Hamlet-like relationship to Miss Havisham. Thus it is apparent that Dickens's references to Julius Caesar in his novels are closely linked to references to Hamlet even as Shakespeare refers to his own play on Caesar in Hamlet (Polonius: "I did enact Julius Caesar: I was killed i' the Capitol; Brutus killed me"; Hamlet: "It was a brute part of him to kill so capital a calf there.-- Be the players ready?"--III.ii.96-100). In his review article on ghosts, Dickens explicitly compares Shakespeare's conception of the Hamlet Ghost with that of a Stoic: "Plutarch, in his life of Brutus, calls the apparition 'a horrible and monstrous spectre, standing stilly, by his side,' and in his Life of Caesar describes it as 'a terrible appearance, in the human form, but of a prodigious stature, and the most hideous aspect.'"[16] So, regardless of whether Shakespeare fully intended Hamlet to be a study in stoic philosophy,[17] it is evident enough that Dickens understood the play to be a

---

[15] Pearson (p. 290) writes that Dickens's friends found Fechter to be a "cad."

[16] Collins, p. 7.

[17] The best recent elucidation of the play as such a study is Rolf Soellner, "'Hang up Philosophy!': Shakespeare and the Limits of Knowledge," Modern Language Quarterly, XXIII (1962), 135-149. An opposing view is that of John W. Draper in "The Prince-Philosopher and Shakespeare's Hamlet," West Virginia Univ. Stud., III (1937), 39-43.

picture of melancholia, of ideality versus reality, perhaps in part because
of Fechter's role on the stage.[18] That Victorian scholars were aware of this
philosophical problem (it appears to have been mainly characteristic of German
theories about the play) is evident from a critical article in Household Words,
which contains such a comment as the following: "Hamlet's Ich accepts his mission,
but his Nicht Ich shudders at it. The play is a tragical development upon a
philosophical basis of the struggle always going on between the Ich and the
Nicht Ich in the Human Soul."[19] That Dickens thought about the play in a serious
manner and very likely cogitated about this point is evident especially from the
following remark by Monroe Engel: "Like most artists, and with good enough
reason, Dickens thought contemporary critics generally hostile to originality.
A burlesque piece in Household Words purported to show how a contemporary
reviewer would review Hamlet if it were a new play; and a similar article in
All the Year Round attacked the tendency of critics to call anything original
'sensational' and showed how one such critic would review Macbeth if it in turn
were new";[20] furthermore, Edgar Johnson has referred to "Household Words and All
the Year Round, the two weeklies over whose pronouncements on all matters he
exercised a rigid control for twenty years. . . . Dickens printed nothing with
which he did not agree."[21]

---

[18]
    The conflict of the ideal and the real is central to stoic philosophy
as is evident with Shakespeare's Brutus particularly.

[19]"Something that Shakespeare Wrote," Household Words, XV (17 January 1857),
49-52.

[20]
    The Maturity of Dickens (Cambridge, Mass., 1959), pp. 24-25. The Macbeth
article is "The Sensational Williams," All the Year Round. XI (13 February 1864),
14-17.

[21]Charles Dickens: His Tragedy and Triumph (New York, 1952), I, viii.

In his article on Dickens's review of Catherine Crowe's The Night Side
of Nature, Philip Collins relates Dickens's concern with ghosts and death to
the idea of the magnetic attraction of opposites, a form of animal magnetism.
This notion played a vital role in the novelist's life and work, especially
as linked to his interest in Dr. Elliotson, a celebrated mesmerizer, and to his
own use of magnetic attraction to relieve the nervous disorder of Mme. De la
Rue.[22] It is revealed particularly in The Mystery of Edwin Drood, wherein
Jasper uses the power of animal magnetism for evil purposes. Dickens was also
stage manager and "The Doctor" in a performance of Mrs. Inchbald's farce
Animal Magnetism. In a letter of 16 September 1850 to Mary Boyle, he remarks
that "Mrs. Inchbald's Animal Magnetism, which we have often played, will 'go'
with a greater laugh than anything else." One knows now that electric adduction
is associated with the magnetic attraction of positive and negative poles;
though relating such magnetism to Physics may go beyond reasonable bounds, the
analogy is at least of historical import.[23] It may thus have been utilized
by Shakespeare in his tragedies: Romeo and Juliet, Antony and Cleopatra, even
Othello and Desdemona represent a certain harmony created out of antithetical
elements. For when Shakespeare wrote his plays, there was growing interest in
the power of magnetic forces: William Gilbert published his De Magnete in 1600,
and Ben Jonson wrote The Magnetick Lady with its puns on loadstones and magnetic
properties. Now, it is of interest that Dickens's very first manuscript (1833)
was an adaptation of Shakespeare's dramatization of the strange, magnetic, yet
disastrous, love of a white woman for a Moor: the O'Thello. Though mainly

---

[22]
    Dickens writes of this in his letters of 26 December 1844 to Emile de la
Rue and of 4 November 1869 to J. S. Le Fanu.

[23] Cf. Edmund Reiss, "Whitman's Debt to Animal Magnetism," Publications of
the Modern Language Association, LXXVIII (1963), 80-88.

a burletta, it none the less revealed the novelist's early preoccupation
with the idea of the attraction of opposites. Later he alluded to this
play in his novels and essays, such as in the "Private Theatricals" section
of Sketches by Boz (Tales, Chapter Nine: "Mrs. Joseph Porter"), and there may
be some influence upon The Mystery of Edwin Drood, which contains similar exotic
and oriental references, like the opium den, and has the same kind of in-
tensity.[24]   In general, the type of animal magnetism with which he was concerned was not so much the purely popular type of "electricity" or of the so-
called "vital force" which, with phrenology, had such an impact in the mid-
nineteenth century; it relates more to the real attraction of opposites, not
just to attraction which is magnet-like but without the magnet's peculiar
power.   In his comment on Crowe's The Night Side of Nature, Dickens writes
on man's speculations about death in a manner reminiscent of Hamlet's to-be-
or-not-to-be soliloquy by referring to "that attraction of repulsion to the
awful veil that hangs so heavily and inexorably over the grave--engendering a
curiosity and proneness to imagine and believe in such things, which proves
nothing but the universality of death, and human speculation on its spiritual
nature." Collins glosses the comment as follows: "Dickens was at this time
very fond of this concept, 'the attraction of repulsion'--'as much a law of
our moral nature, as gravitation is in the structure of the visible world.'"[25]

---

[24] In "The Macbeth Motif in Dickens's Edwin Drood," The Dickensian, XXX
(1934), 263-271, H. Duffield argues for another kind of influence from
Shakespearian tragedy. See also J. Lindsay, Charles Dickens (London, 1950), pp.
403-406.

[25] Collins, p. 8. Cf. also Philip Collins, Dickens and Crime, Cambridge
Studies in Criminology, XVII (London, 1962), pp. 14, 248, and 302.

It is this very "attraction of repulsion" which relates to the magnetic attraction of opposites as revealed in Shakespearian drama.

There is another aspect of Dickens's interest in the non-rational which deserves some of our attention, but it is one that needs to be considered with great caution because of the complex issues involved. This is Dickens's concern with the spiritual order, with religion, and most particularly with the idea that communication with beings of the supernatural realm is possible. If it could be proved that Dickens's belief or interest in ghosts is closely related to the ghost-lore found in Shakespeare's drama, then a valuable link between the two authors might be established. One approach toward such a link is discovering in the works of both a common denominator. It is possible that a common element may be the underlying sympathy, indeed empathy, of both for the pneumatological ideas of the Roman Catholic Church, specifically the notion that it is permissible for a privileged human being to experience apparitions or visitations of beings from another realm. Presumably one has to have a special grace to be able to witness a good spirit whereas the opposite may be true if one is confronted by a devil or evil spirit. Whether or not it is necessary to believe in such things is beside the point, for to see the heart of a writer one must look at his meaning from the standpoint of his age with its beliefs, not from a modern point of view indoctrinated with the idea that anything incapable of being scientifically verified is superstitious. Moreover, in a very real sense, such historical investigation as I propose is indeed scientific in the strictest sense of the word inasmuch as careful observation of phenomena within their chronological context promotes true objectivity. History has to be treated according to Ranke's formula (wie es wirklich geschehen ist) to make sense, but one criterion of what is wirklich is what is determined to be so by the age under consideration.

Both Shakespeare and Dickens had some regard for the Catholic Church and its principles, regardless of their personal religious views or affiliations. This is especially true with the dramatist and King Hamlet's Ghost, for that apparition, derived as it may be from the shade in Belleforest,[26] is presented with all the trappings of the conventional Christian ghost as well as with the usual effects from Seneca and from native superstition. Sister Miriam Joseph Rauh has analyzed Hamlet in terms of the Thomistic doctrine of the discernment of spirits, a mode of analysis which has some application here albeit Shakespeare can hardly be said to have had any direct acquaintance with the writings of Saint Thomas.[27] She points out that Shakespeare was very likely brought up a Roman Catholic,[28] and this pertinent fact may indeed have had some bearing upon the dramatist's intentions; but she does not indicate that, though there are frequent reverent allusions to Catholicism in the plays, there are also many passages that may be traced back to the Book of Common Prayer. Since Shakespeare presumably received an Anglican burial as well as baptism, one may surmise that he accepted the form of Christianity reputed to be the best by the majority

---

[26]
Arthur P. Stabler points this out in "King Hamlet's Ghost in Belleforest?," Publications of the Modern Language Association, LXXVII (1962), 18-20.

[27]"Discerning the Ghost in Hamlet," Publications of the Modern Language Association, LXXVI (1961), 493-502; see also her paper on "Hamlet, a Christian Tragedy," Studies in Philology, LIX (1962), 119-140. Cf. Jean S. Calhoun, "Hamlet and the Circumference of Action," Renaissance News, XV (1962), 281-298; Paul N. Siegel, "Discerning the Ghost in Hamlet," Publications of the Modern Language Association, LXXVIII (1963), 148-149.

[28]His mother, Mary Arden, was from an ancient Roman Catholic family, and his father was listed among the recusants at Stratford.

of English citizens at that time; nominally at least, he appears to have accepted some Protestant tenets. The reverse is true of Dickens. He was not possibly Roman Catholic at all, but there are indications in his maturity that he did respect Catholic ideals, even though he personally reserved his allegiance for the Church of England and, to an extent, Unitarianism. He was a good friend of Clarkson Stanfield's and even wrote once to Forster: "I am delighted to hear of noble old Stanny. Give my love to him, and tell him I think of turning Catholic." After Stanfield died, Dickens eulogized him in All the Year Round (1 June 1867). Theodore Maynard's conclusions, in "The Catholicism of Dickens,"[29] seem to be far-fetched, however; there is no explicit evidence that Dickens actually adopted Catholicism in any sense, either literal or figurative, Maynard's notion that Dickens's apparently anti-Catholic utterances were really political notwithstanding. Yet the novelist's views on Catholic apparitions are another matter. It is significant that the production of Hamlet he liked the best was Fechter's and that Fechter interpreted the tragedy in terms of a Roman Catholic apparition.[30] Then there is the dream Dickens had, on a visit to Italy, about a lady in blue,[31] a dream which, in the light of Freudian interpretations concerning how the unconscious projects conative (or personality)

---

[29] "The Catholicism of Dickens," Thought, V (1930), 87-105.

[30] Thus he even introduced the sign of the cross. For a more extensive treatment of this view with relation to Dickens, see Chapter Four.

[31] Cf. the fact that the Virgin is often depicted in blue garments or drapery even as blue is the color of the heavens and waters when they are clear. Thus blue is symbolic of nobility and purity.

affection, may even reveal a hidden desire of his to become a Catholic.
But such an assumption is purely hypothetical and of interest here only
because of the possible relation to Shakespeare's own thoughts. The account
is recorded in a letter to Forster which is included in Forster's biography.
It is recounted by Maynard as follows:

> Dickens' sister-in-law, Mary Hogarth, whom he had loved and revered as
> a saint during her life, appeared to him in a dream. After some less
> important question had been asked and answered, the dreamer "in an
> agony of entreaty" cried out: "Answer me one other question. What is
> the true religion?" The spirit paused a moment without replying, and
> Dickens "in an agony of haste," lest it should leave him, said, "You
> think as I do, that the form of religion does not so greatly matter,
> if we try to do good?" But, observing that Mary still hesitated, he
> asked again, "Perhaps the Roman Catholic is best? Perhaps it makes one
> think of God oftener, and believe in Him more steadily?" Then, at last,
> in heavenly tenderness the spirit spoke, and the dreamer was so moved
> that he felt his heart would break--"For you, it is the best." He awoke
> with tears running down his face and, rousing his wife, told her what
> he had seen and heard, four times over so that no detail should be for-
> gotten. Later, with characteristic common sense, Dickens analyzed the
> circumstances that might have been the cause of the dream, but commented:
> "And yet, for all this, put the case of that wish being fulfilled by any
> agency in which I had no hand; and I wonder whether I would regard it
> as a dream, or as an actual Vision!"[32]

The dream needs careful scrutiny, for undoubtedly there is something capricious
about the lady: she does not directly answer the question asked; she tells the
dreamer merely what he personally might need to know or perhaps only what it is

---

[32]
Maynard, pp. 88-89. In Forster's _Life_, the word you in Mary's response
is in italic. Perhaps this suggests Dickens's tolerance, or possibly it indicates a note of humor.

his business to know. In terms of modern dream interpretation or oneiro-
criticism, the description may reveal a projection of the dreamer's hidden
wishes; in terms of dream interpretation before Freud, it might even be taken
as a revelation of divine insight (analogous to Joseph's dreams in Genesis).
Dickens himself, by his statement at the end, appears to discount the latter
kind as applicable to him, but he also qualifies his assertion significantly.
In the light of this dream and his statement to Clarkson Stanfield that he
was thinking of turning Catholic (quoted earlier), Dickens's letter to
Forster of 15 September 1840 is of no little interest. It reveals that the
novelist had laid himself open to criticism because of his thoughts on the
possibility of his turning Catholic. Dickens writes: "Would you believe, that
in a letter from Lamert at Cork, to my mother, which I saw last night, he says,
'What do the papers mean by saying that Charles is demented, and further, that
he has turned Roman-catholic?'--!"

C. Sheridan Jones, in "Charles Dickens and the Occult," finds the
most important aspect of this dream in what it reveals about the novelist's
personal pneumatological ideas: "The care and circumspection with which the
narrative is set forth would scarcely have been wasted upon it by a man who
thought it impossible for spirits to revisit the earth, or who regarded the
appearance of every ghost as a further proof of the credulity of the human
judgment."[33] He concludes that Dickens "will pooh-pooh the psychic
as so much fudge as a rule; and at other times he feels it."[34] Though "psychic"

---

[33]
The Occult Review, XXIV (1916), 279.

[34]
Jones, p. 282.

considerations should be treated with extreme caution because too occultist
an interpretation is in danger of contaminating the original meaning with the
imposition of eccentric or quaint notions on an otherwise commonplace imaginative
experience, none the less Jones makes a valuable contribution when he stresses
Dickens's apprehension as revealed in the dream and then in the novels. Claiming
that Dickens's characters are often "saturated with a dread that has no adequate
basis in things purely physical," he goes on to say that "Dickens believed pro-
foundly in the capacity of coming events to influence minds receptive to the
pressure of forces directed against them."[35] He points to "Pip's expectation
of some strange fulfilment of his fate, just before 'his convict' confronted
him in the Chambers at King's Bench Walk" and then to the following description
in The Mystery of Edwin Drood: "Ask the first hundred citizens of Cloisterham,
met at random in the streets at noon, if they believed in Ghosts, they would tell
you no; but put them to choose at night between those eerie Precincts and the
thoroughfare of shops, and you would find that ninety-nine declared for the longer
round and the more frequented way."[36] Thus Jones finds a basis for Dickensian
spirits in the novelist's sense of superstition or psychological make-up. Dickens
himself, in a piece entitled "The Steam Excursion," in Sketches by Boz, comments,
"Sea-sickness . . . is like a belief in ghosts--every one entertains some misgivings on the subject, but few will acknowledge any" (Tales, VII, 392). That

---

[35]
Jones, pp. 281ff.

[36]
XII, 114. In this chapter there is much discussion about whether ghosts
have extra-mental existence. Durdles proposes that there may be ghosts of other
things besides men and women; he argues even for "the ghost of a cry" (p. 116),
though here the line between the mental and extra-mental is slight. The humorous
note is introduced, e.g.: "It was always expressly made a point of honour that
nobody should go to sleep, and that Ghosts should be encouraged by all possible
means" (p. 122).

Dickens himself had misgivings is evident from a letter to Forster: "A horrible thought occurred to me when I was recalling all I had seen that night. What if ghosts be one of the terrors of these jails?"[37] His numerous allusions to the Hamlet Ghost are also relevant, e.g., in a letter of 15 October 1850 to Mary Boyle: "My servant / who has been sneezing, to attract my attention, ever since I began / . . . like an uneducated Ghost in a new Hamlet--so solemn is his warning." A particularly curious reference, perhaps to the same specter, is in a letter of his to Thomas Taylor (4 March 1862): "I meant to have asked you something when I was with you the other day, but the Ghost put it out of my head." Commenting on the elaborate references to apparitions in the novelist's work, Edith M. Davies argues, "though I am not quite certain that he believed in ghosts, I am convinced that he had a great liking for them, judging from the number he introduced into his own books. He also had a wide knowledge of their eccentric behavior and hair-raising histories."[38] Dickens's lady in blue has something in common with the other references to apparitions even though she appeared in a dream; possibly she reflects something of his work, notably the Little Nell episodes in The Old Curiosity Shop, which was written some years before.

Professor K. J. Fielding, in his recent Charles Dickens: A Critical Introduction, writes of the dream in question: "It was probably influenced by the very natural association between the name, Mary, and the Virgin; and

---

[37] The word these is in Forster's biography, the in the Nonesuch Edition.

[38] Davies, "The Cock Lane Ghost," p. 10.

it is strange to notice, what seems to have caught no one's attention before, that on the head of Little Nell's deathbed, also associated with Mary Hogarth, Dickens's artist had pictured the Virgin and child."[39] He observes that Dickens describes the dream in a letter as having been "as real, animated, and full of passion as Macready . . . in the last scene of Macbeth" and that the "blue drapery" of the spirit was like that of the Madonna "in a picture by Raphael." Thus Fielding sets up the Mary-Madonna relationship more distinctly.[40] The picture of the Virgin and Child over the deathbed of the dying girl would confirm the association of Mary, co-redemptrix, with Mary Hogarth, who had a pronounced influence upon the novelist's work.[41] The picture is by no means meaningless in its subject matter, for Nell dies in a vicarage. The allusion to the Virgin sanctifies the demise of the innocent child, as it were, and serves as a kind of literary last rite. Moreover, it puts the scene on a higher level that do those who ascribe sentimentality to Dickens. Even if we believe that excessive sentiment is bad art, we sometimes may concede that religion underlying the seemingly sentimental can make it more meaningful.

It is also possible that Dickens's interest in the preternatural, as exemplified in his dream, relates to the influence of Shakespeare upon him, an influence around which references to ghosts often cluster. One might recall that Shakespeare was himself, according to tradition, the actor who played the part of the Hamlet Ghost. This is of importance inasmuch as he had a son called Hamnet, who died not so long before the play was performed, and in that

---

[39]
London, 1958, p. 87.

[40]Fielding argues that Dickens nevertheless "strongly disapproved" of Roman Catholicism, but I find this judgment somewhat harsh in the light of the evidence. Dickens even wrote a life of Christ that has come down to us as The Life of Our Lord.

[41]I question, however, if we can legitimately contend that Mary's death had the strongest influence upon the death of Little Nell. See Chapter Six of this thesis.

in his will he bequeathed another Hamlet (Hamlet Sadler) funds "to buy him a

ring."[42] Was, one may ask, Shakespeare the man an intended ghost for Shakespeare's

son Hamnet in the guise of Hamlet? The rhyming echo in the names is too obvious

to constitute mere coincidence. In a similar sense, Dickens did most of his own

haunting in his novels. Such a typical Dickensian character as Mr. Dick in David

Copperfield, the shadowy friend of the hero's great aunt and associated with Dickens

also through verbal echo, is ghost-like enough for consideration. The novelist

often signed his name "Dick.," and he had an especial liking for another Dick in

The Old Curiosity Shop: Dick Swiveller. Forster thus writes that "undoubtedly . . .

Dick was his favourite."[43] Some of the most Dickensian of characters, like little

Miss Flite in Bleak House, who haunts, in her way, the Court of Chancery, even as

another unseen character haunts the Ghost's Walk of the Dedlock mansion, may reveal

something spiritually intimate about their creator.

 In the first chapter of David Copperfield, one finds some references to

ghosts and, more particularly, to the Hamlet Ghost. The late T. W. Hill, in

his "Notes to David Copperfield,"[44] has already pointed out that the references

"born on a Friday," "destined to be unlucky," and "privileged to see ghosts" are

---

[42]
 G. B. Harrison, Introducing Shakespeare (Baltimore, 1954), p. 43.

[43]The Life of Charles Dickens (London, 1872-1874), I, 180. Elsewhere the
newer Ley edition is used when specified.

[44]The Dickensian, XXXIX (1943), 79-88, 123-131, 197-201; XL (1943), 11-14.

misleading because "folk-lore ⟨actually, it is nursery rhyme⟩ says that
'Friday's child is loving and giving,' and there is certainly nothing in
the story to suggest that David saw ghosts or was particularly unlucky."
Unfortunately, Hill was sometimes apt to see only the superficial side of
Dickens's allusions, and here he misses richness of meaning by being too
adversely critical. On the one hand, he fails to take into account a point
in his favor, namely that David was born with a caul, which has been said to
be a sign of good luck, but, on the other, he neglects to mention that the
word Friday traditionally commends itself to religion as well as superstition:
Friday the Thirteenth along with Friday the day of fast in commemoration of
Good Friday. The double connotation refers thus to superstitious fate ("destined
to be unlucky") and to disembodied Christian souls ("ghosts").[45] It was indeed
Prince Hamlet's "privilege" to see a ghost, just as it supposedly is David
Copperfield's; but it was also Hamlet's privilege to question the honesty and
morality of the apparition, indeed its very existence, after he had conversed
with it. By alluding to Hamlet's belief in an "undiscover'd country from whose
bourne / No traveller returns," Dickens allows a similar dual privilege for
David. Just as Hamlet was unlucky, tragically so, David was unlucky (Hill's
comment notwithstanding) especially in the loss of his parents and in having a
cruel step-father, in the cruelty he underwent at school and at Murdstone and
Grinby's, and in his first marriage. Though David, literally, sees no ghosts
other than those appearing on Thomas Traddle's Salem House slate, Betsey Trotwood
functions as a kind of ghostly fairy for him even as Magwitch and Miss Havisham

---

[45]
    For the tradition of Friday as a day of bad luck, see Morris Palmer Tilley,
A Dictionary of the Proverbs in England in the Sixteenth and Seventeenth Centuries
(Ann Arbor, 1950), item F 679. It is also traditional that, after the Good Friday
crucifixion, Christ harrowed hell and released unbaptized disembodied souls from
the confinement of limbo.

do for Pip in Great Expectations. Dickens describes Betsey as having such a function as follows: "She vanished like a discontented fairy; or like one of those supernatural beings whom it was popularly supposed I was entitled to see; and never came back any more" (I, 12). Dickens echoes this note later in the novel in his reference to "Hamlet's aunt," a woman who, though no Betsey Trotwood, none the less takes after David's great aunt.

Another deliberate Hamlet allusion in David Copperfield, Chapter One, is that to Chillip, the physician, who "walked as softly as the Ghost in Hamlet, and more slowly" (I, 9). At first glance, the reference may appear to be incidental or a comical simile, but the figure is extended in such elaborations as "he spoke as slowly as he walked," bringing to mind the Ghost's sombre, unhurried parlance, and in reference to "the five minutes or so that Mr. Chillip devoted to the delivery of his oration" (I, 9, 11). The reader recalls King Hamlet's Ghost's long rendition. In other respects, Chillip is the antithesis of the Hamlet specter, thus suggesting the possibility of parody. For he seems to be utterly incapable of wanting harm to befall anyone, since he is "the meekest of his sex, the mildest of little men." Whereas the Shakespearian ghost may not be personally vindictive, it is hardly piously meek or mild in its demands. Chillip might be called a dim reflection of the Hamlet Ghost; he represents a ghostly character comparable to Old Chuffey in Martin Chuzzlewit, the man who has become, as the idiom declares, "a very ghost of his former self." The name Chillip suggests chilliness of the weather in the ghost-scene (Hamlet says, "The air bites shrewdly; it is very cold"), but the doctor is more of a draft than anything else.[46] He serves primarily as a foil to Betsey Trotwood, who herself has something of a ghostly role to play as David's relation.[47]

Indirect references to Hamlet in Chapter One have to be considered with great deliberation, for in some instances the affinity may be only oral, implying a relationship in terms of sound rather than meaning. Moreover, a meaning parallel may be suggested but still not really intended. It is possible, then, that there may be a sound echo coupled with an ingenious, but contrived or insignificant semantic similarity; or there may be an important recoup in meaning without a convincing sound parallel. For example, David's acute admiration of his deceased father, a devotion which makes the hero pay homage in the graveyard and promotes thoughts of death, parallels Hamlet's own grief at the loss of his father. But at that point the possibility of influence seems to pause. The parallel is purely semantic and, in part, thematic. Dickens did have a fondness for alluding to the graveyard scene in the play, in particular for mentioning Yorick's skull; so he may have intentionally wanted to suggest a memento mori parallel. But no sound effects, no real echoes, are prevalent; there is not even a hint of the "chill" in the physician's name. So far this may make relatively good sense. But what about the reference soon thereafter to a "hamlet on the sea-coast"? The literal, denotative meaning is clear and has nothing at all to do with

---

[46] Elizabeth Hope Gordon, in "The Naming of Characters in the Works of Charles Dickens," University of Nebraska Studies in Language, Literature, and Criticism, 1 (Lincoln, 1917), writes, "The lack of exertion with which the name of Chillip is normally pronounced, the ingratiating semi-stop with which it is introduced, the short close vowels, the lack of force in the medial liquid and the final breathed plosive,--all contribute to the general effect of lack of force, characteristic of the depreciatory little doctor. The mention of a possible relation to chill and fillip seems unnecessary" (p. 30).

[47] John Jones, in "David Copperfield," Dickens and the Twentieth Century, ed. John Gross and Gabriel Pearson (London, 1962), pp. 133-143, refers to "the iambic thump and the Victorian-Shakespearian diction (Hamlet, in this case. . .)" (p. 143).

Shakespeare's tragedy. Yet may one entirely ignore the fact that Hamlet has
its setting on a sea-coast too? No, for a true influence must be gauged not
just according to content, but formally; and a possible sound influence is a
formal constituent. Indeed, the reference to the small "hamlet" in the novel
precedes, possibly even prefigures, the reference to a larger Hamlet. One may
have called the other forth naturally; the casual, particular, oral meaning of
"hamlet" produced, through an associative process, the more forceful, dramatic,
universal, even philosophic meaning of "Hamlet." The cumulative effect is not
one resulting from free association alone, but from the principles of Gestalt
Psychology, the tendency of the mind to abstract, and thereby create, in formal
terms.

If "hamlet" relates to "Hamlet," though principally through the effect
of sound, does "Ham" (the name of the young man) also bear a relationship orally?
It would certainly seem possible. In the third chapter David indirectly raises
this question when he bluntly asks Mr. Peggotty, "Did you give your son the name
of Ham, because you lived in a sort of ark?" The answer he receives may be a
reflection of Dickens's own creative imagination. For, instead of a direct
response, David gets one that does not answer the question he asked: he is simply
told that, after all, Ham is not Mr. Peggotty's son. Yet just before this the
reader is informed that "Mr. Peggotty seemed to think it a deep idea." Indeed,
it may have been a deeper idea that one ordinarily might suspect, for it may
connote the point that Dickens was again inspired by Hamlet, that he was incorporating
here an etymological point of contact. One may be reminded of the number of studies
that have been made on the etymology of the word Hamlet, for example R. Meissner's
"Der Name Hamlet."[48] Again the oral resemblance is tantamount: Ham recalls Hamlet

---

[48]
Indogermanische Forschungen, XLV (1927), 370-394.

24

purely in terms of sound, the first phonemic cluster being incorporated in the larger unit. To say that there is any more influence is to go beyond what the text warrants. There is really not a thing that the two figures Ham and Hamlet have in common: one is rustic whereas the other is urbane; one is incidental to the story in every way whereas the other is vital to it.[49]

Allusions to Shakespeare's most interesting revenge tragedy, comparable to the Ham-Hamlet reference, persist throughout Dickens's work; often the ghost-death motif is introduced, the grave-digging scene recurring as with Jerry Cruncher in A Tale of Two Cities and with Durdles in Edwin Drood. The initial description of Durdles recalls the casual rusticity of the Hamlet grave-diggers: "In a suit of coarse flannel with horn buttons, a yellow necker-chief with draggled ends, an old hat more russet-coloured than black, and laced boots of the hue of his stony calling, Durdles leads a hazy, gipsy sort of life, carrying his dinner about with him, in a small bundle, and sitting on all manner of tombstones to dine" (IV, 31). In Martin Chuzzlewit, the reference to Mr. Norris as one who "made a wry face and dusted his fingers as Hamlet might after getting rid of Yorick's skull" (XVII, 293) is much more fastidious. Compare a similar reference in American Notes: "'That, sir,' I replied, 'is a Londonboot.' He mused over it again, after the manner of Hamlet with Yorick's skull" (XVIII, 223).

Aside from David Copperfield, a significant parallel may also be drawn between the early appearances of the Hamlet Ghost and the convict-in-the-

---

49
Cf. the discussion of psycholinguistics in Chapter Five, Part II.

graveyard episode in Great Expectations. There are a number of points of
comparison, not the least important being the suggestion that the Ghost is by
no means free of guilt either and refers to its confinement in a "prison-house."
Is it really unfair to Shakespeare to suggest that just as the convict has
escaped his prison to return and accost the young hero of Great Expectations, so
the Ghost in Hamlet has managed to flee from Purgatory long enough to ask the
Prince to avenge him? The implication is that the Ghost is not entirely pious,
be it ever so "honest" in recounting the murder; however, in stating that it has
been forbidden to disclose certain secrets, the Ghost indirectly reveals that its
return is in keeping with one aspect of the Will of God: in short, God seemingly
permits revenge in this instance, even though He would not condone it. Thus the
Ghost is indeed a "purgatorial spirit," but inverted commas are needed. Is it
actually in its purgatorial state when addressing the Prince? Theologically, it
could not ask for the kind of revenge that Jesus rejected and thereby fail to act
in accord with Christ-like principles if it was in Purgatory. For it is impossible
for a disembodied soul in Purgatory to sin. Then is the Ghost not really in but
rather from Purgatory? It would appear that way: Shakespeare perhaps purposely
invented such a spirit as a dramatic device.

Another parallel is that in both play and novel the hero is confronted
with the image of a man suffering from his past sins and finally determines to
follow the bidding of his revengeful interlocutor: Hamlet stabs Polonius, and
Pip plunders food. With both, attachment to either the Ghost or the convict
leads to awkward relations with young ladies. But whereas in Hamlet the hero
frustrates his beloved to the extent that she becomes demented, in Great Expectations
the reverse is true: Estella succeeds in turning a cold shoulder to Pip, who
thereby feels thwarted in love, a condition that keeps him from an organized

rapprochement to the best morality of the proper Christian life. The Prince's

right to the throne in Shakespeare's tragedy implicitly relates to Pip's great

expectations. Perhaps it is being excessive to suggest that ambition is central

to Hamlet's motivation, that like Bussy D'Ambois he is striving for personal

success, but the Oedipal situation need not be categorically repudiated. For

according to the view that Oedipus marries his mother because a man who wants

to become king would marry the queen (a point that Professor Moses Hadas has suggested

in a lecture to me), and according to the theory that Hamlet's concern with his

mother's sexual life accommodates itself to a legitimate Oedipal interpretation,[50]

it might well follow that personal ambition is a strong motivating factor. Such

considerations, however, though not invalid, are still highly speculative in terms

of the dramatist's intent at least. Shakespeare was primarily concerned with showing

how justice triumphs (the natural appeal his play would have for an Elizabethan

audience); but this moral emphasis does not rule out the point that Hamlet is acutely

aware of his rightful claim to the throne and of his popular support. Thus, he

significantly refers to "the election and my hopes" (V.ii.65). Both Hamlet and Pip

have a natural right to their expectations; this is a donné in each case. The

shortcomings derive from a deficiency on the part of each hero, one resulting not from

inaction but from lack of the appropriate action at precisely the opportune moment.

Contrast Hamlet's disdainful attitude toward Polonius with his final disposal of that

imprudent spy of Claudius's, and Pip's lack of reciprocity, a similar disdain, with Joe

---

[50] I do not wish to present a Freudian interpretation here simply as an additional
fillip. Alfred Harbage, in William Shakespeare: A Reader's Guide (New York, 1963),
writes that the Prince "does indeed display an excessive concern with his mother's
sexual life. The analysts suggest that his passion is interpretable as jealousy
provoked by his unconscious incestuous drives. . . . The suggestion should not be
discounted entirely, but we should try to retain our sense of critical proportion"
(pp. 327-328).

Gargery. If Hamlet had taken thought at the right time, he might have known that the man behind the arras would be an imprudent intruder, not the wily Claudius. And then he would not have struck. If Pip had remembered his sense of duty toward Joe, he would not have been so overtaken by the sense of his own importance. The failings in both heroes are fundamentally comparable; the degree of similitude is what makes them different.

II

Allied to the Dickensian references to ghosts and associated allusions to Hamlet is another area of meaning found in many of the novels: the references to magic or conjuring. In proposing this, I do not mean to suggest that such an appeal to mystification represents a special design with structural dimensions. I am referring only to occasional configurations of meaning or to figures repeating themselves (Wiederholungsfiguren) or just to accumulations. My concern is principally with the occurrence and structure of Shakespearian elements in Dickens: therefore the fact that certain clusters of images, like those relating to ghosts or magic, may be Shakespearian serves me as a point of departure only. Basically my interest is in the Shakespearian links as they relate to the structural development of a particular novel; to be sure, larger categories have a logical relevance, but their significance is more descriptive of material content than essential to literary value and influence.

The references to magic are of special interest for an introductory view because Dickens may have derived them from Shakespeare just, as it seems that he also got his ideas about ghosts from quasi-Senecan apparitions on the stage (as in Richard III and Hamlet). Thus he was under the spell of Prospero, magus of The Tempest.

Indeed, Dickens was especially absorbed in Shakespeare's swan song, as
The Tempest has been called, although the extent to which Prospero stands for the
dramatist himself is in dispute; not only did he refer often to this tragicomedy in
his novels, but his own avocation of conjuring was inspired by the play, at least
in part. He was well aware of the significance of Shakespeare as a Prospero and
of magic as a creative art, and he pointed this out in his article "Stray Chapters:
No. I. The Pantomime of Life":

> Strange tricks—very strange tricks—are also performed by the harlequin
> who holds for the time being the magic wand. . . . The mere waving it
> before a man's eyes will dispossess his brain of all the notions previously
> stored there, and fill it with an entirely new set of ideas: one gentle
> tap on the back will alter the colour of a man's coat completely; and
> there are some expert performers, who, having this wand held first
> on one side, and then on the other, will change from side to side, turning
> their coats at every evolution, with so much rapidity and dexterity, that
> the quickest eye can scarcely detect their motions. Occasionally, the
> genius who confers the wand, wrests it from the hand of the temporary
> possessor, and consigns it to some new performer; on which occasions all
> the characters change sides, and then the race and the hard knocks begin
> anew.
>
> . . . . A gentleman, not altogether unknown as a dramatic poet, wrote thus
> a year or two ago—
>
> "All the World's a stage,
> And all the men and women merely players:"
> and we, tracking out his footsteps at the scarcely-worth-mentioning little
> distance of a few millions of leagues behind, venture to add, by way of new
> reading, that he meant a Pantomime, and that we are all actors in The
> Pantomime of Life.[51]

---

[51] Bentley's Miscellany, I (1837), 297. Dickens here uses meiosis to
establish, not only the point he is making but, indirectly, the fact that he
knows not a little about Shakespeare. The quoted passage is from The Tempest,
and the reference to the magic wand relates to Prospero's magic wand or
"staff" in the same play.

The magical effects used by both men are worth investigating here. In The Tempest, most of Prospero's white magic requires no apparatus: it is meant to appeal mainly to the imagination. An audience could hardly have been expected to observe just how he abated the tempest. None the less, the play contains certain acts of magic and stage properties befitting the magician: the master of the island has his staff or wand,[52] and Ariel, under the direction of his master, makes a banquet of food vanish. There is also Prospero's "book," perhaps a secret volume containing formulae for incantations and such matters. One may recall the popular interest in the magical conjurations of Friar Bacon, such as is reported in Robert Greene's Friar Bacon and Friar Bungay. Shakespeare's white magician, though, has no association with evil spirits; he is not in league with the devil as some Renaissance magic-makers supposedly were. Yet he does recognize the world of appearance as opposed to the real world of eternal truths. And so he offers to "break his staff"[53] at last and confesses that deception was not his final goal. However, the world of the magician, dependent on

---

[52]In view of the numerous references to music in the play, one may wonder if, figuratively, it is not more of a conductor's baton.

[53]The standard interpretation that the staff means a magical wand and that the book is a book of magic has been challenged by H. E. Bowen in "'I'll Break my Staff . . . I'll Drown my Book'" in Renaissance Papers 1961 (Durham, 1961), pp. 47-56. Bowen thinks that the fact that the OED interprets "staff" in this context as the first historical instance of the word meaning "wand" is not significant enough, and cites a number of other instances in Shakespearian drama where "staff" has a different meaning. But Dickens certainly thought of the staff here as a wand; the quotation from "Stray Chapters" indicates that. Moreover, the fact that Shakespeare conveyed the notion of staff-breaking in another context to mean the destruction of a symbol of authority does not preclude the probability that the staff of The Tempest was denotatively a wand, connotatively the same kind of symbol. Cf. Dickens's use of another kind of staff when giving public readings.

appearance as it is, as sphinx-like as Carlyle thought Nature was, has
merits all its own; the art of illusion has thus its technical values.
Consider, for instance, Ariel and the disappearance of the banquet. Harbage
writes that the scene "has great appeal simply as spectacle. We can guess
at the nature of the quaint device 〔one of the dramatist's references to
stage properties〕 . . . with which Ariel makes the banquet disappear; we
have seen stage-magicians use their cloaks in just the miraculous way in which
Ariel uses his harpy-wings."[54] The vanishing act also relates to one of the
most celebrated passages in The Tempest:

> Our revels now are ended. These our actors,
> As I foretold you, were all spirits and
> Are melted into air, into thin air;
> And, like the baseless fabric of this vision,
> The cloud-capped towers, the gorgeous palaces,
> The solemn temples, the great globe itself,
> Yea, all which it inherit, shall dissolve,
> And, like this insubstantial pageant faded,
> Leave not a rack behind.   (IV.i.167-175)

In Renaissance England, the conjuror's trade was just coming into its
own, and noted men like the scientist and magician John Dee exhibited their
accomplishments; the card sharks had their favorite sleight-of-hand effects,
as Greene's "A Notable Discovery of Cozenage" describes in detail. So
Shakespeare did not in any sense depart from his craft when he borrowed some
ideas from the legerdemain of his day in order to make his valediction, if that
is what it was. Something like this is also understandable with Dickens, not

---

[54] Harbage, p. 475.

because this craft appealed to the popular mentality, but because the
conjuror had acquired considerably more finesse by Dickens's time so that
he had more entertainment value, indeed more technical artistic value, than before.

In accepting and adopting the role of the prestidigitator to entertain
his family and friends, Dickens, whenever possible, made a point of attending
the performances of other magicians to get more proficiency.[55] A typical account
of the novelist as parlor magician is that of his eldest daughter:

> At the juvenile parties he was always the ruling spirit, He had acquired
> by degrees an excellent collection of conjuring tricks, and on Twelfth
> Night--his eldest son's birthday--he would very often, dressed as a magician,
> give a conjuring entertainment, when a little figure which appeared from a
> wonderful and mysterious bag, and which was supposed to be a personal friend
> of the conjuror, would greatly delight the audience by his funny stories, his
> eccentric voice and way of speaking, and by his miraculous appearances and
> disappearances. Of course a plum pudding was made in a hat, and was always
> one of the great successes of the evening. I have seen many such puddings,
> but no other conjuror has been able to put into a pudding all the love,
> sympathy, fun and thorough enjoyment which seemed to come from the hands
> of this great magician.[56]

Likewise Jane Carlyle thought Dickens "the best conjuror she ever saw, his tricks
being so good that he could have made a living by performing them in public."[57]
Dickens himself writes as follows:

---

[55]
Forster writes of "a conjuror, who had been called to exhibit twice before
the imperial party, and whom Dickens always afterwards referred to as the most
consummate master of legerdemain he had seen." Life, III, 89. Thus the novelist
must have attended a number of different performances.

[56]"Charles Dickens at Home. With Especial Reference to his Relations with
Children" in Temple Bar, seen only in the Rare Book Collection of the Olin Research
Library of Cornell University. The reference to Twelfth Night may represent another
Dickensian relationship between Shakespeare and magic, i.e., since the birthday was
on Twelfth Night and since Shakespeare happened to entitle a play the same way and
was also a dramatist-magician, two things related to the same thing became related
to each other for Dickens.

[57]
Cited by Pearson, p. 131.

The actuary of the National Debt couldn't calculate the number of
children who are coming here on Twelfth Night, in honour of Charley's
birthday, for which occasion I have provided a magic-lantern and
divers other tremendous engines of that nature. But the best of it
is that Forster and I have purchased between us the entire stock-in-
trade of a conjuror, the practice and display whereof is intrusted to
me. And O my dear eyes, Felton, if you could see me conjuring the
company's watches into impossible tea-caddies, and causing pieces of
money to fly, and burning pocket-handkerchiefs without hurting 'em,
and practising in my own room, without anybody to admire, you would
never forget it as long as you live.[58]

This superlative note is found again in another letter of his: "I have made a

tremendous hit with a conjuring apparatus, which includes some of Doebler's

best tricks, and was more popular that evening after cooking a plum pudding in a

hat, and producing a pocket handkerchief from a Wine Bottle, than ever I have been

in my life."[59] The late Hesketh Pearson, in his account of Dickens's interest in

magic, describes how the novelist and Forster went to such trouble that they costumed

themselves in "demoniacal dresses."[60] In terms of the popular distinction between

the three basic kinds of magician (the mysterious, the humorous, and the natural),

Dickens tried to be the first type, though no doubt he captured some of the

art of the other two. He must have greatly enjoyed producing his mysterious

---

[58]
    Letter to Professor C. C. Felton of 31 December 1842.

[59]
    Letter to Miss Coutts of 27 December 1843. He writes much more on the
subject of his magic in a letter to W. C. Macready of 3 January 1844. That he
describes himself as happier than ever before relates to his indebtedness
to Shakespeare as a stage magician in a different, but sometimes only slightly
different, sense.

[60]
    Pearson, p. 132.

effects and seen in them a major reason for his success, for the elaborate apparatus he chose was designed more for grandiose stage performances than for the intimate gatherings to which he catered. Frank Staff, late Honorable Secretary of the London Magic Circle, disagrees, however, with Jane Carlyle's assessment: "From the description of the tricks presented by Dickens at private gatherings I do not think that he was an expert at sleight of hand, needing only a few simple sleights for his magic with apparatus. There is no doubt, however, that Dickens was a master of magic in another form and that the patter, ancient word meaning muttering, possibly from the Latin pater-noster, the patter or talk with which he presented his tricks equalled and possibly excelled that of the professional magician."[61]

To prove Staff's point that Dickens knew his magical phraseology, one need only examine his playbill with the following caption: "The Un-paralleled Necromancer Rhia Rhama Rhoos, educated cabalistically in the Orange Groves of Salamanca and the Ocean Caves of Alum Bay." Of the effects described, the following is representative: "THE LEAPING CARD WONDER. Two cards being drawn from the pack by one of the company, and placed, with the pack, in the Necromancer's box, will leap forth at the command of any lady of not less than eighty years of age. This wonder is the result of nine years' seclusion in the mines of Russia."[62] Staff may well be doing Dickens an injustice by claiming that the magician of words and characters was not a good performer of magical effects; very likely he was relying upon such

---

[61] "Dickens the Conjuror, and a Mystery Solved," The Dickensian, XXXIX (1943), 61.

[62] Alexander Woollcott, Mr. Dickens Goes to the Play (London, 1922), p. 237.

a playbill rather than upon Dickens's actual repertoire. Furthermore, he does not take into account references to magic in the novels, indications that the novelist had more than a casual interest in the effects of conjuring. For example, in David Copperfield there is a reference to a sword-swallowing act (Micawber says, "I should probably be a mountebank about the country, swallowing a sword-blade, and eating the devouring element"), to magical incantation ("this last repetition of the magic word," HEEP), and most intriguing of all with regard to Shakespeare, to tables "cleared as if by art-magic," surely an allusion to Ariel's removal of the banquet in The Tempest.[63]

Many of Dickens's characters seem to call forth magical analogies by their very "tags" or descriptions. Edgar Johnson writes of Pickwick: "His very existence and personality represent a kind of magic; if not that of the ugly duckling turned into a swan, a very foolish goose transformed into an angel in gaiters"; "Mr. Pickwick, bursting out of his green covers, had beamingly played the fairy godfather in actual fact, and magically transfigured the life of his own creator."[64] Quilp, in The Old Curiosity Shop, is a kind of magician without tricks, in that he consumes boiling water and can accomplish other feats worthy of an Indian fakir. Thus F. Dubrez Fawcett, in his Dickens the Dramatist on Stage, Screen, and Radio, calls Quilp "essentially a stage figure, compounded of Puck and Caliban."[65] In the American Notes, Dickens purposely compares his trip to the New World with that to an unknown (though probably Mediterranean) isle in The Tempest, using the term

---

[63] Compare the title of Chapter Fifty-five of the novel: "Tempest."

[64] Johnson, I, 174, 194.

[65] London, 1952, p. 17.

term "sea-change" and remarking at one point, "You seem to have been transported back again by magic." In Our Mutual Friend, an early reference to "local habitation" recalls Prospero's speech in which he promises to break his staff, and the allusion to a "Golden Age" calls to mind Gonzalo's attempt to visualize the enchanted island as existing at an ideal time. Dickens's final work, Edwin Drood, evoked Chesterton's comparison of it with "the performance of a dying magician making a final splendid and staggering appearance before mankind,"[66] another reminder of Shakespeare as Prospero. Finally, Dickens's repudiation of the "Noble Savage" myth in Household Words for 11 June 1853 suggests an influence of Shakespeare's Caliban, who is in some ways the antithesis of savage nobility. Thus he writes: "My position is, that if we have anything to learn from the Noble Savage, it is what to avoid. His virtues are a fable; his happiness is a delusion; his nobility, nonsense. We have no greater justification for being cruel to the miserable object, than for being cruel to a WILLIAM SHAKESPEARE or an ISAAC NEWTON; but he passes away before an immeasurably better and higher power than ever ran wild in any earthly woods, and the world will be all the better when his place knows him no more."[67] Is it too much here to remember Caliban, who, demon that he is, decides at the end of the drama after Prospero renounces his magic that he will turn over a new leaf and "seek for grace"?

To sum up, there are numerous ways in which the magic of Shakespeare influenced the magic of Dickens. No doubt the magical imagery of Othello, as

---

[66] See Johnson, II, 1116.

[67] Apparently Dickens was unacquainted with Guiderius and Arviragus of Cymbeline.

vividly described in Robert B. Heilman's recent volume on the Moorish drama, _Magic in the Web: Action and Language in "Othello,"_[68] had an effect on the novelist, especially in relation to his interest in mesmerism mentioned earlier. Since Edgar Johnson emphasized that "Dickens printed nothing with which he did not agree" (cited previously), the various articles on magic in the weekly journals he edited and to which he contributed ought to be examined also. For example, one might profitably look into an article on the Elizabethan scientist-magician Dr. Dee, entitled "The Magic Crystal,"[69] or a paper on Robert-Houdin, the master of escape, called "Out-Conjuring Conjurors"[70] or even a study of American ingenuity with the title "A Californian Conjuring Trick."[71] A final word from an anonymous paper, "Dickens, the Great Magician," offers the most fitting closing tribute: "Emerson has said: 'The poetry of the vulgar has yet to be written.' Dickens found that poetry in the hearts of the people, and has done more, save _Shakespeare,_ than any other author to show the whole world is kin."[72]

III

Aside from the influence of the Shakespearian apparitions and the

---

68

Lexington, 1956. Cf. the most recent study on this subject: Evert Sprinchorn, "The Handkerchief Trick in _Othello,_" _Columbia University Forum,_ VII (1964), 25-30.

[69]_Household Words,_ II (1850), 284-288.

[70]_Household Words,_ XIX (1859), 433-439.

[71]_All the Year Round,_ XXXIX, n.s., XIX (1877), 253-261.

[72]_The Dickensian,_ IV (1908), 145-147. The italics are mine.

interest in magic, there are a large number of other references that
have to be cataloged. In my master's thesis, "The Lear-Cordelia Motif
in Dickens's The Old Curiosity Shop,"[73] I made a study of statistical
data thus far analyzed, namely the frequency-tables set up by James S.
Stevens, in Quotations and References in Charles Dickens,[74] and by
Earle Davis in "Literary Influences upon the Early Art of Charles
Dickens."[75] Stevens concludes that, out of 845 allusions he has tabulated,
365 are to the Bible, 103 to modern authors, 71 to the Classics, and 69
to Shakespeare. Davis manages to put his list of references to Shakespeare
out in front, but both tabulators fall short of the most accurate kind of
analysis. Indeed, there are such a large number of oblique references
to the dramatist that it would be exceedingly difficult to arrive at a
scientifically reliable estimate. Davis claims that there is an "overwhelming use of Shakespearean references,"[76] but he then goes on to find
the greatest influence in the Fielding-Smollett tradition, alluding in
passing to George Gissing's rather questionable assertion that "oddly
enough, Dickens seems to have made more allusions throughout his work to
the Arabian Nights than to any other book or author."[77] But if the
principal number of references to a single author is to Shakespeare and

---

[73] The Catholic University of America, 1958.

[74] Boston, 1929.

[75] Unpubl. doctoral diss. (Princeton, 1935). Later, in his published
work, he revises his views.

[76] Davis, p. 10.

[77] Davis, p. 10n. Cf. W. F. D. Curtoys, "Tobias Smollett's Influence on
Dickens," The Dickensian, XXXII (1936), 249-254; Frank Wilson, Dickens in
seinen Beziehungen zu den Humoristen Fielding und Smollett, publ. doctoral
diss. (Leipzig, 1899).

not to Fielding or Smollett, why should not Shakespeare's influence upon him
be recognized as the supreme one? To be sure, the eighteenth-century novel did
have a prominent influence if for no other reason than that it preceded Dickens's
historically and thereby served as a forerunner, but a general influence of that
nature is often so very vague. One's discernment of it is usually thematically
oriented, without a real basis in concrete fact; it may actually amount to little
else than an analogue. Besides, many of the picaresque features ascribed to the
earlier form of the novel, derivative from the Renaissance narratives of Thomas Nashe
and Deloney, have a basis in Shakespearian drama, not just in terms of character
involvement, but with regard to monologues and episodic situation.

     We may assume, for a hypothetical case in point, that the greatest influence
upon Shakespeare was pre-Shakespearian English drama, notably the fifteenth-century
morality plays and interludes. Indeed, the similarity in speech patterns, in moral
action and reaction, even in humor and dramatic intent, is worthy of study. But,
given these affinities, what can we say about the influence on Shakespeare? No doubt
he had some vital familiarity with past plays, for actors still performed them at
Stratford, but can one rightly conjecture that their mere proximity in terms of the
indigenous dramatic tradition made them spiritually closest to his work? The main
influences on Shakespeare were, most likely, chronicle histories and the Bible. Likewise,
the major influence upon Dickens was neither Fielding nor Smollett but rather that
which has had the most pervasive effect upon English writers after their own history
and biblical writings, namely the plays of Shakespeare. Indeed, even as Dickens
was sufficiently influenced by the eighteenth-century novel to name one of his sons
after Henry Fielding, he was also inspired by a Shakespearian

actor of the age, William Macready, to the extent that he not only dedicated
Nicholas Nickleby to him but entrusted his children to the actor's care when
he went to America, naming another son after him. For an intimate account of
his identification of Macready with Macbeth, consider the following recollection
by Eleanor E. Christian:

> One sunny morning we were standing on the sands watching the young
> Macreadys at play with the Dickens children. The son of the great
> actor was defending a mimic fort of piled-up sand, against a storming
> party headed by the son of the great author. As young Charley advanced,
> the little Macready threw himself into an attitude of defiance, with
> head erect, and spade grasped like a martial weapon.
>
> Dickens broke into a hearty laugh, and, pointing to the boy, cried out,
> in imitation of the great actor's Macbeth, "Lay on, Macduff! and dashed
> be he who first cries, hold! enough!"[78]

Along with Macready's friendship, Dickens's theatrical ability, his stagecraft
as revealed in his being director, playwright, and actor,[79] made him especially
receptive to the creative genius of England's greatest dramatist.

A contemporary of Dickens's, R. H. Horne, provides an important comment
on the novelist's work: "Never in the world of theatres was a better manager
than Charles Dickens. Without, of course, questioning the superiority of Goethe

---

[78]"Recollections of Charles Dickens. His Family and Friends," Temple Bar,
LXXXII (1888), 481-506, seen in the Olin Research Library without page references.

[79]The following volumes are essential for a good perspective of Dickens's
knowledge of the stage: F. Dubrez Fawcett, Dickens the Dramatist (London, 1952);
S. J. Adair Fitz-Gerald, Dickens and the Drama (London, 1910); Ethel Keresztes,
"Dickens and the New York Stage," unpubl. Master's thesis (New York University,
1946); T. Edgar Pemberton, Charles Dickens and the Stage (London, 1888); J. B.
van Amerongen, The Actor in Dickens: A Study of the Histrionic and Dramatic Elements
in the Novelist's Life and Works (New York, 1927); Alexander Woollcott, Mr. Dickens
Goes to the Play (New York, 1922).

(in the Weimar theatre) as a manager in all matters of high-class dramatic literature, one cannot think he could have been so excellent in all general requirements, stage effects, and practical details. Equally assiduous and unwearying as Dickens, surely few men ever were, or could possibly be. He appeared almost ubiquitous and sleepless."[80] F. Dubrez Fawcett adds to the conventional theatrical meaning in commenting upon Ruskin's allocation of Dickens to a magical circle: "Dickens," he says, "always moved in a circle of stage fire, and seldom exhibited himself in public without first 'making an entrance.'"[81] R. F. Dibble, in "Charles Dickens: His Reading," remarks that "his interest in the drama, as shown by the writing of four plays and by his acting, was very keen. His works contain many references to characters and scenes in Shakespeare's plays, and his admiration for him is expressed in a letter from America to Forster: 'I continually carry in my great-coat the Shakespeare you bought for me in Liverpool. What an unspeakable source of delight that book is to me!'"[82] Dickens's participation in a group of so-called "Strolling Players," which produced Jonson's Every Man in his Humour and Shakespeare's The Merry Wives of Windsor, is relatively well-known. Less known is his early experience with private theaters. Edgar Johnson supplies back-

---

80
   Pemberton, p. 121. R. H. Horne and Dickens were collaborators. They worked on a number of articles together—including "Shakespeare and Newgate," which appeared in Household Words, IV (4 October 1851), 25-27.

81
   Fawcett, p. 17.

82
   Modern Language Notes, XXXV (1920), 337 (Dibble's italics). He falls drastically short in saying that only "four plays" were written: Dickens composed a good nine. They are as follows: Misnar, the Sultan of India; The O'Thello; The Strange Gentleman; The Village Coquettes; Is She His Wife? Or, Something Singular; The Lamplighter; Mr. Nightingale's Diary; The Frozen Deep (with the help of Wilkie Collins); No Thoroughfare. He contributed his talents to others as well. There are no mentionable Shakespearian influences evident in these plays, except of course for The O'Thello.

ground information: "In Wilson Street, Gray's Inn Lane, Catharine Street, Strand, and other places, there were 'private' theaters. In these, which were even cheaper than the other theaters, stage-struck amateurs were allowed for a fee to play Shylock, Captain Absolute, Charles Surface, or Macbeth"; he concludes that "the knowing backstage description of all this $\sqrt{\ }$ in Sketches by Boz $\sqrt{\ }$ makes it clear that Dickens's experience of the private theaters was not limited to the spectators' side of the proscenium."[83] In demonstrating Dickens's love for the stage, William Miller and T. W. Hill write, "He can have been never so happy as when his pen was in his hand, or he would not have taken the trouble to write his own prompt-books, stage-directions, and even the bills of the plays for his private theatricals."[84] Edgar Johnson provides more detail: "With characteristic energy he began a business-like campaign. He had been going to the theater almost every night for the preceding three years, always seeking the best acting. He had been especially devoted to Charles Mathews, and had sat in the pit whenever that actor played. He now started practicing industriously, even such things as walking in and out, and sitting down in a chair, $\sqrt{\ }$ as Dickens says $\sqrt{\ }$ 'often four, five, six hours a day: shut up in my own room, or walking about in the fields. I prescribed to myself, too, a sort of Hamiltonian system for learning parts; and learnt a great number.' Besides this self-training, he took a series of lessons from the well-known actor Robert Keeley."[85] Compare Frederick G. Jackson, in "Dickens as Actor":

---

[83] Johnson, I, 56-57. Cf. Malcolm Morley, "Private Theatres and Boz," The Dickensian, LIX (1963), 119-123.

[84] "Charles Dickens's Manuscripts," The Dickensian, XIII (1917), 181.

[85] Johnson, I, 60.

Mrs. Cowden Clarke says of his acting: "The 'make-up' of Dickens as Justice Shallow was so complete that his own identity was almost unrecognizable. . . . His impersonation was perfect: the old, stiff limbs, the senile stoop of the shoulders, the head bent with age, the feeble step, with a certain attempted smartness of carriage, characteristic of the conceited Justice of the Peace, were all assumed and maintained with wonderful accuracy; while the articulation, part lisp, part thickness of utterance, part of a kind of impeded sibilation, like that of a voice that 'pipes and whistles in the sound' through loss of teeth, gave consummate effect to his mode of speech."[86]

Allusions to the stage abound in the novels too, of course. T. Edgar Pemberton provides a good summary in the second chapter of his Charles Dickens and the Stage. The theatrical company of Vincent Crummles in Nicholas Nickleby stands out particularly as does the character of Wopsle in Great Expectations.[87] With both, the plays produced are Shakespeare's. Performances of Richard the Third, Macbeth, and Othello are described in the Sketches. There is an account of a Julius Caesar performance in David Copperfield which may anticipate the account of Hamlet in Great Expectations. This relationship is subtle but should not be discounted by the literary historian probing into the depths of Dickens's intent. The assumptions are that Dickens was somehow cognizant of the fact that Hamlet is a maturer play than Julius Caesar but that it follows on the heels of the Roman play in several respects (for example, the Senecan element is similar, the ghost references being analogous; the theme of revenge is dominant in both with Stoic overtones, such as Hamlet's reference to Horatio as "more an antique Roman than a Dane"; Julius Caesar is implicitly referred to in Hamlet at least three times: I.i.113-120, III.ii.92-100, V.i.202), and that the clear Hamlet

---

[86] The Dickensian, III (1907), 174. It is significant that Mrs. Clarke, author of the nineteenth-century Shakespeare concordance, thus refers to Dickens as Shallow. According to Van Amerongen, Dickens took the role of Falstaff too (p. 16).

[87] See V. C. Clinton-Baddeley, "Wopsle," The Dickensian, LVII (1961), 150-159; John Archer Carter, "The World of Squeers and the World of Crummles," The Dickensian, LVIII (1962), 50-53; Malcolm Morley, "More about Crummles," The Dickensian, LIX (1963), 51-56.

references in both David Copperfield and Great Expectations partake analogously
of a similar developing maturity—even as the Julius Caesar performance in the
earlier novel reflects the influence first taking shape. It is, I think, significant that David Copperfield himself recognizes the difference between the
stoic austerity which the Romans represented for him in school and their effect
upon him in the play: "To have all those Roman nobles alive before me, and walking
in and out for my entertainment, instead of being the stern task-masters they had
been at school, was a most novel and delightful effect" (p. 273). As the novel
progresses, Hamlet references are evident with increasing frequency, but only
in the case of Micawber's reflections; the Hamlet influence in general does not
reach its peak before Great Expectations. Thus Dickens may have put together his
raw materials in the character of David, but without shaping it as he did in the
case of Pip. Tucker Brooke writes similarly of Shakespeare: "Brutus in Julius
Caesar, though a fine and effective stage type, is not a thoroughly harmonized
portrait. He is a preliminary drawing for Shakespeare's Hamlet, who has many of
the same difficulties to face and is of similar mental fiber. It is perhaps not
too rash to assume that the unresolved doubts which half appear in the stage-character
of Brutus drove Shakespeare to attempts at deeper introspection, and so to higher
and somewhat extra-dramatic triumphs. Shakespeare's standard play is Hamlet."[88]

The many theatrical character types in Dickens's novels may be glanced at,
but there is little point in considering their function in detail isolated from
the structure of the novels in which they appear. Such figures as Jingles in

---

88
"The Renaissance: 1500-1660," A Literary History of England, ed. Albert C.
Baugh et al. (New York, 1948), p. 527.

Pickwick Papers, Smike in Nicholas Nickleby, Little Swills in Bleak House, and
Old Frederick Dorrit in Little Dorrit may be mentioned. Some characters are
"walk-ons," like Miss Flite in Bleak House. Some theatrical episodes exploit
character to the full. One wonders if perchance Hamlet's turning the tables
on Rosencrantz and Guildenstern so that they would be "hoist" with "their own
petar" did not have an effect upon Krook's sudden destruction by "spontaneous
combustion," for in symbolizing Chancery, Krook represents the very powder of
beaurocracy that blew itself up. Dickens's own dramatic heights were reached on
the stage when he acted Captain Bobadill in Jonson's comedy, and one might be
tempted to indulge in the fancy that the influence of Jonsonian humours on Dickens
was greater than the influence of Shakespeare. But Dickens knew little of Jonson's
work outside of this play, and even his role as Bobadill is less significant in
itself than it is when related to Dickens's love of Falstaff, for the Captain is
a miles gloriosus type directly in the commedia dell'arte tradition which produced Shakespeare's obese knight. And, if J. B. van Amerongen is right, Dickens
played Falstaff as well as Shallow.

Finally, there is the question whether or not Dickens's propensity for
theatricality always helped or sometimes hindered his work. Might not even the
influence of the greatest English dramatist have had a partly adverse effect upon
the novelist?

To find the answer, one should take into account several things. First of
all, Shakespeare was more dramatic than theatrical, Elmer Edgar Stoll notwithstanding.
Secondly, Brantz Mayer has reported as follows on Dickens's reading in Baltimore:
"Much as we esteem and applaud the histrionic art we cannot avoid feeling that Charles
Dickens descends from the author to the actor; yet, we pardon him when he is pathetic

and pity when he is farcical. Still, in the selfishness of our curiosity, there
is an appreciable delight in the display; for, who is there who would not go far
to hear Shakspere read his plays or Scott his novels?"[89] In thus commenting on
the "magician who has swayed the public for the third of a century,"[90] Mayer raises
the critical point that Dickens sometimes overdid his dramatic effects. In the same
vein, Earle Davis concludes that "it is . . . the sincere belief of the present writer
that the reasons for the occasional modern reaction against Dickens is caused mostly
by Dickens's use of dramatic technique in his narrative method."[91] The question,
then, narrows: Is Dickens sometimes too "dramatic"?

Robert Erwin Garis provides a suitable answer. He writes: "I would like
to define Dickens' relationship to his reader as a 'theatrical relationship,' and
to define the mode of Dickens' works, early and late, as the 'theatrical mode'";[92]
he elaborates on this as follows:

> It is my contention that Bleak House is not a dramatic work of art. I will
> show that Bleak House presents judgments--very powerful ones--about moral
> attitudes and moral behavior without dramatizing the conflicts between them.
>
> While in reading the sensational suspenseful "actions" in a Dickens novel we
> find ourselves consciously saying to ourselves, "This is not drama, but
> theatre," in the comic writing we are so completely in cooperation with the
> method that no self-reminders are necessary.

---

[89] From an undated manuscript in the Fales Collection of New York University, p. 2.
The phrase "pity when" may be a careless error for "pity him when."

[90] Mayer, p. 4.

[91] Davis, p. 136.

[92] "Moral Attitudes and the Theatrical Mode: A Study of Characterization in
'Bleak House,'" unpubl. doctoral diss. (Harvard, 1956), p. 29.

Lady Dedlock's actions are presented to us, not dramatically, but
theatrically; not for understanding and moral involvement, but for
nervous excitement.

Dickens' symbols in Bleak House are illustrative and amplifying,
almost never analytical or completely defining. They are the
vehicles of very powerful and very simple value judgments and
emotional identifications. The wealth of detail within them is
agglomerative, hardly ever more complexly organized than a simple
series. They are not, in a word, dramatic symbols.[93]

These statements are suggestive; Garis is using the word theatrical largely

in a figurative sense to mean showmanship as not restricted to stage trappings.

One may be reminded of T. S. Eliot's remark that "Dickens's figures belong to

poetry, like figures of Dante or Shakespeare, in that a single phrase, either

by them or about them, may be enough to set them wholly before us."[94] The

poetry has now become theater, both being resolved under the larger heading of

poetics. So, in answering the question of whether Dickens was too "dramatic,"

one can legitimately state that, as Garis says, he was not really dramatic, but

theatrical. It appears to me that his knowledge of the aesthetic components of

Shakespeare's drama (the delineation of character, the speech patterns, and the

use of set phrases or theatrically effective lines) was by no means superficial;[95]

however, more often than not, his awareness of the total moral effect of Shakespeare's

---

[93]
 Garis, pp. 1-2, 34, 184, 321.

[94]Selected Essays, 1917-1932 (New York, 1932), p. 375.

[95]
 Edward P. Vandiver, in "Dickens' Knowledge of Shakspere," The Shakespeare
Association Bulletin, XXI (1946), 124-128, points this out, but his own treatment
is too brief to be very helpful.

drama was, if not exactly on the surface, at least not especially influential on his work. Ironically, Dickens himself refers to Shakespearian drama as having had a powerful moral effect upon him. For example, he refers to the catharsis of King Lear, proclaiming that Macready's role was "stupendously terrible." But when all is said and done, such an influence of one or the other of the plays upon Dickens himself or one of the novels does not yet establish basic structural kinship. This may be partially owing to the fact that the two genres are separate, that there could hardly be as significant an influence as, say, there is of both the Oresteia and Freudian psychology upon Eugene O'Neill's Mourning Becomes Electra. The separate works of Shakespeare and Dickens are far too individualized within their separate modes. Moreover, Dickens apparently had not as much tragic sensibility.[96]

Is there any way, in conclusion, by which the Shakespearian influence had an ameliorating effect on Dickens? Did he, in any sense, recompose the plays as George Harry Ford said that he tried to write another King Lear in The Old Curiosity Shop?[97] We may conclude that the effect of the dramatist upon the novelist was not adverse, excepting the rather ludicrous idea that a comparison automatically deflates Dickens because Shakespeare overshadowed him dramatically. Indeed, inasmuch as Dickens utilized Shakespearian themes in his work, he almost surpassed the dramatist in the sense that he built upon the thematic framework Shakespeare provided for him. In this connection, one might consider J. H.

---

[96] As J. H. McNulty points out in "An Imaginary Conversation between Dickens and Shakespeare," The Dickensian, XXXIII (1937), 122-125, though the matter is in dispute.

[97] Dickens and his Readers (Princeton, 1955), p. 69.

McNulty's description of a meeting held to determine whether Dickens might not have been a greater writer than Shakespeare. He reports that a piece of inferior verse was examined and the verdict pronounced that "if Dickens had written thus he would never have been forgiven but all faults are overlooked in Shakespeare."[98]

Finally, a few closing remarks on this chapter of the relationship ought to take into account the universal quality the two authors shared. Though some scholars have tried to see this only in terms of their humor,[99] others have found it in their appeal to mankind at large. It is no accident that they have been supremely admired by the Russians, not basically because of any hidden proletarian motifs, I suspect, but because of the way they both point to the very core of human personality.

---

[98] "A Most Ingenious Debate," The Dickensian, XXXI (1935), 201.

[99] See, for example, the anonymous article "Shakespeare and Dickens," The Dickensian, I (1905), 146-147.

CHAPTER TWO:

HOW SUBSTANTIAL WAS THE SHAKESPEARE INFLUENCE?

The Concise Cambridge History of English Literature contains a comment
that, at first blush, might affect too sensitive a literary scholar adversely:
"Shakespeare depicts his mechanicals with a Dickensian understanding."[100] The
reference is clearly to some of Dickens's characters who have finely chiseled
exteriors but who do not permit searching internal analysis; since Dickens is
more known for creating such individuals than Shakespeare is, it is not really
inappropriate to apply the figurative term Dickensian to the dramatist's art.
But let one now consider what evidence there is perhaps for a reversal of the
above statement, for claiming that Dickens depicted his characters with a
Shakespearian understanding. What made Edward Fitzgerald, for example, call the
novelist the "Cockney Shakespeare"? To begin with, just what did Dickens know
of Shakespeare?

I

The first source of information regarding the Shakespearian influence upon
Dickens is the novelist himself. It should not be what commentators have said,

---

[100]
Cambridge, 1959, p. 294. Cf. "With Shakespeare, Dickens is the most English
of writers, and, like Shakespeare, he has conquered the world" (p. 776). Cf. a
letter to TLS of 6 Feb. 1964 by Robert Gathorne-Hardy, from which the following is
excerpted: "Shakespeare's characters, in correct verse, talk themselves alive as
powerfully as do those of Dickens"(p. 107).

49

whether they be contemporary or not; it should not be even what the novelist
has indicated in his novels. Influence is, after all, a highly personal kind
of relationship, evidence for which largely depends upon explicit acknowledgment
by the person upon whom the influence is supposed to have been exerted. Thus
the obvious place to look first is in Dickens's correspondence.

The letters furnish a rich store of Shakespearian allusions, particularly
in their references to performances Dickens attended and to outstanding actors of
the day (for example, Macready, Kean, and Fechter), with whom he was intimately
acquainted. To put some kind of order in an examination of the letters, I shall
adhere to the following table of analysis:

A. References to King Lear
B. References to Macbeth
C. References to Hamlet
D. References to Othello
E. Reference to Antony and Cleopatra
F. References to the comedies (As You Like It,
                              Much Ado about Nothing, A Mid-
                              summer Night's Dream)
G. References to Falstaff
H. Mixed references
I. General references

As I have already indicated in the preface, my references are apt to be in-
conclusive inasmuch as I do not have complete access to the letters (there remain,
for example, a large number in the Huntington Library which I have not seen);
consequently, I am able to cite only those allusions evident in the Nonesuch
Edition and in other letters available in individual collections which I have
seen. None the less, the list is very substantial.

(A) The references to King Lear, specifically to Macready's restoration

of the play on the English stage, come first for two main reasons: Dickens
was particularly impressed by this production, even to the point of writing
a review of it for the "Theatrical Examiner" section of The Examiner.
Furthermore, I can present the best account of allusions to this tragedy in
the letters since I have been assisted in this respect by Mrs. Madeleine House,
wife of the late editor of the forthcoming Pilgrim Edition, and by Mr. J. C.
Thornton, indexer. Thus the references on Lear which follow may be nearly
complete. There are six significant references to Macready's production I
have come across. Two additional references, more indirect but nevertheless
significant, also deserve mention; they do not relate as such to Macready's
performance. The allusions are as follows in terms of chronological order:

1. "What has come to Macready? Has management driven
    him mad? . . . He'll play Lear to the life if he
    goes on like this" (to Forster, January 1838).

2. "Nickleby is finished. . . . I begin again (God
    willing) on Monday!!! But I hope to see Lear
    on Monday night" (to Forster, July 1839).

3. Macready "is one of the noblest fellows in the
    world; and I would give a great deal that you
    ⟨should sit⟩ and I should sit beside each other
    to see him play Virginius, ⟨Leare⟩ Lear, or
    Werner" (to Felton, 1 September 1843).

4. "Of course you like Macready. Your name's
    Felton. I wish you could say ⟨i.e., see⟩ him
    play Lear. It is stupendously terrible" (to
    Felton, 2 January 1844).

5. "Among the multitude of sights, we saw our
    pleasant little bud of a friend, Rosa Cheri,
    play Clarissa Harlowe the other night. I believe
    she did it in London just now, and perhaps you
    may have seen it? A most charming, intelligent,
    modest, affecting piece of acting it is: with
    a Death superior to anything I ever saw on the
    stage, or can imagine, except Macready's in Lear"
    (to the Countess of Blessington, 24 January 1847).

6. "I yearn for the Drury days. --I want King Lear--
   I want everything--I want 'em all at once" (to
   Macready, n.d., beginning "Kate will be delighted").

7. "I am as infirm of purpose as Macbeth, as errant as
   Mad Tom, and as ragged as Timon" (to Leigh Hunt, 4
   May 1855).

8. "The serpent's tooth" (to Mrs. Elliot, 4 July 1867).[101]

These letters deserve careful scrutiny. The reference in (1) to
Macready being driven mad perhaps by managing and playing the leading role
in King Lear significantly indicates one aspect of that tragedy which impressed Dickens: the mad scenes. Since Dickens also had a propensity for
describing eccentric and demented persons, the fact that he was strongly aware
of the madness as described by Shakespeare should not be taken lightly. I
have discovered a possible source of "He'll play Lear to the life if he goes
on like this" apart from Macready's production. The Monthly Magazine for
February 1834 contains an unsigned article entitled "The Monomaniac," which
specifically tells of someone having been so overcome by a performance of the
tragedy that he was actually driven mad himself (thus he played "Lear to the
life"). Since Dickens was contributing to this periodical at that time, the
influence of the article is plausible. Here are a few pertinent excerpts from
it:

One evening Mr. Hill . . . took his family to Drury-lane Theatre, for

---

101
   Felix Aylmer, Dickens Incognito (London, 1959), queries whether "Dickens's
reference to 'the serpent's tooth' was meant to convey that Fanny Trollope was
a thankless child with whom he wanted nothing to do" (p. 35). The allusion is to
King Lear's exclamation "How sharper than a serpent's tooth it is / To have a
thankless child!" (I.iv.289-290). Cf. "Sharp-toothed unkindness" (II.iv.131).
The allusion has some bearing upon the Lear references in Martin Chuzzlewit.

the purpose of witnessing the unrivalled Kean, and scarcely less gifted
Rae, in the characters of King Lear and Edgar, and that evening afforded
a striking testimony to the knowledge our Shakspeare possessed of nature.
In that scene where the banished king falls a victim to Edgar's deceit,
Hill felt strangely and painfully interested; he drank in every visionary
word, he watched every turn of countenance, until, as the eye of Kean
brightened with the lurid ray of madness, his soul, mind, reason and all
rocked with fearful motion in his brain; his ideas ran riot after strange
and wild imaginings; and, casting a maniac's glare upon his wife, he
muttered, "Take me away! I, too, am mad."

. . .

I found him in his library reading a volume of Shakspeare, open at the
tragedy of Lear.[102]

The anecdotal quality of this incident probably amused Dickens, and he retained

it in the recesses of his mind when he referred to yet another Shakespearian actor,

Macready. The reference to "Drury-lane Theatre" invites comparison with Dickens's

enthusiastic response to King Lear at Drury Lane in (6); here again the theme

of madness in the play furnishes a possible basis for a happily intense or

even rather explosive personal reaction ("--I want King Lear--I want everything--

I want 'em all at once"). In (2) the reference to Nicholas Nickleby along with

Macready's production of the tragedy is of note inasmuch as Dickens dedicated

the novel to Macready (though the novel itself is best known here for its Romeo

and Juliet description). The letters to Professor Felton (3 and 4) are highly

commendatory of Macready's Lear. In (4), the use of the epithet terrible

indicates the extent to which Dickens wanted to promote an understanding of the

terrifying quality which the tragedy provoked in him. For an understanding of what

the Victorians understood by such catharsis, a few remarks by their foremost critic,

---

102
   "The Monomaniac," The Monthly Magazine, XVIII(1834), 201, 210. The phrase
"fearful motion in his brain" is misprinted as "fearful motion in in his brain"
(p. 201).

Matthew Arnold, are relevant here. In his Preface to Poems, 1853, Arnold wrote, "In presence of the most tragic circumstances, represented in a work of Art, the feeling of enjoyment, as is well known, may still subsist; the representation of the most utter calamity, of the liveliest anguish, is not sufficient to destroy it; the more tragic the situation, the deeper becomes the enjoyment; and the situation is more tragic in proportion as it becomes more terrible."[103] Though this was written almost a decade after Dickens's remark, it no doubt reveals the basis of Dickens's far from adversely critical reference to Lear as "terrible." Probably the novelist, like the esteemed critic, looked back to Aristotle's Poetics for the idea that a tragedy can purge the emotions through a cathartic experience involving pity and terror (or awe). The real basis for the terror of Lear is evident in (5), where Dickens refers to its "Death" scene as "superior to anything I ever saw on the stage, or can imagine" (a statement, incidentally, gravely misquoted in the Nonesuch Edition, where the entire phrase "or can imagine," for instance, is deleted). In (7), the allusion to "Mad Tom" is clearly to Tom o' Bedlam as depicted by Shakespeare in Lear.[104]

(B) Philip Collins has recently written, "It is clear that, on murder, Dickens was haunted by Macbeth, as, when writing about fathers and daughters, by

---

[103]
   Matthew Arnold: A Selection of his Poems, ed. Kenneth Allott (London, 1954), p. 252. The critic specifically singles out King Lear for discussion in his Preface. (The italics are mine.)

[104] He is referred to as such in Morgann's famous essay on Falstaff, which Dickens knew well.

King Lear."[105] But before one can point with any authority to a Macbeth
motif in his novels, one should examine the references to this "Scottish"
tragedy in Dickens's letters. The following are noteworthy:

1. "--the Theatre opens at Margate--all manner of
   breeziness, freshness, and waviness going on--
   and no Beard! Again I ask, when does Fir Grove
   come on to Dunsinane?" (to Thomas Beard, 8
   September 1842).

2. "Macbeth, especially the last act, is a tremendous
   reality; but so indeed is almost everything he
   $\underline{/}$Macready$\underline{/}$ does" (to Professor Felton, 1 September
   1843).

3. "I have slept as badly as Macbeth" (to Thomas Mitton,
   12 February 1844).

4. "He $\underline{/}$Scott$\underline{/}$ saw Macready play Macbeth in Boston,
   and gave me a tremendous account of the effect"
   (to Mrs. Charles Dickens, 26 February 1844).

5. "In the ghostly unrest of going to begin a new
   book my time is like one of the Spirits of Macbeth
   and 'will not be commanded'--even by me" (to Mrs.
   Winter, 10 March 1855).

6. "I must harden my heart, like Lady Macbeth" (to
   Thomas Beard, 1 May 1858).

7. "Macready came to the Murder at Cheltenham on
   Friday night, and delivered his criticism in the
   brief words:--'Two Macbeths'" (to Mary Boyle, 24
   January 1869).

8. Macready is again quoted: "'it comes to this--er--
   TWO MACBETHS!' with extraordinary energy" (to James
   T. Fields, 15 February 1869).

105
  Dickens and Crime, p. 300.

There can be no doubt that, on the strength of the same number of allusions in the letters and the more explicit references in the novels, Macbeth had as much influence on Dickens as King Lear did. There is no evidence that the influence of the Scottish tragedy was greater artistically, for the parts of Dickens's novels which most reveal this influence are sometimes criticized as melodramatic. Not that melodrama as such is artistically inferior, for it developed historically and naturally from the French melodrame, and I daresay that some of the modern adverse reaction to the dramatic form is derived from its association with the so-called western "horse opera" as well as from excessive cinematic mystery stories. What attracted Dickens to Macbeth at the start was probably the witchcraft in it. One might remember that his first acquaintance with the stage was with apparitions (for instance, he saw Richard III with its specter at an early age).[106] In his description of the "Madonna" dream (letter to Forster of 30 September 1844), Dickens commenced with a reference to Macbeth, probably because an oblique reference to the Ghost of Banquo and to the train of apparitions Macbeth sees seemed like an interesting point of departure. The most arresting aspect of the influence here in the letters is Macready's comment on Dickens's "Reading" of Oliver Twist. That the novelist was well aware of the effect he was creating with the murder of Nancy is evident from a letter to Kent (16 November 1868): "You have no idea of the difficulty of getting to the end of Sikes. . . . My Dear fellow believe me, no audience on earth could be held for ten minutes after the girl's death. Give them time, and they would

---

[106] See Johnson, I, 22-24. Cf. the references to performances of Macbeth and Richard III in the "Dullborough Town" section of Dickens's The Uncommercial Traveler.

be revengeful for having had such a strain put upon them." Thus the pathos surrounding Nancy's death was akin to that about Nell's. But one has to be cautious in interpreting Macready's high praise of the death scene as equal to "two Macbeths" (possibly he meant that then, in effect, there were two Macbeths, namely Shakespeare's and Dickens's), for the actor was advanced in years at the time and probably was more anxious to commend the novelist's dramatic public reading than to offer a fair comparison. Dickens himself stressed that Macready doubtlessly did not get everything. J. W. T. Ley remarks, "It is pretty clear that Dickens's eagerness to help Macready rather embarrassed the actor. He offered him also The Strange Gentleman [one of Dickens's dramatic efforts conceded to be not on a par with his novels]; he also offered to dramatize Oliver Twist for him, upon which Macready commented 'Nothing can be kinder than this generous intention of Dickens, but I fear it is not acceptable.'"[107] Perhaps Macready's later remark relating Oliver Twist to Macbeth was intended as a polite way of atoning for his earlier refusal. It is difficult to judge; certainly there is not very much in the novel to remind one of that tragedy. If it relates to Shakespeare at all, it does so more to Othello, where there is at least a similar episode of a lover killing his beloved for reasons of jealousy. Othello kills Desdemona, who has been kind to Cassio; Sikes kills Nancy, who has been kind to Oliver. Just as the Moor thinks that his wife is unfaithful and she is not, so Sikes has similar thoughts about Nancy when he slays her. The comparison points out that Othello is a tragedy and that the murder in Oliver Twist may be more "pathetic" but still is really no less

---

107
 John Forster, The Life of Charles Dickens, ed. J. W. T. Ley (London, 1928), p. 137, n. 138. Besides Oliver Twist, Nicholas Nickleby and The Old Curiosity Shop were dramatized by Dickens. Cf. note 82. Scholars and critics have largely contended that in these adaptations, as well as in his other dramatic efforts, he was not successful as in his novels. The influence of Shakespeare in these plays is slight if it is present at all.

dramatic. But Dickens's episode is none the less highly effective in a theatrical way. The assassination and subsequent victory of justice was influenced by Macbeth (Nancy's demise somewhat relates to the murder of Macduff's wife), as Macready seems to have indicated, but was also influenced by Othello, a tragedy which had haunted Dickens ever since he was impressed enough by the play to write a burletta of it as a young man. Such a double influence was certainly not uncommon, because a number of the novelist's characters may be traced back to more than one Shakespearian representative. Quilp, the dwarf of The Old Curiosity Shop, for instance, has ancestors in Caliban, Iago, and even Puck.

(C) Whereas Macbeth had the most obvious influence upon Dickens of all the Shakespearian plays and whereas King Lear had the most penetrating one (Dickens's enthusiastic reception of the death scene also points that way), Hamlet had the most substantial in terms of the quantity and quality of allusions. The following list of references to Hamlet in the letters is representative:

1. "There's the rub" (to Daniel Maclise, 2 September 1840).

2. "I have a great diffidence in running counter to any impression formed by a man of Maclise's genius, on a subject he has fully considered. But I quite agree with you about the King in Hamlet. Talking of Hamlet, I constantly carry in my great-coat pocket the Shakespeare you bought for me in Liverpool. What an unspeakable source of delight that book is to me !" (to Forster, 22 March 1842).

3. "He wears a cloak, like Hamlet" (to Forster, 3 May 1842).

4. "Maclise's picture from Hamlet is a <u>tremendous</u>
   production. There are things in it, which in their
   powerful thought, exceed anything I have
   ever beheld in painting. You know the subject?
   --The play scene in Hamlet. The murderer is
   just pouring the poison into the ear of the mimic
   king. But what a notion is that, which hoods this
   murderer's head, as who should say to the real
   king--'<u>You</u> know what face is under that!' What
   an extraordinary fellow he must be who so manages
   the lights in this picture, that on the scene
   behind, is an enormous shadow of this group--as
   if the real murder were being done again by
   phantoms! And what a carrying-out of the pre-
   vailing idea, it is, to paint the very proscenium
   of the little stage with stories of Sin and
   Blood--the first temptation--Cain and Abel--and
   such like subjects--crying murder! from the very
   walls" (to Forster, 31 July 1842).

5. "If I had no Dombey, I could write and finish
   the story with the bloom on--but there's the rub.
   . . Which unfamiliar quotation reminds me of a
   Shakspearian (put an e before the s; I like it
   much better) speculation of mine. What do you
   say to 'take arms against a sea of troubles'
   having been originally written 'make arms,' which
   is the action of swimming. It would get rid of a
   horrible grievance in the figure, and make it
   plain and apt" (to Forster, 19 September 1847).

6. "My servant / who has been sneezing, to attract
   my attention, ever since I began / . . . like an
   uneducated Ghost in a new Hamlet--so solemn is his
   warning--" (to Mary Boyle, 15 October 1850).

7. "At the theatre last night I saw Hamlet, and should
   have done better to 'sit at home and mope' like the
   idle workmen. In the last scene, Laertes on being
   asked how it was with him replied (verbatim) 'Why,
   like a woodcock--on account of my treachery'" (to
   Forster, 29 January 1854).

8. "It is curious to see London gone mad. Down in the Strand here, the monomaniacal tricks it is playing are grievous to behold, but along Fleet Street and Cheapside it gradually becomes frenzied, dressing itself up in all sorts of odds and ends, and knocking itself about in a most amazing manner. At London Bridge it raves, principally about the Kings of Denmark and their portraits. I have been looking among them for Hamlet's uncle, and have discovered one personage with a high nose, who I think is the man" (to Frederic Ouvry, 5 and 7 March 1863).

9. "You ask me about Fechter and his Hamlet. It was a performance of extraordinary merit; by far the most coherent, consistent, and intelligible Hamlet I ever saw. Some of the delicacies with which he rendered his conception clear, were extremely subtle; and in particular he avoided that $\langle$ $\lceil$ illegible $\rceil$ $\rangle$ brutality towards Ophelia which, with a greater or less amount of coarseness, I have seen in all other Hamlets. As a mere tour de force it would have been very remarkable in its disclosure of a perfectly wonderful knowledge of the force of the English language; but its merit was far beyond and above this. Foreign accent, of course; but not at all a disagreeable one. And he was so obviously safe and at ease, that you were never in pain for him as a foreigner. Add to this, a perfectly picturesque and romantic 'make up', and a remorseless destruction of all conventionalities, and you have the leading virtues of the impersonation. In Othello he did not succeed. In Iago he is very good. He is an admirable artist, and far far beyond anyone on our stage. A real artist and a gentleman" (to W. F. de Cerjat, 16 March 1862).

10. "I don't wonder at your finding it difficult to reconcile your mind to a French Hamlet; but I assure you that Fechter's is a very remarkable performance, perfectly consistent with itself (whether it be my particular Hamlet, or your particular Hamlet, or no), a coherent and intelligent whole, and done by a true artist. I have never seen, I think, an intelligent and clear view of the whole character so well sustained throughout. . . . He obviously knows English so thoroughly that you feel he is safe. You are never in pain for him. This sense of ease is gained directly and then you think very little more about it" (to W. F. de Cerjat, 21 May 1863).

What can be gleaned from this profusion of references, surely only a sampling of Dickens's remarks about the tragedy, and a meager sampling at that? One may notice at the outset that even minor phrases such as "There's the rub" were intended to relate to the play; thus the reference in (1) is repeated in (5) with a comment that he liked to use the expression often enough (notice the slight humorous tone in the phrase "Which unfamiliar quotation") and that it reminded him of Shakespeare. One might generalize from this and affirm that the reason that the expression was indeed familiar to Dickens was that he liked to use it frequently as a kind of touchstone to remind himself of the dramatist.

The reference in (2) relates to (4) directly, but since the picture referred to is not at my disposal, I cannot comment upon it satisfactorily. Forster, however, in quoting the letter of 22 March 1842, writes that Dickens is "referring apparently to some remark by myself on the picture of the Play-scene in Hamlet, exhibited this year."[108] The allusion is obscure. The reference in (5) to a Hamlet emendation is worth examining, if not for the value of the scholarly comment at least because it shows that Dickens had a sustained interest in the play and scrutinized its language closely. That he also had a critical interest in it is evident from his article on Fechter in The Atlantic Monthly, which treats of the actor's Prince but also of his Iago. Forster wrote Dickens that the novelist's proposed emendation did not make too much sense since "it would hardly give him the claim he thought of setting up, for that swimming through your troubles would not be 'opposing' them."[109]

108
    Forster, I, 336.
109 Forster, II, 360.

Strictly speaking, though, the action of swimming does amount to a kind of opposition, for the human body has to pit itself against the forces of the waves in order to surmount them and pass through them. Swimming thus involves tension. It is reasonable to assume that Shakespeare wanted to incorporate the idea of "making arms" in his metaphor but that he chose to improve upon that ordinary figure of speech by adding to it the notion of "taking arms" and thereby setting up a more powerful image. Dickens's observation, then, would not be basically wrong; he just did not pursue his analysis far enough.

The recurrence of the Hamlet Ghost in (6) was to be expected. As usual, Dickens adds a note of humor to the allusion. Indeed, he plays up the humor in a manner that is out of proportion for a fitting comparison with the real Ghost of the play. That he was aware of this tendency to turn a probably well-meaning disembodied soul into a sprite is perhaps shown in his casual reference to "an uneducated Ghost in a new Hamlet." In (7) the reference to moping may just mean that the performance was a poor one, but it might be indicative of the romantic interpretation of the tragedy which tended to over-stress the melancholy nature of the Prince. We know from Dickens's remarks on Fechter's Hamlet, which he so very much admired, that the hero was by nature "pensive"; Mr. Micawber, furthermore, significantly refers to "the philosophic Dane" (David Copperfield, LII, 733). With regard to (8), it is by no means un-usual that the idea of madness associates itself in Dickens's mind with the idea of the play Hamlet. The reference to finding the portrait of Hamlet's uncle is a natural one; even as a mad London "raves . . . about the Kings of Denmark" such as Claudius, so Shakespeare's Prince pretended to rave also about

Claudius. Dickens's very word monomaniacal recalls the title of the article
mentioned in The Monthly Magazine: "The Monomaniac." Yet he may not have been
conscious of this association and probably was only making a humorous quip about
London's frenzy at some exhibit of royalty.

The letters concerning Fechter (9 and 10) show the extent to which Dickens
really was enamored of the tragedy. From what he writes, it is clear that he had
seen a number of other performances of the drama, certainly Macready's, and that
he is conscious of having his particular view of Hamlet the Dane as well. As I
shall show later in detail, his version found expression in at least two novels:
David Copperfield and Great Expectations. (In passing, one may compare a similar
influence on Germany's leading modern dramatist, Gerhart Hauptmann. After
struggling with intellectual and theatrical problems he saw in the drama, Hauptmann
suggested various solutions. Then he wrote his own play based on the Hamlet
legend entitled Hamlet in Wittenberg and even composed his own Hamlet-novel.)
That Dickens thought in terms of different kinds of Hamlet interpretations was,
then, not peculiar with him. Indeed another prominent Victorian, Alfred Lord
Tennyson, was also very much impressed with the play and noticeably inspired by
it in his creative work; thus he called his monodrama Maud his "little Hamlet"
because many of the ideas reflected therein are derived from the play, though from
a Victorian more than an Elizabethan reading of it. This does not mean that
Tennyson thought that he in any way wrote another Hamlet in the way that Ford has
said that Dickens was trying to write another King Lear in The Old Curiosity Shop;
on the contrary, he stated that his poem was only "slightly akin to 'Hamlet.'"[110]

110
   H. McLuhan, ed. Alfred Lord Tennyson: Selected Poetry (New York, 1956), p. 221.

The two statements do not contradict each other when seen in a proper light:
"Maud" can be Tennyson's own "little Hamlet" and yet be but "slightly akin"
to the play Shakespeare wrote. Another parallel is worth citing, T. S. Eliot's
"The Love Song of J. Alfred Prufrock," which has been dubbed Eliot's Hamlet
in spite of the fact that the central figure denies, without the least hesitation,
that he was intended as a Hamlet-figur ("No! I am not Prince Hamlet, nor was meant
to be"). So how, one may wonder, could Archibald MacLeish, in his essay on "Poetry
and the Public World," have written so poignantly of Shakespeare's Hamlet, Laforgue's
Hamlet, and then Eliot's own Hamlet, even to the extent of referring to a Hamlet-
grinning skull of Eliot's? Evidently he felt that Eliot was influenced by the
play when composing Prufrock, whether conscious of it or not. As if to prove this
point, MacLeish has written a poem, which is related in form and style to Laforgue's
adaptation of Shakespeare's tragedy as well as to Prufrock, entitled "The Hamlet
of A. MacLeish." In his monograph T. S. Eliot, Leonard Unger writes that "Prufrock
is himself already a Laforguean Hamlet, an early Eliotic Hamlet,"[111] and Rudolf Germer
refers to Prufrock as a modern Hamlet type, comparing "I should have been a pair of
ragged claws / Scuttling across the floors of silent seas" with Hamlet's remark to
Polonius: "You yourself, sir, should be old as I am, if like a crab, you could go
backward" (II.ii.202-203).[112]

But, we may ask, what would this revelation have to do with Dickens? Is it
not just an elaborate attempt to foist an unconventional view of the play upon the
unsuspecting reader? The answer is that it is not if we consider it in terms of Dickens's

---

[111]
    Minneapolis, 1961, p. 16.

[112]
    "Die Bedeutung Shakespeares für T. S. Eliot," Jahrbuch der Deutschen
Shakespeare-Gesellschaft, XCV (1959), 112-132.

artistic creativity. It is no accident that he referred to the possibility of having different kinds of Hamlet in mind in his letter to De Cerjat. For, when he had written the letter, he already had composed novels which bore the impress of the influence. In the process of inspiring him, the original works had, to be sure, undergone a vital change (the basic one being the formal shift in genre); the result was not so much an actual influence of Shakespeare's play as an aesthetic and structural whole or even a clustering of incidents. It was, instead, a new creation, a re-creation. The influence was primarily a spiritual communion on a literary level, and so it is better to speak, not just of the "influence" of Shakespeare's plays on Dickens's novels, but of "the Shakespearian element in Dickens."

(D) References to Othello are far less numerous than to the other tragedies and should take up little space in this analysis except as a way of completing the survey of Dickens's relationship to the four major tragedies the dramatist composed. As indicated earlier, Othello may well have had some influence or effect on Nancy's demise in Oliver Twist; in this connection, it may also be of passing interest that in a letter to Forster of 3 November 1837 Dickens mentions the play ("Charles Kean was advertised for Othello") along with his work on Oliver Twist and a reference to Defoe's History of the Devil. The letter has been cited by Marie Hamilton Law as revealing Dickens's debt to his predecessor,[113] but one may also recall references to Shylock as devil in The

---

113 "The Indebtedness of Oliver Twist to Defoe's History of the Devil," Publications of the Modern Language Association, XL (1925), 892-897.

Merchant of Venice. The mentioning of Othello may likewise help to support
a suggestion of inspiration drawn substantially from other considerations.

(E) A single allusion to Antony and Cleopatra that I have found in the
letters is worth citing if for no other reason than that it relates to the portrayal of Mrs. Skewton as Cleopatra in Dombey and Son, though no influence as
such is possible since the novel was written much earlier. The letter to
Wilkie Collins of 4 March 1855 indicates that Dickens was familiar enough with
the play to serve as a critic of a particular performance of it:

> I have to report another failure on the part of our friend Williams
> last night. He so confounded an enlightened British audience at the
> Standard Theatre on the subject of Antony and Cleopatra, that I clearly
> saw them wondering towards the end of the Fourth Act, when the play
> was going to begin.
>
> A man much heavier than Mark /Lemon_7 . . . played Caesar. When he
> came on with a map of London--pretending it was a scroll. . . and said
> "He calls me Boy"--a howl of derision arose from the audience which
> you probably heard in the Dark, without knowing what occasioned it.
> All the smaller characters, having their speeches much upon their minds,
> came in and let them off without the slightest reference to cues. . . .
> It was very brightly and creditably got up, but /as I have said_7
> Williams did not carry the audience. . . .
>
> You will have the goodness to picture me to yourself--alone--in pro-
> found solitude--in an abyss of despair--ensconced in a small managerial
> Private Box in the very centre of the House--frightfully sleepy. . . .

A few passages from Dombey and Son prove a worthwhile contrast:

> "Mr. Dombey and the major found Mrs. Skewton arranged, as Cleopatra,
> among the cushions of a sofa: very airily dressed; and certainly not
> resembling Shakespeare's Cleopatra, whom age could not wither" (XXI, 280).

The Major pointed out "that it was hard in Cleopatra to require the world to be all heart, and yet to appropriate to herself the hearts of all the world; which obliged Cleopatra to remind him that flattery was insupportable to her, and that if he had the boldness to address her in that strain any more, she would positively send him home" (XXI, 282).[114]

(F) From Dickens's own propensity for humorous situations, it would seem evident that he was on the whole more influenced by Shakespeare's comedies than by his tragedies. However, this is scarcely the case. The allusions to the comedies are infrequent compared with the references to the major tragedies, but they are none the less important in revealing the extent of the novelist's acquaintance with Shakespearian drama. For example, on 10 September 1847 Dickens wrote Forster that he had seen a performance of "As You Like It really very well done." Compare two letters to Wilkie Collins:

"Macready went on Friday to the Rehearsal of Comme il vous plaira, which was produced last night. His account of it was absolutely stunning. The speech of the Seven Ages delivered as a light comedy joke; Jacques at the Court of the Reigning Duke instead of the banished one, and winding up the thing by marrying Celia! Everything as wide of Shakespeare as possible, and confirming my previous impression that she [Georges Sand] knew just nothing at all about it" (13 April 1856).

114
  The representation of Mrs. Skewton as Cleopatra forms an integral part of the novel, and therefore these random, though representative, excerpts do not do full justice to the influence of Shakespeare here.

"Comme il vous plaira--which is a kind of theatrical representation
that I think might be got up, with great completeness, by the Patients
in the asylum for Idiots. Dreariness is no word for it, vacancy is no
word for it, gammon is no word for it, there is no word for it. Nobody
has anything to do, but to sit upon as many grey stones as he can. When
Jacques had sat upon seventy stones and forty two roots of trees (which
was at the end of the second act), we came away. He had by that time
been made violent love to by Celia, had shewn himself in every phase of
his existence to be utterly unknown to Shakespeare, had made the speech
about the Seven Ages out of its right place and apropos of nothing on
earth, and had in all respects conducted himself like a brutalized, be-
nighted, and besotted Beast" (22 April 1856).

Again, Dickens's ability to criticize an adaptation of a Shakespearian play as
being "utterly unknown to Shakespeare" implies that his acquaintance with the
true comedy, As You Like It, as well as with Shakespeare's other plays was by no
means inattentive in the sense that Edward Wagenknecht once determined.[115]

Three letters bearing allusions to Much Ado about Nothing are likewise
worth evaluating. In a letter to Miss Coutts of 28 February 1843, he wrote, "I
hope you liked the Much Ado--and the Comus--and that you will go to see Virginius
next Monday." The allusion is, as Edgar Johnson indicates,[116] to Macready's
portrayal of Benedick in Much Ado, a performance which inspired Dickens's article
on "Macready as Benedick."[117] Thus it is safe to claim that this comedy, as produced by Macready, had a special meaning for Dickens; I shall examine the influence
in some detail when I come to an analysis of Martin Chuzzlewit in Chapter Five.
Finally, a minor reference to "that Much Ado about Nothing" (letter to W. H. Wills,

---

[115] Earle Davis comments: "How Edward Wagenknecht, The Man Charles Dickens, 1929,
can say that Dickens was not too familiar with Shakespeare is beyond me" (p. 105n).
Davis is in part correct. Not only did Dickens himself jocularly refer to a
particular Shakespearian quotation as "unfamiliar," but he also played on this "un-
familiarity" in the Shakespearian caption for Household Words ("familiar . . . as
household words").

[116] The Heart of Charles Dickens, as Revealed in his Letters to Angela Burdett-
Coutts; Selected and Edited from the Collection in the Pierpont Morgan Library (New
York, 1952), p. 41n.

[117] The Examiner, 4 March 1843, p. 132.

15 November 1855) is of interest because it probably suggests, in a whimsical
way, that Dickens was fond of the title of Shakespeare's comedy and was influenced,
directly or indirectly, by it when he proposed the following title for an article
in Household Words: "A Journey in Search of Nothing."[118] Thus in another letter
to W. H. Wills several years later, Dickens writes, "I have altered the names
thus: A Journey in Search of Nothing . . ." (13 August 1857). He lists several
other titles, but the fact that the above title comes first is perhaps suggestive.
Whether or not he himself wrote at least a part of the article is unknown, but
since he went so far as to change the title, one can assume that he had a hand in
it. However, he also revised much of what was submitted to him and collaborated
in various ways with other contributors; so we cannot be certain. At least it is
safe to say that he had definitely read the article in question and had passed
favorable judgment on it (Johnson, one recalls, maintains that "Dickens printed
nothing with which he did not agree"). That he altered the title is no indication
of disapproval; on the contrary, it shows that he took sufficient interest in the
paper to think of a better title. I shall consider it again in my discussion of
the nil-factor in Chapter Five; suffice it to say at present that Dickens's
deliberate endorsement of Nothing as the end-word of the title reflects influence,
albeit slight influence, of Much Ado about Nothing. The allusion to "that Much
Ado about Nothing," perhaps an intentionally amusing use of the word that to
indicate that the title was indeed a comic one and thus appropriate for a comedy,[119]
substantiates this point.

Another reference to Much Ado, though comparatively incidental, is

---

[118]
Household Words, XVI (5 September 1857), 217-223.

[119]Thus Falstaff, the obese rogue, has been described as "that Falstaff." Cf.
the familiar English colloquialism "all that." The use of the demonstrative
adjective in this fashion suggests that the user purposely declines to provide a
more descriptive adjective since he believes that the reader can guess his meaning.

in a letter to Professor Felton of 2 March 1843: "I am in great health and spirits, and pondering[120] away at Chuzzlewit, with all manner of facetiousness rising up before me as I go on. . . . My little captain . . . has been in London. . . . We took him to Drury Lane Theatre to see Much Ado about Nothing. But I never could find out what he meant by turning round to Kate after he had watched the first two scenes with great attention; and inquiring 'whether it was a Polish piece?'!" Perhaps this captain was trying to make a facetious remark relating the title of the play to its content, thereby contributing a form of "nonsense"[121] all his own, but the reference is rather obscure. The allusion in a letter which also mentions Chuzzlewit in a stage of completion is suggestive because it relates to the possible influence of the comedy, indeed of the "nothing" motif itself, upon that novel, a consideration to be developed in a later chapter.

Another instance of what Forster terms Dickens's "droll glimpse of Shakespeare at the theatre"[122] is evident in a letter of 24 July 1853 to the biographer: "We went to the theatre last night, to see the Midsummer Night's Dream--of the Opera Comique. It is a beautiful little theatre now, with a very good company; and the nonsense of the piece was done with a sense quite confounding in that connexion."

---

[120] So reads the original. The Nonesuch Edition has "powdering."

[121] There is a clear relationship between the title of Shakespeare's romantic comedy Much Ado about Nothing and the colloquialism used to designate talk between lovers: "sweet nothings." That Dickens was aware of this affinity ought to be evident from his acquaintance with William Jordan's article, "Nonsense! A Miscellany about Love," Bentley's Miscellany, IV (1838), 167-172, when Dickens was editor. Cf. his use of the word nonsense to describe the love situation in a version of A Midsummer Night's Dream (letter to Forster, 24 July 1853). One may also compare or contrast the commonplace used in describing pastoral indolence: dolce far niente.

[122] Forster, III, 81.

(G) No account of Shakespearian allusions in the letters would be adequate without due consideration of references to Falstaff, Dickens's favorite comic character in the plays as is evident from his purchase of Gad's Hill Place (the scene of the famous Falstaff robbery across from the Falstaff Inn) for retirement. The following list is representative:

1. "I really don't know how I can make way for Darby the Swift in the next no., unless by the omission of Falstaff" (to Richard Bentley, March 1837).

2. "Have you done with my Maurice Morgann on Falstaff. I want to lend it" (to T. J. Serle, 29 January 1844).

3. "There happened to be living here at that time a stately English baronet and his wife, who had two milksop sons, concerning whom they cherished the idea of accomplishing their education into manhood coexistently with such perfect purity and innocence, that they were hardly to know their own sex. Accordingly, they were sent to no school or college, but had masters of all sorts at home, and thus reached eighteen years or so, in what Falstaff calls a kind of male green-sickness" (to Forster, August 1846).

4. "A poet named Willyim Shay Kes Peer gets drunk in company with Sir John Foll Stayffe" (to Macready, 24 July 1853).

5. "Down at Gad's Hill near Dorchester in Kent-- Shakespeare's Gad's Hill, where Falstaff engaged in the robbery--is a quaint little country house of Queen Anne's time" (to W. F. de Cerjat, 17 January 1857).

6. "We will have 'Of Gad's Hill Place' attached to the title of the Baronetcy, please--on account of the divine William and Falstaff" (to Arthur Helps, 3 March 1870).

The reference in (1) is to an obscure publication which appeared in April 1837

called Magazine Falstaff. In (2), the scholarship referred to is Maurice
Morgann's An Essay on the Dramatic Character of Sir John Falstaff, which first
appeared in 1777 and was a landmark in the history of scholarly treatises on
Shakespeare's corpulent knight. That Dickens was familiar with it speaks very
favorably of his scholarly acquaintance with Shakespearian drama. There is no
question, however, that although Morgann's work has been known mainly for his
view that "this Character was not intended to be shewn as a Coward,"[123] the notion
persists that Morgann perpetuated the idea of Falstaffolatry by romantically
raising the image of the Knight to an almost godlike level. But the value of the
work here is purely to be considered in terms of its being a historical document
for Dickens. There can be no question that the novelist's love of Gad's Hill (see
5 and 6) was directly related to his knowledge of Morgann's work which dealt
largely with the question of Falstaff's "courage" during the Gad's Hill incident
in Henry IV, Part I. Thus Morgann writes, "The surprize at Gads-hill might have
betrayed a hero into flight."[124] Morgann ends his essay with a comment on
Falstaff's death, which I quote below in full since it is possible that Dickens's
ideas on this scene and on Morgann's views about it may have influenced his novels:

> Shakespeare . . . knew that this character could not be completely dis-
> missed but by death.--'Our author, (says the Epilogue to the Second Part
> of Henry IV.) will continue the story with Sir John in it, and make you
> merry with fair Catherine of France; where, for any thing I know, Falstaff
> shall dye of a sweat, unless already he be killed with your hard opinions.'
> If it had been prudent in Shakespeare to have killed Falstaff with hard
> opinion, he had the means in his hand to effect it;--but dye, it seems, he
> must, in one form or another, and a sweat would have been no unsuitable

---

[123]
    From Shakespeare Criticism: A Selection, introd. D. Nichol Smith (London,
1953), p. 153.

[124]
    Smith, p. 182.

catastrophe. However we have reason to be satisfied as it is;--his death was worthy of his birth and of his life: 'He was born,' he says, 'about three o'clock in the afternoon with a white head, and something a round belly.' But if he came into the world in the evening with these marks of age, he departs out of it in the morning in all the follies and vanities of youth;--'He was shaked (we are told) 'of a burning quotidian tertian;--the young King had run bad humours on the knight;--his heart was fracted and corroborate; and a' parted just between twelve and one, even at the turning of the tide, yielding the crow a pudding, and passing directly into Arthur's bosom, if ever man went into the bosom of Arthur.' --So ended this singular buffoon; and with him ends an Essay, on which the reader is left to bestow what character he pleases: An Essay professing to treat of the Courage of Falstaff, but extending itself to his Whole character. . . .[125]

The passage also had an influence upon W. Maginn in his article,"Sir John Falstaff," which appeared in Bentley's Miscellany when Dickens was editor of that periodical. Maginn writes, "'Falstaff shall die of a sweat, unless already he be killed with your hard opinions.' The audience was not cloyed with fat meat, Sir John was not killed with their hard opinions; he was popular from the first hour of his appearance; but Shakspeare never kept his word. It was the dramatist, not the public, who killed his hero in the opening scenes of Henry V."[126] Some of Maginn's commentary relates strikingly to a Dickens-Falstaff parallel; for example, consider "he must always be a dweller in clubs and taverns, a perpetual diner-out at gentlemen's parties, or a frequenter of haunts where he will not be disturbed by the presence of ladies of condition or character."[127]

But the most interesting thing about Morgann's account of the death of Falstaff is that it might have inspired Dickens's own treatment of his heroes

---

[125] Smith, p. 189. The phrase "something a" is apparently a misprint for "something of a."

[126] "Sir John Falstaff," Bentley's Miscellany, I (1837), 508.

[127] Maginn, p. 505.

and heroines, particularly Little Nell and Paul Dombey, who are likewise
executed by their creator against the wishes of their admirers. Quite
possibly the death of Nell was prompted, at least in part, by the Falstaff demise
rather than just by the death scene in Lear, which George Harry Ford considers
a major influence[128] and which thereby inspired my master's thesis.[129] Certainly,
in terms of the novel itself, the Lear-Cordelia parallel is more appropriate. But
that Dickens was, as he himself admits, inundated with letters imploring him
to save Nell and that he then deliberately had her succumb suggests to me, not
so much that he was thinking of Cordelia or that he was hard-hearted, but that
he had hidden in the recesses of his mind the idea of Falstaff's dying.[130] If
Falstaff was Shakespeare's most loved character, no one wanted to see him "put out
of his misery," and yet Shakespeare could not find it decorous to have the clownish
Knight appear at Agincourt with Henry V. So, no doubt against the wishes of his
admirers, of whom Queen Elizabeth according to tradition was one here, he chose
to have the Knight die; likewise, Dickens decided that it was time for Nell to
die even though his readers implored him to keep her alive. The effect in both
cases was a sad one, but very likely that is just what both Shakespeare and Dickens
wanted.

There is no link between Falstaff and Nell in any other sense except
perhaps one: the Knight does not die on stage, and the audience hears about his
demise at second hand through Nell Quickly; true to tavern tradition, this Nell
is a heavy-set woman, a considerable contrast to Little Nell. That the Hostess's

---

[128]Dickens and his Readers (London, 1955), pp. 69 and 193. Collins (Dickens
and Crime, p. 300) agrees with Ford.

[129]The possibility of a Falstaff influence is suggested not to repudiate the
conclusions of the thesis, but to add to them.

[130]This is not considered in Chapter Six, which largely represents a summary
of findings in the thesis.

account of Falstaff was perhaps influential is not surprising since scholars
suspect that Dickens was influenced by Shakespeare's characterization of the
same woman when he invented Mrs. Gamp;[131] so if there was influence in one novel,
there could have been some in another. The Old Curiosity Shop first began to appear
in print in Master Humphrey's Clock just a few years prior to the comment on Morgann's
Essay; one may argue that Dickens did not know of Morgann when he wrote his novel,
but one cannot be sure of it. There is insufficient evidence that Dickens did know
Morgann when he composed his chapter on Nell's death in January 1841. But that
Dickens was at least well acquainted with Shakespeare's play at a very young age is
evident from Forster's report of an early conversation with him: "'This is Gads-hill
we are coming to, where Falstaff went out to rob those travellers, and ran away.'
'You know something about Falstaff, eh?' said I. 'All about him,' said the . . .
boy. 'I am old (I am nine), and I read all sorts of books.'"[132]

But whether or not the death of Nell was prompted by Shakespeare's decision
to have Falstaff die, the account of the Knight's passing away, as reported in
Morgann's Essay, very likely had a profound effect on Dickens in other ways. In
glossing references to the Hamlet Ghost in the initial chapter of Copperfield, John
Jones adds, "Not that it is necessarily a bad thing to plunder Shakespeare, of
course. If Dickens got the idea of Barkis going out with the tide from Falstaff's

---

[131]Thus F., in "Shakespeare and Mrs. Gamp," The Dickensian, V (1909), 164,
believes that Nell Quickly influenced Dickens and refers specifically to the following
line with its suggestive "malapropism": "I' faith, sweetheart, methinks now you
are in an excellent good temperality; your pulsidge beats as extraordinarily as
heart would desire" (Henry IV, Part II, II.iv.24). Martin Chuzzlewit was written
at the very time that Dickens mentioned Morgann in his letter (1843-1844).

[132]Forster, I, 5.

dying 'just between twelve and one, ev'n at the turning o' th' tide', the
idea is still a good one."[133] In all likelihood, if the idea is Shakespearian,
it is taken from Morgann's Essay rather than directly from a reading of the
play itself. But the influence of Henry V itself should not be discounted.

The allusion in (3) to "what Falstaff calls a kind of male green-
sickness" is of considerable interest to me, although its import might escape
the casual modern reader. In a paper wherein Falstaff's death of a broken
heart is considered, I suggest that at least a secondary cause of the weakness
precipitating his condition, and possibly the first cause, was that he himself
had the very "kind of male green-sickness" that he talks about in his panegyric
on the virtues of sack as a preventive measure.[134] Though Dickens does not
link up Falstaff's panegyric and later death, he significantly indicates in (3)
that the sickness of which the Knight speaks is indeed not just a jest but quite
in keeping with reality. This corroborates an important point I have made
in the Falstaff article: in opposition to the common medical belief that chlorosis
was not really possible in the male, I cited numerous treatises (mainly French)
which point to the fact that, not only can there be a form of male chlorosis, but
the disease of chlorosis itself, when accompanied by side effects and other ailments
but possibly even when alone, can be fatal.[135] No doubt the influence of drink
was a contributing factor in Falstaff's case in spite of his assertion that drinking
sack may be a means of guarding oneself against "catching" the green-sickness.
And it is of no little interest that the novelist also points various times to

---

[133] "David Copperfield" in Dickens and the Twentieth Century, ed. John Gross
and Gabriel Pearson (London, 1962), p. 143n.

[134] "Falstaff's Green Sickness Unto Death," Shakespeare Quarterly, XII (1961),
47-55.

[135] Ibid., p. 49, nn. 14-15.

the Knight's capacity for drink (as opposed to his enjoyment of food). This is obvious, not only in the farce mentioned in (4), but from another reference to the panegyric on sack, one recorded in Pictures from Italy: the allusion to "the sugar-plums, like Falstaff's adulterated sack, having lime in their composition" (p. 111). One may refer to Maginn's article again, since Dickens probably had read that: "I see no traces of his being a glutton. . . . The sack and sugar Falstaff admits readily; of addiction to the grosser pleasures of the table neither he nor his accuser says a word. . . . The bottle supplies an endless succession of jests; the dish scarcely contributes one."[136] Dickens, himself, however, loved food very much indeed (as George Orwell has taken pains, perhaps too many, to point out in Dickens, Dali, and Others); therefore we may say with assurance that the novelist probably did think of the fat Knight as, if not necessarily gluttonous, at least very fond of good food.

A final reference to Falstaff and Dickens, though not in the letters, is appropriate as a closing note. In Household Words for 15 April 1854, an article entitled "Legs" is significant in pointing out part of the human anatomy that captivated Dickens and his circle. There are several comments on legs in the novels and often in relation to Shakespeare (especially with the Wopsle Hamlet performance in Great Expectations). The following commentary serves as a fitting tribute to the dying Knight:

> It has always struck me that a great void exists in popular physiology, from the comparative neglect with which it has treated the legs of mankind. . . .

---

[136] Maginn, p. 504.

Yet only consider the immense importance of legs! What should we be
without them? Ask that infinitely poor and miserable person, a bed-
ridden man. To be deprived of the blessed faculty of locomotion at
will--not to possess that glorious privilege of riding "Shank's mare,"
or of taking the "marrow-bone stage" . . . .

If the heart be the stronghold of vitality, the legs are the outposts
of life. The legs die first. The outposts are captured before the
citadel is stormed. Mrs. Quickly put her hand upon poor dying Sir
John Falstaff's legs, and they were "as cold as a stone."137

Falstaff died of a broken heart, as the play tells us, but his legs gave way first.

Yet Shakespeare did not have sufficient leg references to suit the Victorians, it

appears, as Dickens tells us in Martin Chuzzlewit:

"Shakespeare's an infernal humbug, Pip! What's the good of Shakespeare,
Pip? I never read him. What the devil is it all about, Pip? There's
a lot of feet in Shakespeare's verse, but there ain't any legs worth
mentioning in Shakespeare's plays, are there, Pip? Juliet, Desdemona,
Lady Macbeth, and all the rest of 'em, whatever their names are, might
as well have no legs at all, for anything the audience know about it,
Pip. Why, in that respect, they're all Miss Biffins to the audience,
Pip. I'll tell you what it is. What the people call dramatic poetry
is a collection of sermons. Do I go to the theatre to be lectured? No,
Pip. If I wanted that, I'd go to church. What's the legitimate object
of the Drama, Pip? Human nature. What are legs? Human nature. Then
let us have plenty of leg pieces, Pip, and I'll stand by you, my buck!"
(XXVIII, 460).

(H) Some letters contain references to more than one play at a time, and

a few of these deserve mention next:

137
     "Legs," Household Words, IX (15 April 1854), 209, 210, 212. The quotation
from Henry V contains what is probably a typographical error: "as cold as a stone"
should read "as cold as any stone." Also, it is better to refer to Nell Quickly
here as Mistress Pistol rather than Mistress Quickly.

1. "Our straw-hatted friend . . . ! Oh my stars! To
   think of him, all that time--Macbeth in disguise;
   Richard the Third grown straight; Hamlet as he
   appeared on his seavoyage to England. What an
   artful villain he must be, never to have made any
   sign of the melodrama that was in him! What a
   wickedminded and remorseless Iago . . . ! raging
   to murder you and seize the part! Oh fancy Miss
   Kelly 'getting him up' in Macbeth" (to Forster,
   22 November 1846).

2. "I think we had better postpone the visit to
   Islington until Richard III comes on which is
   next week, with an entirely new cast. I've seen
   the Othello" (to Mark Lemon, June 1854).

3. "I am as infirm of purpose as Macbeth, as errant
   as Mad Tom, and as ragged as Timon" (to Leigh
   Hunt, 4 May 1855).

The reference in (1) is to an aspiring actor whom Dickens previously had left alone

during rehearsals at Miss Kelly's Theatre and who turned out to be "a gentleman in

training for the tragic stage," as Forster says. Dickens's temperament is very much

in evidence here; he takes off from Macbeth in a flurry of humorous speculation, as

he does in a similar fashion in his novels. Frequently he takes fanciful excursions

on the spur of the moment if a simile or the like inspires him to exhibit his Spiel-

trieb. The reference to Richard III in (2) is noteworthy because it points out once

again the novelist's knowledge of that retributive tragedy. One might compare what

Forster tells us: how Dickens could "recollect how his young heart leapt with terror

as the wicked king Richard, struggling for life against the virtuous Richmond, backed

up and bumped against the box in which he was."[138] One might similarly recall how

Richard III influenced Quilp's wife to call her husband a "second Richard Crookback."[139]

---

[138] Forster, I, 12.

[139] Mark Spilka makes a point of this in "Little Nell Revisited," Papers of the
Michigan Academy of Science, Arts, and Letters, XLV (1960), 429. Cf. Ernest E.
Polack, "Humorous Villains: A Comparison between Daniel Quilp and Shakespeare's Richard
the Third," The Dickensian, VI (1910), 182-184.

(I) Finally, a number of general allusions to Shakespeare present themselves:

1. "I have been reading a soul-stirring Drama called the Larboard Fin, which looks to me like an undiscovered play by Shakespeare, surreptitiously modernized" (to W. H. Wills, 13 April 1854).

2. "I hope you are enjoying yourself at Broadstairs-- holding on by your great advance in health--and getting into the condition . . . morally, of William Shakespeare" (to Wilkie Collins, 1 August 1858).

3. "Apart from the knowledge and ingenuity it $\lfloor$ Campbell's Shakespeare $\rfloor$ evinces, it is so exceedingly graceful and pleasant, that I have read it with uncommon satisfaction. It will always hold its place on the shelf in my mind where I keep Morgann's essay on the character of Falstaff; a delicate combination of fancy, whim, good heart, good sense, and good taste, which I am pretty confident is a favorite of yours" (to Lord Campbell, 27 January 1859).

The allusion in (1) may, of course, be passed over without comment; the reference in (2) is worth contrasting with the quotation on "legs" cited from Martin Chuzzlewit a few pages earlier; for whereas previously, in his novel, Dickens had spoken in favor of the aesthetic character of the drama, here he points instead to Shakespeare's moral appeal. The change may indicate a new insight on Dickens's part and probably shows that he is thinking more of Collins than of his own ideas (Collins was known for moralizing in his detective stories, as The Moonstone shows particularly in the characterization of Miss Clack). In (3) the reference once again to Morgann shows the very great esteem in which Dickens held Morgann as well as Falstaff. John Campbell was Lord Chancellor and had written a volume entitled Shakespeare, which he sent to Dickens; the novelist stated earlier in the letter that he had read the work. If it were not

for the fact that he only on occasion refers to a particular scholarly volume
in his letters, this particular tome might be of little import; but the fact
remains that there are preciously few allusions to books of merit or to books
at all. Of the ones he does mention, the volume of Shakespeare's plays that
Forster gave him when he came to the United States for the first time stands out
and was highly influential (if we can take what Dickens says about it at face
value); Morgann's Essay is also noteworthy; and, finally, Campbell's Shakespeare
serves to combine the three works in a kind of trilogy of Shakespeare scholarship.

II

After the letters, the next most important source of Shakespearian
allusions outside of the novels themselves is in the articles, both those which
we know Dickens wrote and those which he knew of or which he revised or helped
write. Of the papers in which we know that he had a hand or which he finally
composed himself, a number in Bentley's Miscellany signed "Boz" are relevant
here. The article entitled "Stray Chapters" is of note because it shows how
Dickens's fondness for magic related directly to his reference to Shakespeare
as magician in The Tempest, as I have pointed out earlier. And the allusion
to magic is also noticeable in Morgann's Essay. For example, Morgann comments,
"With what a Magic hand does he /Shakespeare_7 prepare and scatter his spells!"[140]
and then makes a critical distinction in pointing out that "True Poesy is magic,
not nature; an effect from causes hidden or unknown. To the Magician I

---

[140]Smith, p. 175.

prescribed no laws; his law and his power are one; his power is his law."[141]
He elaborates on this with the longest footnote in the essay. It commences with
a reference to "Poetic magic," a consideration of a "feeling of propriety and truth,
supposed without a cause, or as seeming to be derived from causes inadequate,
fantastic, and absurd,--such as wands, circles, incantations, and so forth," which
"we call by the general name magic, including all the train of superstition, witches,
ghosts, fairies, and the rest."[142] In the course of the discussion, Morgann remarks
that "the magic of the Tempest is lasting and universal"[143] and closes with the
following point: "The whole play of the Tempest is of so high and superior a nature
that Dryden, who had attempted to imitate it in vain, might well exclaim that

> '--Shakespeare's magic could not copied be,
> Within that circle none durst walk but He.'"[144]

The footnote contains many other views that undoubtedly impressed Dickens since
he thought so highly of Morgann's work, for example a few remarks on "the machinery
in Macbeth," a comparison of three "mad" figures in King Lear: "the real madness
of Lear . . . the assumed wildness of Edgar . . . the Professional Fantasque of
the Fool," and commentary on the Tempest characters Caliban, Ariel, and Miranda.
The entire discursus of the difference between Nature and Magic derives from Renaissance
and pre-Renaissance sources. Of these, Arabian writers ought to be mentioned for their
contributions to the general subject of magia (we should not forget Dickens's great

---

[141] Smith, p. 176.

[142] Smith, p. 177n.

[143] Smith, p. 178n.

[144] Smith, p. 179n. Dryden could not foresee the genius of Dickens, however,
whose magic is surely in part based on much of Shakespeare's.

love of The Arabian Nights, to which he often refers in his novels and which
relates to his interest in magic); also Pico della Mirandola's treatise on The
Dignity of Man represents a standard Renaissance view of the distinction between
so-called "natural" magic and that produced by Art.

But the major articles by Dickens which have some bearing on the Shakespeare
influence are the two papers concerning Macready in The Examiner and the paper on
Fechter's acting in The Atlantic Monthly. The first of these was entitled "The
Restoration of Shakespeare's Lear to the Stage" and appeared in the "Theatrical
Examiner" section, for which Forster usually provided material. It was printed on
4 February 1838 and served as a review of Macready's production, one close to
Shakespeare's original play after more than a century of the amputated version of
Nahum Tate's. The eighteenth century had found Shakespeare's version of the Lear
legend too harsh; Tate had insisted that the Fool's function was largely extraneous,
that Lear should be able to return to his throne at the end, and that Cordelia ought
to have a happy ending by marrying Edgar. So the Fool was entirely omitted.
Possibly one reason for this was the low humor in a number of the lines (though
the eighteenth-century stage was licentious at times, it tried to avoid being crude)
and such seeming irrelevancies as the King's pronouncement at the end of the play
when he carries in Cordelia: "And my poor fool is hang'd!" The attribution of
poor fool here either to Lear's wandering mind confusing his daughter with the Fool
or to his sentimental nature, his using the phrase as a term of endearment, was a
product of nineteenth-century scholarship and does not need to represent Shakespeare's
intent. (Elsewhere in the play when Lear says "poor fool" he means literally his
Fool, so why not here also?) Since Cordelia had been associated with the jester
(Shakespeare writes that when Cordelia left, the Fool pined away because of his past
fondness for her), it may not seem unusual that Tate had her marry Edgar, the

legitimate son of Gloucester's who feigns madness as "poor Tom o' Bedlam," bringing
the subplot and main plot together more closely. Even Macready found the role of
the Fool difficult to manage, as Carol Jones Carlisle has pointed out in her paper
on "William Macready as a Shakespearean Critic."[145] Dickens, in his review, tries
to cope with Macready's version, which was indeed closer to the original play by
far than Tate's; in so doing, he claims that the Fool "is interwoven with Lear--
he is the link that still associates him with Cordelia's love, and the presence
of the regal state he has surrendered" (italics his). This leads him to provide
a gloss for the crucial line "And my poor fool is hang'd!" He comments: "Can
there be a doubt, after this, that his love for the Fool is associated with Cordelia,
who had been kind to the poor boy, and for the loss of whom he pines away?" In
other words, Dickens is maintaining that, in some way, Shakespeare intended a deliberate
ambiguity (which seems unlikely) or, if not that, at least a two-fold association:
poor fool could then literally be the Fool as well as, say by connotation, Cordelia.
Her body could also have made the King think of the Fool's death by means of a
Gedankensprung, and indeed Dickens does comment on the jester's last line as a
possible premonition of his death (what Harbage calls a "comic prophecy") in the
review. The dramatic effect of the double reference is instantaneous: Lear, in
his exclamatory statement, "unites" the two who have loved him so dearly.

But there is a difficulty with this interpretation. We may recall briefly
Dickens's proposed emendation for a line in Hamlet, a suggestion that goes entirely
too far to be taken seriously by the Shakespeare scholar.[146] Now, is the novelist not
going too far here as well? Is there not something absurd in claiming that the King

---

[145] Renaissance Papers 1954 (Durham, 1954), pp. 31-39. Cf. Lewes, "Was Macready a
Great Actor?" in The Leader (8 Feb. 1851) and Forster, "Macready as Macbeth" in The
Examiner (4 Oct. 1835) for Victorian estimates.

[146] See I, C, 5 of this section of the dissertation. Though Mr. Roger Gard has
berated me for being contemptuous toward Dickens in saying something similar
(Essays in Criticism, XIV, 209; see my reply, XIV, 425), I cannot agree with such
an emendation and neither could Forster. I take Dickens very seriously indeed--so
seriously that I do not want him to be seen as the Shakespearian scholar that he is not.

is connecting his dead daughter (and a queen at that) with the court jester?
There is not if one considers that Cordelia's very association with the Fool
prompted her initial, heart-felt but foolish, responses to the King during the
love-test in the first scene. Thus George Sampson writes with some force, in
commenting on the eighteenth-century "happy ending": "Those who feel the need
for some kind of 'happy ending' are incapable of tragedy and should recline at
ease upon sentimental novels. Cordelia, often feebly represented, is a piece
of stubbornness—her own father's daughter, and they fall, as they should, together.
In its unsparing purgation of the spirit, Lear is the greatest of Shakespeare's
tragedies."[147] It is, furthermore, possible that Dickens was aware of the implications
of the double reference of poor fool so far as Cordelia is concerned, that he saw
in her the picture of an imprudent young lady (the influence of the play upon
Martin Chuzzlewit supports this, as I shall show later). One would be on unsafe
grounds in asserting that Dickens believed, with most nineteenth-century
commentators as represented in Furness's Variorum Edition, that the phrase poor
fool referred only to Cordelia. Many of these scholars do not see it as an
allusion to the Fool at all; they maintain that since Lear is holding his dead
daughter in his arms when he enters and presumably when he makes the later
exclamation, he must be referring strictly to Cordelia and to her alone. As
I show in a recent note in "The Critical Forum" section of Essays in Criticism,[148]

---

[147] The Concise Cambridge History of English Literature, p. 266. The view that Cordelia shares some of her father's obstinacy may have been first suggested by Heinrich Heine. Recently John Wain has written, "Even Samuel Johnson, whom I regard as the greatest English literary critic, lapsed for a moment into sadly muddled thinking when debating the propriety or otherwise of Cordelia's death in King Lear. . . . The poet who decided that Cordelia must die, knew also that Miranda must live." The Times Literary Supplement, 26 July 1963 , p. 561.

[148] "Lear's 'Poor Fool' as the Poor Fool," Essays in Criticism, XIII (1963), 425-427.

they do not take "poor fool" in the literal way Shakespeare very likely intended.

The main piece of evidence supporting the contention that Dickens believed that the phrase refers to Cordelia and not to the Fool as such is the novelist's own essay, his review of Macready's production. Commenting on the jester's departure from the mainstream of the play's action, Dickens writes: "When all his attempts have failed, either to soothe or to outjest these injuries, he sings, in the shivering cold, about the necessity of 'going to bed at noon.' He leaves the stage to die in his youth, and we hear of him no more till we hear the sublime touch of pathos over the dead body of the hanged Cordelia." From this, one can say that Dickens may not have thought that the Fool was hanged unless he hanged himself (which is unlikely) or unless the phrase "going to bed at noon" was recognized as a premonition. Yet why did Shakespeare bring in a reference to the jester at the moment when attention is supposedly riveted on the King and his dead daughter? Dickens has an answer: "We may fancy him, while planning his immortal work, feeling suddenly, with an instinct of divinest genius, that its gigantic sorrows could never be presented on the stage without a suffering too frightful, a sublimity too remote, a grandeur too terrible—unless relieved by quiet pathos, and in some way brought home to the apprehensions of the audience by homely and familiar illustration. At such a moment that Fool rose to his mind, and not till then could he have contemplated his marvellous work in the greatness and beauty of its final completion."[149] It appears, then, that Dickens believed that Shakespeare deliberately introduced the Fool to provide a form of fellow feeling for the suffering monarch. But it is also by no means unlikely that he may have

---

[149]
    Reprinted in the Miscellaneous Papers, ed. B. W. Matz (London, 1908), p. 72—hereafter, Matz. Cf. "that Fool" with the phrase "that Much Ado about Nothing" cited earlier; in each case a facetious quality is tinged with a hint of affection. Dickens may not have meant his comment here to refer to the "poor fool" reference specifically, however.

introduced the reference to soothe, perhaps disperse somewhat, the tragic effect

of Cordelia's death. In this connection, a hitherto unnoticed article is worthy

of mention: Ingleberry Griskin's "Merrie England in the Olden Time: Her Gambols,

Songs, and Flashes of Merriment, with the Humours of her Ancient Court-Fools, Will

Summers, Dick Tarlton, and Archibald Armstrong." Based in all probability upon

Macready's production of King Lear in part, though also perhaps voicing disagreement

with his interpretation, Griskin's article shows how even a nineteenth-century writer

found the main reference (the denotation) of "poor fool" to be the Fool himself:

> Another joyous remnant of the olden time was the court-fool. "Better be
> a witty fool than a foolish wit." What a marvellous personage is the
> court-fool of Shakspeare! . . . And that glorious fool in Lear! How
> touching is his devoted attachment to the distracted old king, and its
> grateful return! In the intensity of his sorrows and in the agony of
> death, he remembers his faithful servant:
> > --"And my poor fool is hang'd!"
> Shakespeare never showed himself a more profound master than in harmonising
> and uniting in beautiful contrast these transcendent pictures of human
> wit and human woe.[150]

One may recall that Dickens also made much of the role of the Fool in his review

article and that he probably read Griskin's article, since it appeared in Bentley's

Miscellany. Here is what he says about the same passage: "And are we not even then

prepared for the sublime pathos of the close, when Lear, bending over the dead body

of all he had left to love upon earth, connects with her the memory of that other

gentle, faithful, and loving being who had passed from his side--unites, in that

moment of final agony, the two hearts that had been broken in his service--and

exclaims--'And my poor fool is hanged!'"[151] He describes the apparent incongruity of

the scene (incongruous in terms of logic, if not psychology), very likely as Macready

---

[150]
    Bentley's Miscellany, V (1839), 101.

[151]
    Matz, p. 73. Dickens's italics. The punctuation here is from The Examiner,
however, which is closer to the author's original work. Note that whereas Dickens
writes "unites," Griskin (following him?) has "uniting."

played it; if he had believed that poor fool refers to Cordelia as well as to the
actual jester, he would have been going a step beyond nineteenth-century scholarship
limited largely to the "poor fool" / Cordelia identification and would have been
anticipating recent scholarship dealing with "ambiguity" (or multiple meaning). This may
indeed be so, for there is a very interesting passage in David Copperfield which seems
to echo the Lear passage and, if it really does, surely reveals something about Dickens's
intentions concerning how the crux should be solved:

> "And when you had made sure of the poor little fool," said my
> aunt--"God forgive me that I should call her so, and she gone where you
> won't go in a hurry--because you had not done wrong enough to her and hers,
> you must begin to train her, must you? begin to break her, like a poor
> caged bird, and wear her deluded life away, in teaching her to sing
> your notes?"
> "This is either insanity or intoxication," said Miss Murdstone.   (XIX, 207)

The first line, "And when you had made sure of the poor little fool," refers directly
to a female and is used as a term of endearment. That Dickens had Lear in the back of
his mind seems evident enough from other parallels here; for instance, "poor caged bird"
not only underscores the first line but relates to the King's remark to Cordelia concerning
"birds i' th' cage" (V.iii.9), even as the allusion to "insanity" reflects indirectly
upon the King's madness. Therefore Dickens probably interpreted "And my poor fool is
hang'd" as connoting--if not denoting ("God forgive me that I should call her so")--
Cordelia. But he found the principal reference to the Fool as Griskin did (Griskin's
"And that glorious fool in Lear" paralleling "And my poor fool is hang'd"). They both
discerned Shakespeare's true meaning here, for if the dramatist had meant poor fool
in this particular play to refer to a female, to Lear's queenly daughter, he would most
likely have written "My poor fool Cordelia! Hanged!" or something similar and not have
included the initial And, which clearly implies that he thinks that the Fool is as dead
as Cordelia. Dickens may have had some awareness of this, even though few would claim

that he was much of a Shakespeare scholar. The Einfluss was largely creative.

After "Stray Chapters" and "The Restoration of Shakespeare's Lear to the Stage," the next important article of Dickens's on Shakespeare is his paper entitled "Macready as Benedick," which appeared in The Examiner on 4 March 1843. The review is a highly laudatory one. Thus he writes:

> We can imagine no purer or higher piece of genuine comedy than Mr Macready's performance of the scene in the orchard after emerging from the arbour. . . .
>
> Refer to any passage in any play of Shakespeare's, where it has been necessary to describe, as occurring beyond the scene, the behaviour of a man in a situation of ludicrous perplexity; and by that standard alone (to say nothing of any mistaken notion of natural behaviour that may have suggested itself at any time to Goldsmith, Swift, Fielding, Smollett, Sterne, Scott, or other such unenlightened journeymen) criticize, if you please, this portion of Mr Macready's admirable performance.[152]

There is not much in the review which offers material for serious scholarly debate; though Dickens probably would not have easily admitted the word, the paper is mainly expository. Its prime significance is in showing the novelist's earnestness about Much Ado about Nothing, which his letters also reveal. Possibly the parenthetical remark beginning "to say nothing" may be an oblique Dickensian allusion to the play's very title; especially since he is so fond of playing with the word nothing, or the nil-factor, in his novels (see Chapter Five). Unconscious influence is certainly possible in this instance.

---

[152] Reprinted in Matz, pp. 91-94. Though "refer to any passage in any play of Shakespeare's" may be pure rhetoric and therefore should not be taken literally, one should not discount the possibility that it strongly implies that Dickens knew the dramatist's work rather well.

Dickens's article "On Mr. Fechter's Acting"[153] is important for the description of "Fechter's Hamlet, a pale, woe-begone Norseman, with long flaxen hair, wearing a strange garb"; it also eulogized the Frenchman's portrayal of Iago. But not only Dickens's own works should be considered here. Inasmuch as the author was editor of two weekly journals which circulated for many years, Household Words and All the Year Round, one is warranted in gleaning from these sources pertinent information regarding his Shakespearian interests. And one might note from the very beginning that the titles he chose were derived from Shakespeare. Household Words came from "'Familiar in their mouths, as Household Words' --Shakspeare" (letter of 4 February 1850); All the Year Round was adapted from "the story of our lives from year to year"--again Shakespeare.[154] An investigation of these weeklies should prove elucidating, for as Johnson says, "Dickens printed nothing with which he did not agree. This journalistic activity is significant not only in itself but for the light it throws on his development and on the themes of his novels. But the nineteen volumes of the first and the even more numerous volumes of the second have represented an intimidating bulk of material which few commentators have even

---

[153]
Reprinted in Matz, pp. 63-67.

[154]
The references are as follows: "Our names, / Familiar in his mouth as household words" (Henry V, IV.iii.52); ". . . question'd me the story of my life, / From year to year" (Othello, I.iii.130). Dickens has been criticized for adapting both quotations inexactly (or for misquoting Shakespeare), but surely he was consciously intending to accommodate the lines to his purpose and not really misquoting. To cite these adaptations as instances of Dickens's superficial acquaintance with Shakespeare is to misunderstand Dickens's intent; it would be like judging Shakespeare in terms of what he "borrowed" from Plutarch.

attempted to study."[155] In reference to Household Words in particular, Johnson

states, "Though none of the articles were signed, the signature of his style was

so obvious that readers often imagined the entire magazine to be written by Dickens.

(Sometimes, in fact, they were not far from the truth--John Hollingshead says that

in 1854 Dickens read nine hundred unsolicited contributions and used eleven after

entirely rewriting them.)"[156]

Of the articles in these weeklies known to have been written by Dickens

himself, few are germane to this discussion, however. The little essay entitled

"Nobody, Somebody, and Everybody"[157] is interesting with regard to the novelist's

use of the nil-factor and will be considered in Chapter Five. The paper called

"Shakespeare and Newgate" in Household Words for 4 October 1851 is not especially

pertinent here; it was written in part by R. H. Horne. One of the most suggestive

contributions was "Mr. W. Shakespeare, Solicitor" in Household Words for 23 October

1858. It commences with an unusual statement meant to capture the attention of the

reader: "My own private belief is that W. Shakespeare was a hydropathic doctor, as

I mean to prove from his works, and display to the world in a work of considerable

magnitude that has been lately sent to press. In the mean time I interest myself

about the opinions of others, and have just been buying two new publications on the

subject of our mutual friend." (It is of note that although the writer obviously

is not Dickens, the reference to "our mutual friend" might not have escaped the

imagination of the novelist, who employed the same expression as the title of his

last full-length novel four years later.)[158] The principal interest of this paper,

---

[155]Johnson, I, viii.

[156]
   Johnson, II, 712.

[157]
   See Matz, pp. 599-602.

[158]
   Cf. a casual reference of Dickens's to a "mutual friend" in Johnson, I, 572.

however, is that it reveals Shakespeare's acquaintance with legal language,
as the title indicates. Dickens, one may recall, was also well versed in
such legal terminology and employed it outspokenly in his novels, notably
Pickwick Papers and Bleak House. The article also contains some comments
on water as a cure-all that have suggestive implications regarding Shakespeare.
and, to an extent, Dickens. The two clear-cut instances in the former are the
storm scene in Lear and the initial storm in The Tempest; in both cases, the
purging effect of water is evident. But can one justly consider the shower
in The Old Curiosity Shop in this respect? Inasmuch as the storm in Lear had
some influence on the shower in the novel, one can; but probably the significance
of the parallel is so slight that further elucidation would be of little account.

Then there is the paper called "Something that Shakespeare wrote,"
one incorporating the facetious suggestion that Shakespeare was not so well known.
Dealing with Hamlet, it contains three possible mid-nineteenth-century reviews
of the tragedy considered as if it had been just discovered:

> 1. The plot of Mr. Shakespeare's tragedy, though, on
> the whole, well constructed, is exceedingly in-
> volved, and it is made more difficult to follow by
> the circumstance that two of the principal characters
> are mad, a third is foolish, and a fourth is a ghost.
> This is a most talkative ghost. . . .
>
> We lay this work down--immature as it is--not without
> expression of the pleasure we have had in its perusal.
> If we have appeared to dwell upon its faults, we have
> done so because we believe Mr. Shakespeare competent
> to understand them, and still, with a promising career
> before him, young enough to succeed in their correction.

2. Unaccustomed to spirits, Hamlet becomes light-headed.

Hamlet, who leads his friend Horatio--a noble development--
to believe that he is assuming the cloak of madness for a
purpose. . . .

Happening to enter the churchyard at the time of Ophelia's
burial, Hamlet has an interesting scuffle with Laertes
in her grave, which is pourtrayed by the poet in his most
pathetic manner.

Hamlet's Ich accepts his mission, but his Nicht Ich
shudders at it. The play is a tragical development upon
a philosophical basis of the struggle always going on between the Ich and the Nicht Ich in the Human Soul.

3. Hamlet is a melodrama. . . . Let it suffice to say that
of the dozen characters it contains, exclusive of the
supernumeraries, eight are killed by sword, drowning, or
poison, during the course of the piece; and one appears
as a ghost because he was killed before the play began. . . .

The comment in (1) applies as well to the Hamlet motif in David
Copperfield; thus at least one individual is mad (Mr. Dick) and a number
are decidedly neurotic (Betsey Trotwood with her donkey-mania, for instance),
Micawber is foolish, though in his good-natured way, and Chillip as the Hamlet
Ghost in Chapter One displays the talkative nature with an "oration." To some
extent, the parallel or analogy may be traced in Great Expectations, too,
where Miss Havisham is eccentric enough to be mad as well as a ghost in her
own right (a point to be expanded on in Chapter Four), Old Orlick is also
fanatically mad, and Pumblechook is foolish. The allusion to the drama as
"immature" probably is meant as a thrust at revenge as grossly pagan and at
ghosts as products of superstition. As such, there does not seem to be likely
influence; but it may also relate to the relative youth of the hero, and one
may compare the youth of both David and Pip.

The comments on insanity in (2) relate to Dickens's views on the subject. His pneumatological ideas are also related ("Unaccustomed to spirits") and two articles in Household Words may be compared: "The Spirit Business" in the issue for 7 May 1853 and "A Haunted House" in that for 23 July 1853. The humorous reference to Hamlet having "an interesting scuffle with Laertes" in Ophelia's grave relates, of course, to Dickens's own propensity for referring to the skull of Yorick, as mentioned earlier. The comment on "Hamlet's Ich" as opposed to his "Nicht Ich" obviously reflects German idealism and therewith German scholarship on the play (Goethe's in particular); the stress on the "Ich" compares with Dickens's use of first-person development in his novels, particularly in the novel containing the greatest amount of Hamlet influence: Great Expectations.[159]

In (3), the allusion to Hamlet as melodrama recalls once again the melodramatic effects Dickens achieved, for better or for worse, in some of his later novels. And it is not so unfair to Shakespeare for his most mysterious play, if you will, to be termed an "old-fashioned melodrama." In a letter to Forster of 22 November 1846, Dickens calls it that by implication: ". . . Hamlet as he appeared on his seavoyage to England. What an artful villain he must be, never to have made any sign of the melodrama that was in him!" (The principal allusion is, to be sure, to the celebrated straw-hatted friend at Miss Kelly's Theatre.) Other articles on Hamlet may be related here: "Mr. Irving's Hamlet" for 5 December 1874 and "How Old was Hamlet?" for 3 November 1877, both in All the Year Round. Then there are the incidental references to the play, occurring almost at random. Thus, in "The Great Coffee Question," Household Words for 12 April 1851, the writer

---

159
    Cf. Robert B. Partlow, Jr., "The Moving I: A Study of the Point of View in Great Expectations," College English, XXIII (1961), 122-131. There are other prominent influences of Shakespearian drama other than that of Hamlet here, though.

commences with a playful reworking of the to-be-or-not-to-be soliloquy:
"Coffee or chicory--that is the question. Whether is it /‾sic‾7 better
for mankind to suffer the stings and subtleties of outrageous frauds, or,
by opposing, end them?" A paper called "Eatable Ghosts" in All the Year
Round for 17 October 1863 introduces the exciting but none the less rather
quaint notion that such beings as quasi-disembodied souls may exist (though
why they should be "eatable" is difficult to grasp). One may be reminded of
Daniel Defoe's account of ambulatory dead spirits in his Journal of the Plague
Year, for Dickens was influenced by Defoe (at least by his History of the Devil,
as has been pointed out earlier). "Like the ghosts of other nations," the
author of "Eatable Ghosts" speculates, "they are the spectres of deceased persons,
and they have the generic quality of vanishing at cock-crow /‾like the Hamlet
Ghost as compared earlier with the Ghost of Marley‾7. . . . They can put on
various shapes; they are not without a certain degree of acquisitiveness, and
they can produce palpable effects, as though they were not altogether incorporeal."
In the light of this article, is it any wonder that Dickens accommodated his
ideas on the Hamlet Ghost to his own purposes by consciously humanizing the
apparition and employing it for humorous effects? One may recall that John Gay
(and possibly Alexander Pope along with him) thoroughly enjoyed similar bizarre
ghost references in The What D'Ye Call It, even dreaming up the concept of "a
ghost from an embryo." Such eighteenth-century fancy easily lent itself in the
nineteenth century to romantic notions of more grotesque creatures. Fortunately,
Dickens avoids the excesses of the grotesque imagination in discussing characters
who remind him of ghosts; the lightness of his style is a great asset to him here.

Then there are the articles relating to Macbeth, such as "The Witches of Scotland" in Household Words for 25 July 1857 and "Worse Witches than Macbeth's" in All the Year Round for 15 March 1862. An article on "Meat and Drink in Shakespeare's Time" in Household Words for 13 March 1858 offers another reference to Falstaff's diet, recalling the article on the Knight in Bentley's Miscellany and Dickens's own comments on Falstaff as a drinker: "Falstaff was right in his choice of nectar, for says Doctor Venner [a contemporary of Shakespeare's], sack 'is most accommodate for old men, for gross men,' but as to his halfpenny-worth of bread, Sir John was wrong, for sack, we learn, 'is chiefly to be drunken after the eating of meats of gross substance, and such as consist of an excremental moisture, as pork, fish, etc. . . .'" Other typical articles on Shakespeare, to round out the list, are "Shakespeare's Music" in All the Year Round for 28 March 1863 and "Shakespeare not a Man of Parts" in the same weekly for 23 April 1864.

III

After the allusions in the letters and the references in articles which Dickens either wrote, helped write, or undoubtedly read, the next step in determining the extent of the Shakespeare influence, before one begins examining representative novels themselves, concerns the views of other scholars and critics. What did Dickens's contemporaries, his biographers, and his readers say with regard to the nature of the Shakespearian influence on him?

John Forster's biography is of immediate interest, and though many of its comments have already been cited in connection with the letters, from which he freely quotes, it is remarkable that there are almost as many comments of Forster's on the letters to Dickens, comments which relate to Shakespearian drama, as there are Shakespearian allusions in the novelist's letters. Since Forster and Dickens were

remarkably close friends, much closer (Ley observes) than Boswell and Johnson,
Forster's own Shakespeare references ought to be considered here. Thus in
commenting on <u>Pickwick</u> Papers, Forster sets up the character parallel which had
influenced Dickens ("Sam Weller and Mr. Pickwick are the Sancho and the Quixote
of Londoners, and as little likely to pass away as the old city itself");[160] he
then goes on to remark about "his difficulty in <u>Pickwick</u>, as he once told me,
having always been, not the running short, but the running over: not the whip but
the drag that was wanted. Sufflaminandus erat, as Ben Jonson said of Shakespeare."[161]
Another such reference, though by no means a distinguished one, is Forster's report
of the end of one of Dickens's letters: "His letter ended abruptly. 'I am going
for a long walk, to clear my head. I feel that I am very shakey from work, and
throw down my pen for the day. There! (That's where it fell.)' A huge blot
represented it, and, as Hamlet says, the rest was silence."[162] Finally, a long
reference to Dickens and the Lear-Cordelia motif is so striking that it needs to
be quoted in its entirety. Though Forster was alluding to Dickens's short story
"The Haunted Man," his remarks are applicable to the motif as evident in certain
novels as well:

> Critical niceties are indeed out of place, where wildness and strange-
> ness in the means matter less than that there should be clearness in
> the drift and intention. Dickens leaves no doubt as to this. He
> thoroughly makes out his fancy, that no man should so far question the
> mysterious dispensations of evil in this world as to desire to lose
> the recollection of such injustice or misery as he may suppose it
> to have done to himself. There may have been sorrow, but there was

---

[160]Forster, I, 111. Cf. <u>Pickwick</u> and Sp. <u>picaro</u>.

[161]Forster, I, 151.

[162]Forster, II, 132.

the kindness that assuaged it; there may have been wrong, but
there was the charity that forgave it; and with both are connected
inseparably so many thoughts that soften and exalt whatever else
is in the sense of memory, that what is good and pleasurable in
life would cease to continue so if these were forgotten. The old
proverb does not tell you to forget that you may forgive, but to
forgive that you may forget. It is forgiveness of wrong, for
forgetfulness of the evil that was in it; such as poor old Lear
begged of Cordelia.[163]

Complementing Forster's quotations and observations, Edgar Johnson's
comments, in his compendious twentieth-century biography, deserve consideration
next. Johnson follows Forster to a great extent, quoting him at length as well
as supplementing the nineteenth-century biography with pertinent new data.
Incorporating more commentary on the Shakespearian element in Dickens than any
other writer I have come across, Johnson flatly remarks, "When Keats was near
the point of death, 'Perhaps,' he was heard to say, 'I may be among the English
poets after my death.' Matthew Arnold gave the world's reply: 'He is; he is
with Shakespeare.' Of what English novelist can that be said except Charles
Dickens?"[164] I should like to be "one up" on Professor Johnson, however; for
who has been influenced by Shakespeare more than Dickens has? Surely no other
English novelist has been. So I submit that Dickens was influenced the most.

It is of special interest that Johnson's critical estimation is followed
with perspicacity by the majority of contributors to the recent collection of
essays entitled Dickens and the Twentieth Century,[165] as well as by Lauriat Lane,
Jr., in his edition of The Dickens Critics.[166] It almost appears as if the

---

[163] Forster, II, 416.

[164] Johnson, II, 1141. He does not specify Shakespearian influence, though.

[165] Ed. John Gross and Gabriel Pearson, London, 1962.

[166] Ithaca, 1961.

Shakespearian label or parallel is used as a basic argument for Dickensian apologetics. The idea seems to be that if Dickens is relating to or following the Shakespeare tradition, and he himself heads the list of followers, why should he not be great, even "the greatest"? A list of quotations from the first of these modern collections might be interesting to peruse:

For even if one holds (again with Dr. Leavis) that Dickens was-- in a Pickwickian, that is, a Shakespearian sense--more of a pop- ular entertainer than a great novelist, it is still as a writer of fiction that he must be judged.[167]

Like Macbeth, Sikes "bends up each corporal agent to this terrible feat." An animal kills naturally, like a cat killing a bird; and in Dickens's other murders the murderer's animality is increased by the deed.[168]

The Sikes in grey cotton stockings is the same man who goes to murder like Macbeth.[169]

Scott had helped him towards his concept of the Fool; but he wanted to make his fool-figures more integrally connected with the historical theme of convulsion and change than they are in Scott's work. He was trying to return to the Shakespearian Fool, but couldn't assume a folk-tradition. As a result, his Barnaby and Gordon lack the realistic basis of Scott's figures; for he makes them carry a far greater philosophic burden.[170]

It seems an easy thing to say "a mist rose between Mrs. Creakle and me." But no English novelists except Scott and Dickens do say it easily. It is Shakespearian.[171]

---

[167]John Killham, "Pickwick: Dickens and the Art of Fiction," in Gross and Pearson, p. 41.

[168]John Bayley, "Oliver Twist: 'Things as They Really Are,'" in Gross and Pearson, p. 60.

[169]Bayley, p. 63.

[170]Jack Lindsay, "Barnaby Rudge," in Gross and Pearson, pp. 94-95.

[171]John Jones, "David Copperfield," in Gross and Pearson, p. 136.

The iambic thump and the Victorian-Shakespearian diction (Hamlet
in this case--"bourne of all such travellers"--which Dickens no
doubt has at the back of his mind because of his description of
Doctor Chillip, walking "as softly as the Ghost in Hamlet," three
pages earlier). . . .

Not that it is necessarily a bad thing to plunder Shakespeare, of
course.[172]

Were Esther to be complicated the novel would have to be correspondingly
simplified and the Dickens world depopulated. Who would wish it so?
If the real subject-matter of a novel is a subtly dramatized consciousness then the objects of that consciousness will tend to the sparse
refinements of the closet drama. Dickens is the opposite of this;
he is to Shakespeare as James is to Racine.[173]

The important image or gesture or word should owe its existence to
some non-symbolic necessity (as it almost always does in Shakespeare)--
to plausible characterization, say, or likely incident.[174]

I think Jack Lindsay is doing the novel no more than justice when he
describes it as one of the greatest works of prose ever written, a
work which finally vindicates Dickens's right to stand, as no other
English writer can stand, at the side of Shakespeare.[175]

Thus, in summing up the various critical estimations in his prefatory note to

the collection, John Gross writes, "It has become a commonplace to bracket him

with Shakespeare: what other comparison could convey his strength, his scope,

his range of sympathy? If the parallel is pushed too far, it inevitably harms

him, however, since we are bound to conclude that he wasn't Shakespeare, that

finally there is something stunted about his genius."[176] Gross's estimate

---

[172] Jones, p. 143 and p. 143n.

[173] W. J. Harvey, "Chance and Design in Bleak House" in Gross and Pearson, p.
150.

[174] Christopher Ricks, "Great Expectations" in Gross and Pearson, p. 200.

[175] Arnold Kettle, "Our Mutual Friend" in Gross and Pearson, p. 225. The
reference is to Lindsay's Charles Dickens (London, 1950), p. 308. Lindsay,
like Johnson, is not considering the influence of Shakespeare as such, however.

[176] "Dickens: Some Recent Approaches" in Gross and Pearson, p. xvi.

follows from Johnson's statement and serves as a positive endorsement of it:
Dickens deserves a place next to Shakespeare whether or not he was influenced
by the dramatist. One may, however, take exception to some of Gross's
qualifications; for if the implication that his not being Shakespeare means
that there is something stunted about his genius, Gross is being illogical.
One might well compare Gross here with Lane (the second critic mentioned above),
who writes, "In ranking Dickens with Shakespeare most critics obviously have
in mind the Shakespeare of Falstaff and Bottom. . . . They see Dickens and
Shakespeare as great humorists, creating characters of wit, vivacity, earthiness,
gusto, above all unforgettability, that embody and appeal to certain basic human
needs and desires and at the same time charm us toward moral sympathy and
awareness. Yet the best of such critics also see both Dickens and Shakespeare
as great poets."[177] Lane here is not going back to Johnson particularly, rather
to Santayana. In his Soliloquies in England and Later Soliloquies, Santayana
had propounded that "Dickens could don the comic mask with innocent courage; he
could wear it with a grace, ease, and irresistible vivacity seldom given to men.
We must go back for anything like it to the very greatest comic poets, to
Shakespeare or to Aristophanes"; "the most grotesque creatures of Dickens are not
exaggerations or mockeries of something other than themselves; they arise because
nature generates them, like toadstools; they exist because they can't help it,
as we all do."[178] Lane's final judgment, that the greater Dickens critics also
look to the "poetic" aspect of the novelist's creativity, has a basis in the

---

[177] "Introduction: Dickens and Criticism" in Ford and Lane, p. 18.

[178] New York, 1922, pp. 68 and 69.

writings of Lionel Stevenson: "Most critics now recognize that the novel
shares in the emotional and imaginative objectives of poetry and hence that
distortions of reality are justifiable for symbolic or 'mythopoeic' purposes.
Hence acclamation of Dickens as the greatest English novelist has become almost
unanimous."[179] Here again there appears to be an echo of Johnson's statement.

Returning to Johnson's biography after this brief excursion into
derivative critical writings, one finds that he includes a great number of
Dickensian references to Shakespeare gleaned, to a large extent, from the
letters. There are miscellaneous references, such as "Forster hastened to them
$\angle$ Kate and Charles Dickens $\angle7$ with the exciting news that almost seventy thousand
copies of the Clock had been sold. Jubilant at another triumph, they prolonged
their holiday somewhat longer than they had expected to, and . . . made
excursions to Shakespeare's house at Stratford and Johnson's at Lichfield."[180]
Here the connection between Shakespeare and Johnson suggests possibly the dual
influence of these two giants upon Dickens. Pickwick comes to mind first. As
the head of the celebrated club named after him, he recalls Samuel Johnson and
the circle over which he presided with Garrick, Murphy, and the like. But he
also recalls, perhaps first, the circle of rogues headed by Falstaff in The
Merry Wives of Windsor. Pickwick, being by no means as learned as Johnson, yet
having respect for such obscure subjects as tittlebats, and being not at all as
roguish as Falstaff and yet in the picaresque tradition none the less, is a

---

[179]
"The Victorian Period" in Contemporary Literary Scholarship: A Critical
Review, ed. Lewis Leary (New York, 1958), p. 144.

[180]
Johnson, I, 219, 297. See here Paul Hookham, "Samuel Johnson and Samuel
Pickwick: A New Point of View," The Dickensian, VII (1911), 126-128.

kind of compromise rather than a compound. Inasmuch as Pickwick was intended
as a comic character, the Falstaff influence is uppermost. One recalls that
Dickens's love for the fat knight knew no bounds. Forster writes of the novelist's
"last . . . appearances . . . in April /̄1870--as a reader_7̄. On the 5th he took
the chair for the Newsvendors, whom he helped with a genial address in which even
his applogy for little speaking overflowed with irrepressible humour. He would
try, he said, like Falstaff, 'but with a modification almost "as large as himself,"
less to speak himself than to be the cause of speaking in others.'"[181] And Johnson,
time and time again, introduces a Falstaffian reference, such as: "But suddenly the
title came, and he announced it to Forster in a letter consisting only of a quotation
from Falstaff: 'We have heard THE CHIMES at midnight, Master Shallow!'"[182] Johnson,
of course, remarks on the Falstaff influence upon Pickwick--though somewhat indirectly. Thus he entitles his chapter on the novel "Knight of the Joyful
Countenance," denotatively an allusion to Cervantes's Don Quixote, but connotatively
a reference to Shakespeare's fat knight. He remarks that "Seymour . . . had trouble
producing illustrations to the publishers' liking. His first sketch of Pickwick
was a tall, thin man. Edward Chapman at once protested. Pickwick must be fat: 'good
humor and flesh had always gone together since the days of Falstaff.'"[183] And he
concludes, "Pickwick Papers had swiftly ripened to an affectionate hilarity that
made Dickens a master of luminous humor unexampled by any writer since Shakespeare."[184]

After considering Dickensian references to Shakespeare that reveal the
novelist's love of the corpulent Knight and that lend themselves to parallels with,

---

[181]Forster, III, 494.

[182]Johnson, I, 519. In the writing of the story, Dickens found a more relevant
parallel in Macbeth, however.

[183]
Johnson, I, 119.
[184]
Johnson, I, 273.

or influences on, Pickwick and similar Falstaffian figures, Johnson makes spot
references to such comedies as Twelfth Night (Dickens had told of Forster's being
"in the clouds like Malvolio")[185] and The Comedy of Errors (Dickens had remarked,
"We have seen the Comedy of Errors played so dismally like a tragedy that we
really cannot bear it").[186] As for the allusions to Shakespearian tragedy itself,
the number of references to Hamlet cited by Johnson is outstanding. For instance, there was the time that "Dickens arranged a benefit performance of
Hamlet at the Haymarket, to which Macready and other actors donated their
services," for the children of Edward Elton, an actor who drowned in the Irish
Sea.[187] One can well say, then, that Dickens's eulogy of Fechter's Hamlet
performance as the best he had seen was by no means merely a rhetorical flourish.
For if he knew the play well enough to urge that a special performance be enacted,
he doubtlessly witnessed a variety of different productions and had probably
intimate reading knowledge of the tragedy. Thus even his occasional allusions
to "there's the rub" in his letters (e.g., to Maclise, 2 September 1840, and
to Forster, 19 September 1847) are meaningful with respect to his Hamlet interest.
One may compare the time that Dickens visited an institution for the blind where
the director told about a man who had an unusual dream; when this person was informed that his story was based on a dream he had, he inquired "whether dead
people ever dreamed while they were lying in the ground." Dickens recounted the
experience and Forster documented it; then Ley provided the following note to
his revised edition of the biography: "Ay, there's the rub; / For in that sleep
of death what dreams may come, / When we have shuffled off this mortal coil."[188]

---

[185] Johnson, II, 1051.

[186] Johnson, II, 844.

[187] Johnson, I, 457.

[188] Ley, p. 397. See Hamlet, III.i.65-67.

The dream-association was indeed important for Dickens; relating to his keen interest in pneumatology, as especially shown in his attendance at the occult proceedings of Home, in the lady-in-blue dream, and in his references to apparitions, the dream here referred to is especially meaningful in that it suggests further affinity of the pneumatology in Hamlet to Dickens's own ideas. To be sure, the allusion cited may be Ley's only and not Dickens's, but the very fact that such parallels were easily drawn in Victorian times suggests that Ley's comment may even be taken as an insight into the workings of Dickens's own mind. Consider the following excerpt from an article in a journal with which Dickens was associated and to which he contributed: ". . . the persuasion that there are troops of ministering spirits haunting our path, employed as agents in the unseen world, or as instruments through means of which the Deity, in whom we live, and move, and have our being, is pleased to employ in our behalf, is neither unreasonable or wanting in probability. Taken in this light, I say that the idea is calculated rather to inspire devotion, and a religious sense of the goodness of our Maker, than a superstitious dread of those phantoms which owe their origin to the harsh appalling rites of our pagan ancestors."[189] One might ask whether the fact that Dickens arranged the Hamlet performance as a benefit for children of an actor who was drowned had any particular relationship to the pneumatological ideas inherent in the drama and incorporated by Dickens in David Copperfield, a novel which likewise contains a drowning incident. With this note of watery death comes the additional note of a world of the spirit beyond the realm of death. Hamlet's to-be-or-not-to-be soliloquy inaugurates this.

---

[189] F., "Speculation on Ghosts!: With the Singular Circumstance of a Dream," The Monthly Magazine, XVIII (April 1834), 426.

Another Hamlet reference cited by Johnson is that in Dickens's
speech for the Metropolitan Sanitary Association in 1850. The novelist
announced that "the state of public health in London . . . was 'the tragedy
of Hamlet with nothing in it but the gravedigger.'"[190] Recalling the numerous
allusions to the graveyard scene and Yorick's skull, this reference is typical
of Dickens's interest in the more macabre aspects of the tragedy, as well as its
humorously grotesque effects. Whether or not it proves anything about what T.
S. Eliot, in the essay of his mentioned earlier, called the decadence of Dickens
is a moot point; the usual designation of the term decadence, in its pejorative
sense, is to a compulsive, even distorted concern with the decaying, and in that
sense the Baudelairean reference would have no meaning here. Probably all that
the gravedigger-skull allusions indicate is Dickens's natural, and religiously
commendable, concern with a memento mori or, if you please, eschatological tonic.
There is no need to see more in the suggestion than that.

Further references to Shakespeare's revenge-tragedy as reported by Johnson
are of lesser import perhaps. He writes that "in May the Guild company swooped
down upon Shrewsbury and Birmingham, where Dickens kept everything 'under the
Managerial eye,' played Lord Wilmot and Gabblewig, which together were 'something
longer,' he said, 'than the whole play of Hamlet—am dressed fourteen times in
the course of the night—and go to bed a little tired.'"[191] The length of
Hamlet was a factor for Dickens, as it would naturally be for a Shakespearian: it
is the dramatist's longest work. A much more interesting reference, with regard

---

190
  Johnson, II, 715.
191
  Johnson, II, 754.

to what I should call Dickens's first "Hamlet" novel, David Copperfield,
is the following as quoted by Johnson: "My mother, who was also left to
me when my father died (I never had anything left to me but relations), is
in the strangest state of mind from senile decay; and the impossibility
of getting her to understand what is the matter, combined with her desire
to be got up in sables like a female Hamlet, illumines the dreary scene
with a ghastly absurdity that is the chief relief I can find in it."[192]
Here one recalls Sarah Bernhardt's nineteenth-century production of a female
Hamlet, but Dickens's description of "Hamlet's aunt" in David Copperfield is
more closely related. For the aunt is yet another Hamlet, one inclined to
dress in black and to deliver orations on sundry topics relating mainly
to this "quintessence of dust."

After Forster and Johnson, a leading scholar one should consider
is the foremost advocate of "historical criticism," namely, the late Elmer
Edgar Stoll. Stoll was concerned with the theatrical as opposed to what he
termed the psychological; his emphasis has met with considerable recent disapproval because of its so-called "anti-intellectual" approach, but no one
would dispute the point that he was a realist first and last. It is, then,
of primary import that Stoll draws our attention to the Shakespeare-Dickens
relationship on other than "psychological" grounds. In a leading article,
"Heroes and Villains: Shakespeare, Middleton, Byron, Dickens," Stoll remarked
that "for the likes of Sairey Gamp, as Gissing avers, one must go to the very

---

[192] Johnson, II, 959.

heights of world literature, to him who bodied forth Dame Quickly and Juliet's nurse."[193] He thus saw a kinship between the two authors that cannot easily be dismissed. Walter Donald Head, in a recent dissertation, uses Stoll's conclusions as a basis for an extended investigation into Dickens's novels and for pointing out parallels between the two writers. Commenting that "Sairey Gamp and Falstaff have been compared by Professor Stoll, in reference to Shakespeare's and Dickens's dramatic treatment of them, as ' . . . representative of their authors in that so much of their vitality resides in their speech,'" Head quotes Stoll's statement to the effect that "no third author in English or perhaps the world has successfully distinguished and differentiated so many characters, in so large a measure, by 'the tone of voice, the trick of utterance.'"[194] Taking the lead from Stoll, Head continues: "More obvious in Dickens's novels is the tendency for characters to explain themselves in soliloquy. The influence of Shakespeare is apparent in Dickens's treatment of certain villains, and no doubt the influence descended partly through Scott, who contributed to Dickens's use of the dramatic device."[195] Head then refers to "the Iago-like Varney soliloquies" in Dickens's favorite Scott novel, Kenilworth;[196] "for other examples of soliloquy," he notes, "see Fagin's . . . to reveal his character and to point the moral of the evils /sic/ of capital punishment; Chester's soliloquies . . . clumsily advancing the plot and explaining his motives; and lastly, the Grandfather's soliloquy about Nell's

---

[193]Review of English Studies, XVIII (1942), 264.

[194]"An Analysis of the Methods Used by Dickens in Presenting his Characters," unpubl. doctoral diss. (Vanderbilt, 1958), pp. 69-70.

[195]Head, p. 78.

[196]Head, p. 79.

death in The Old Curiosity Shop . . . probably intended to rank with Lear's lament for Cordelia."[197] Deriving the stress on clear-cut hero-villain contrasting from Stoll's historical criticism, Head develops his description of the conflicts in Dickens's novels;[198] his comment on the novelist's reaction to Maclise's picture from Hamlet is worth citing in full: "The basis for the growth of Dickens's symbolism is that ever-present desire to use all possible means of expressing character and to echo and re-echo his themes. One of the most enthusiastic comments that he ever made on a painting illustrates his theory clearly. . . . What an over-crowded canvas that must have been! But its appeal for Dickens was in its combinations of the particular subject of the play scene with the general idea of murder and violence, and in its symbolic echo and re-echo of the theme."[199]

If Dickens got his ideas for villains from Shakespeare, as Stoll and now Head largely believe, then one might speculate validly enough about the possible Shakespearian prototypes of various wicked-minded characters in the novels. Fagin comes to mind immediately; Dickens made of him a "melodramatic" figure, one who out-Shylocks Shylock in his ignominious cruelty. (However, one should remember that the real villainy, murder, is performed by Sikes and that, with all his treachery, Fagin is aided by Monks, who carries through much of the intriguing.)

---

[197] Head, p. 81, n. 35. In his final reference to the Lear-Cordelia motif in The Old Curiosity Shop, he corroborates the underlying idea of my Master's thesis mentioned earlier; his comment was arrived at when mine was, in 1958. His references are to Oliver Twist, IX, 68; Barnaby Rudge, XXIII, 196; XXVII, 254; The Old Curiosity Shop, LXXI, 583. See Chapter Six of this present dissertation.

[198] "Stoll in his comparison of Dickens's villains to Shakespeare's referred to Chesterton's remark that Dickens 'wished to have an obstreperous incalculable enemy . . .' wished to keep alive the idea of combat. Stoll added, 'So did Shakespeare.'" Head, p. 222.

[199] Head, pp. 132-133.

Dickens called such a villain an "out-and-outer," presumably one whose evil fascination transcended, artistically, the superficial values of the common melodramatic stereotype. Head comments that when Dickens "was going to see MacReady act, he sent him a one-sentence note. 'Please be an out and out villain tonight.' And he described Fagin to Forster as 'such an out and outer that I don't know what to make of him.'"[200] The relationship between Quilp and Richard III is a ready-made parallel, but I have found evidence enough to conclude that the relationship was also between Quilp and Edmund, who has been in turn often compared with Richard and who fits the Lear-Cordelia motif in that novel better. Head refers to Vholes of Bleak House as "'very respectable,' perhaps with a hint from 'honest' Iago."[201] Finally, there are other parallels upon which Head draws (he considers that "Dickens used such conventional structures as the Romeo and Juliet theme"[202] in Barnaby Rudge and Martin Chuzzlewit). But the main import of his thesis is its vindication of Stoll's approach. Adapting Chesterton's phrase that both Shakespeare and Dickens attempted "to make the incredible credible,"[203] Stoll went far to prove that both authors were after a certain theatrical concern in many of their characterizations and that avoidance of this consideration would amount to neglecting their intent.

Along with E. E. Stoll, J. B. Priestley deserves mention as elaborating upon the comic effect in the two authors. In The English Comic Characters, Priestley puts Falstaff at the top of his list, ranking Micawber second. This classification suggests that whereas Pickwick is more Falstaffian than Micawber,

---

[200] Head, p. 221.
[201] Head, p. 160.
[202] Head, p. 201.
[203] New York, 1925 (quoted by Stoll, loc. cit.).

nevertheless Micawber is funnier--better as a new comic creation than being a
second-rate Falstaff: "He $\underline{/}$Micawber$\underline{/}$ is not only the greatest of Dickens' comic
figures, but with the one exception of Falstaff, he is the greatest comic figure
in the whole range of English literature, a literature supremely rich in such
characters."[204] But, one may justly ask, is there not something reminiscent of
Falstaff in Micawber too? Are not both inclined to be garrulous, obese, and
though on the edge of rascality (Micawber, for instance, prefers to live on his
pretended laurels than work), at heart innocuous, thus heightening their humorous
impact? True, but Micawber has a propensity for referring to Hamlet and therefore
would better be put in the same camp with his favorite "philosophic Dane"; his
sententiousness argues that he is really more of a Polonius type than a Falstaffian
figure. One might object to a Polonius type quoting the Prince, who after all
kills the old spy; but the counselor of the tragedy does refer to (and quotes)
Hamlet in the play by telling the King and Queen of the presumed madness of the
Prince, and there is not a word in the entire drama to prove that Polonius ever
fully disliked his potential son-in-law. Priestley also compares Falstaff's
Ancient, Pistol, with Dick Swiveller of The Old Curiosity Shop. I submit,
though, that there is a joint influence of Falstaff, Shallow, and Pistol upon
Swiveller. Doubtlessly, Dickens was well acquainted with all three, but the
chances of a "Shallow" influence is more notable since he assumed the role
of the splenetic Justice in the Strolling Players's production of The Merry Wives.
Now, even though these performances came after the publication of Master Humphrey's
Clock and The Old Curiosity Shop, the possibility of the influence of Shakespeare's
Shallow should not be underestimated. Dickens, we may recall from Forster's

---

[204] Priestley, p. 243.

biography, already knew all about Falstaff and his friends when he was yet
a "queer small boy."[205]

But there has been dispute on just how learned Dickens was in his
knowledge of Shakespeare. The main point of attack has supposedly been Edward
Wagenknecht's assertion in his Cavalcade of the English Novel that Dickens
"knew . . . Shakspere (superficially)"; fortunately, Edward P. Vandiver has
challenged the remark and claimed that "Dickens was deeply interested in Shakspere
and . . . his knowledge of Shakspere was more than 'superficial.'"[206] Yet, to some
extent, I am inclined to believe that Vandiver is setting up a straw man, for
Wagenknecht also asserts, in The Man Charles Dickens, that he thinks "there is
abundant evidence in the frequency with which Dickens refers to Shakespeare and
the interest he takes in the performance of his plays, both that he valued the
great dramatist and had a good general knowledge of his work."[207] Indeed, Wagenknecht refers to the Shakespeare impact upon Dickens, on their similar immortality,
in a manner that could hardly be ascribed to one who minimized the importance of
the relationship. Here is a representative excerpt of his from the Cavalcade of
the English Novel:

> Dozens of characters make but one brief appearance in Dickensland, yet,
> like Shakespeare's First Gravedigger in Hamlet, in that instant they talk
> themselves into immortality. . . . He had a great knack for "tagging"
> his characters. . . . It may be a speech-tag, like "I never will desert
> Mr. Micawber" or John Jarndyce's frequent references to the east wind.
> Or it may take the form of a characteristic action, as when Traddles draws
> skeletons all over his slate. Shakespeare, it will be recalled, speaks
> of Juliet's habit of blushing, and Hamlet has the trick of repeating words

---

[205]Forster, I, 5.

[206]Vandiver, p. 128.

[207]New York, 1929, p. 98.

and phrases--"very like, very like." Such things do not necessarily "mean" anything, but they do cause a character to come alive on the printed page.[208]

Earle Davis writes, "How Edward Wagenknecht, The Man Charles Dickens, 1929, can say that Dickens was not too familiar with Shakespeare is beyond me. He (pp. 8-9) apparently bases his opinion upon that instance where Dickens had difficulty remembering a favorite passage."[209] But compare this with Wagenknecht's own words in the volume Davis cites:

> But, of course, his _/Dickens's_/ knowledge was not scholarly or exact in any way, and Percy Fitzgerald has pointed out conveniently that the very mottoes used for both "Household Words" and "All the Year Round" are inaccurate quotations _/Dickens may not have intended the quotations to be exact but might rather have wanted to accommodate Shakespeare's meaning to his own, to assimilate what the dramatist wrote, as it were, since the actual words of Shakespeare's cannot be adapted here very easily/_. Holman Hunt records that on one occasion, when Dickens was asked to name his favorite passage in Shakespeare, he replied "that the question was one difficult to answer, for that he loved so many," and then went on to speak of Falstaff's recruiting scene with Shallow. Well, there is a good deal implied in that. _/Is it possible that this suggested to Wagenknecht that Dickens was "Shallow" in more ways than one, not just as Justice Shallow on the stage but also in his lack of learning with regard to Shakespeare, his knowledge being "not scholarly or exact in any way"? If so, the motivation seems somewhat perverse for a proper scholarly method. Anyway, Shakespeare himself only had "small Latine."/_
>
> The burlesque of research in "Pickwick" and the account in "Nicholas Nickleby" of Mr. Curdle, who "had written a pamphlet of sixty-four pages, post octavo, on the character of the Nurse's deceased husband in Romeo and Juliet, with an inquiry whether he really had been a "merry man" in his lifetime, or whether it was merely his widow's affectionate partiality

---

208
    New York, 1943, p. 223. Cf. a much more recent statement of his wherein he elaborates on the "immortality" he mentions above: "Immortal Memory," The Dickensian, LVIII (1962), 133-141. The article contains numerous Shakespeare-Dickens references (the phrase in the title, a common one with Dickensians, may derive from Hamlet, I.ii.2: "The memory be green").

209 Davis's diss., p. 105n.

that induced her so to report him," and who "had likewise proved,
that by altering the received mode of punctuation, any one of
Shakespeare's plays could be made quite different, and the sense
completely changed"--these things are so amusing. . . .[210]

The late T. W. Hill provides a good critical compromise: "It is not
surprising that Dickens, in appealing to the English, should be influenced by
his great predecessor." He then qualifies the statement:

By this is not meant his literary style, which was indeed peculiarly
his own. Nowhere does he attain to flights of rhetoric and
eloquence reached by Shakespeare, but his appeal is none the less
effective because it is more simple and intimate. Nor is there in any
/sic/ conscious imitation, although in places a likeness may be traced
where similar types of character are dealt with. . . . Dickens's references
to Shakespeare and his works are numerous and he evinces a thorough
knowledge of some of Shakespeare's plays, but chiefly of those that
would be familiar to a theatregoer and not to a student. . . . he
appreciated to the greatest extent the genius of the great dramatist,
as is shewn by his masterly analysis of "King Lear" in the Miscellaneous
Papers.[211]

Surely an author capable of producing such a "masterly analysis" of perhaps

Shakespeare's greatest play, most awesome tragedy, and most far-reaching

---

210
New York, 1929, pp. 93-99, 228. For an account of the content of the pamphlet,
see Irving Browne, Iconoclasm and Whitewash and Other Papers (New York, 1885), pp.
75ff. The idea that "by altering the received mode of punctuation, any one of
Shakespeare's plays could be made quite different, and the sense completely changed"
is exaggerated but perhaps not so bizarre as it may first appear. In Hamlet, for
example, the Ghost's command to the Prince, "Taint not thy mind" (I.v.85), has a
different meaning when the semicolon after the passage in the Folio version is given
full weight that it has if there is modernized punctuation. The whole question of
whether Hamlet's mind is already tainted, for instance, may hinge on the interpretation
of the syntax here. See Chapter Four. (The word amusing above is not used contemptuously.)

211"A Dickensian's View of Shakespeare," The Dickensian, XII (1916), 96. See as
well Dickens's paper "Haymarket Theatre," which also treats of a production of
King Lear by Macready. See the Appendix.

poetic structure has a knowledge of Shakespeare that far transcends a
layman's acquaintance. Indeed, from the account of King Lear on the stage since
Shakespeare's time which Dickens provides in his "masterly analysis," and
especially from his penetrating discussion of the role of the Fool in the drama,
one may even affirm that he was a Shakespeare scholar in his own right as
well as a critic.

My method of classification is not chronological here but rather in
accord with the relative importance of the scholar or critic to be considered.
Thus Hill is important, not just because of his single article offering a
Dickensian's view of Shakespeare, but for his Notes on the individual novels,
comments to which I shall refer later when they are relevant. They point to a great
deal of Shakespearian influence. Now I should like to turn to one of the most
distinguished continental writers on Dickens, Wilhelm Dibelius, whose two major
studies to be considered here are Charles Dickens[212] and "Dickens and Shakespeare"
in the Shakespeare Jahrbuch.[213] In a previous work,[214] I have referred to
Dibelius's points under five headings: (1) direct influence of Shakespeare on
Dickens; (2) indirect influence and similarities; (3) their analogous attempts
to relate melancholia in tragedy or melodrama to grotesque comedy; (4) their
attempts to combine realism and a kind of mysticism; and (5) their common literary
milieu. To recapitulate these points here in detail would be supererogatory;
Dibelius, though recognized as a very important Dickens scholar, need not

---

[212]
Leipzig, 1916.

[213]Jahrbuch der Deutschen Shakespeare-Gesellschaft (Berlin, 1916), pp. 76-83.
[214]
"The Lear-Cordelia Motif," pp. 2, 9-13.

be taken so very seriously since his point of departure is mainly that of
the literary generalizer. He refers, for example, to a large body of material
on the Shakespeare-Dickens relationship but declines to cite it in particular,
as if to do so would be too condescending; he glosses over a large number of
resemblances without fully coming to grips with them. But his investigation was
relatively new at the time, in spite of the feuilleton essays to which he refers
in passing; not much real scholarship on the subject was in print. It might
be interesting, however, to compare in brief the views of Dibelius with those of
Cumberland Clark in a monograph entitled "Shakespeare and Dickens: A Lecture"[215]
and published two years after Dibelius's article. Claiming that "Swinburne often
associated Shakespeare and Dickens," Clark provides a number of parallels of his
own: (1) He notes that both men started out poor and died rich, that both were
born in country towns and retired to country estates; (2) both suffered from
pirates (Dickens's concern with copyright came to the fore during his excursion to
the United States, and possibly Hamlet's fight with pirates reflects Shakespeare's);
(3) both were actors and wrote plays; (4) "many of Dickens's characters are highly
theatrical: Wemmick, Dick Swiveller, Sleary in 'Hard Times,' Tappertit, Turveydrop,
Micawber, Crummles, and Wopsle"; (5) "Shakespeare and Dickens both made Gadshill
immortal" (the former with Falstaff and the latter with devotion to Falstaff); (6)
"in sense of humour Shakespeare and Dickens may perhaps be counted as equals."
Now, there is very little to go by with these more-or-less chance resemblances;
for the most part, they seem superficial. Thus Clark does not hesitate to remark

---

[215] London, 1918.

that "I do not for a moment mean to say that there is any critical value
in these coincidences," as he calls the parallels he cites, for "they are
simply interesting curiosities of literature." He then presents a number
of critical contrasts, for example: "there is no touch in Dickens of that
keen wit for which Shakespeare is so distinguished"; "Dickens' stories
meander along in an indefinite way and frequently are more than improbable"
(though he adds here that "as with Shakespeare we can forgive all defects
in this direction because of the delight and interest we take in the characters");
"Dickens rarely resorts to psychological analysis in his delineation of
character as Shakespeare does. Shakespeare shows us two Macbeths, the outer
one known to the gracious King Duncan and his subjects and the inner one known
to Lady Macbeth and the spectator." Finally, he compares Falstaff with Sairey
Gamp in order to point up the difference in comic portrayal: "Shakespeare
exposes Falstaff's nature to us through and through; Sairey Gamp is comic
not in herself, and not on account of any sense of humour possessed by her, but
because of the funny things she said." With regard to the nature of their
respective sense of humor, Clark may have a point; but his remarks on Dickens's
lack of psychological motivation as contrasted to Shakespeare's "two Macbeths"
seems unsubstantiated and relatively meaningless. Stoll would have thought
that neither author was particularly psychological, except perhaps in terms
of given psychological methods of the age in which they lived. (Thus Dickens's
interest in mesmerism might be called that.) It may even be slightly ironic
that the very "two Macbeths" which Clark opposes to Dickens have been, in
effect, related to Oliver Twist by William Macready when he called the Nancy-

Sikes episode therein equal to "two Macbeths."[216]

The principal biographers and critics of Dickens have now been mentioned: Forster, Johnson, Stoll, Priestley, Wagenknecht, Vandiver, Dibelius, and Clark. And there are a host of others who accompany them in some minor capacity. As these writers point out, the Shakespearian influence on Dickens as public entertainer and letter-writer was prominent. There remain the allusions to the dramatist in Dickens's private life, in his speeches and daily events. Here are a number of such additional facts: (1) Dickens was an original member of the Shakespeare Society founded in 1842 and attended meetings diligently; he also attended other activities bearing on his theatrical interests. Thus Johnson writes that the novelist "presided at the first annual dinner of the General Theatrical Fund, an organization founded seven years previously to help aged or invalid actors not eligible for aid under the Drury Lane and Covent Garden funds. . . . Covent Garden had become a scene of political meetings. 'You might play the bottle conjuror with its dramatic company,' Dickens said in his speech, 'and put them all into a pint bottle.' Drury Lane was so exclusively devoted to opera and ballet 'that the statue of Shakespeare over the door' only served 'emphatically to point out his grave.'"[217] (2) Dickens revered Shakespeare's birthday, considering it the birthday of the English novel. Those who might suspect that he would never have contemplated such a genre influence as that of the drama upon the novel should

---

[216] See Dickens's letters to Mary Boyle (24 January 1869) and to James T. Fields (15 February 1869). Macready, however, was most likely not using his expression ("TWO MACBETHS") in anything like the particular manner in which Clark is.

[217] Johnson, II, 591.

give this statement of his some thought. He made the claim in a speech for
the Garrick Club in April 1854; it is recorded by Harry Furmiss, in "A Shakespeare Birthday: A Reminiscence of Charles Dickens,"[218] and mentioned by Dibelius.[219]
(3) In 1848 he took an active role in securing a curator for the Shakespeare
house in Stratford. Johnson writes, "There was already a project on foot to
purchase Shakespeare's house at Stratford-on-Avon for the nation. Why not combine
this, Dickens thought, with an endowment for a perpetual curatorship of the house,
and make Knowles the first incumbent of the post? The amateur group /of actors_7
should be revived to raise money for these purposes."[220] (4) There is considerable evidence that Dickens read Shakespeare avidly. The late T. W. Hill,
in "Books that Dickens Read,"[221] specifies that "at Gad's Hill there was, of
course, his, and our, prime favourite, Shakespeare, of whom I find several editions,
including a reprint of the First Folio of 1623, besides many commentators." He
lists twenty-four items in Dickens's library under Shakespeare and Drama. One
cannot take Hill's word for it, however, for he was inclined to be inaccurate in
his manner of tabulation. The more competent Catalogue of the Library of Charles
Dickens[222] from Gadshill lists forty-nine volumes of the Shakespeare Society
publications. In a paper about "Dickens Reading at the British Museum,"[223]
William Miller considers six photographic copies of library indents of books

---

218
   The Pall Mall Magazine, XXXVII (1906), 423-428.

219"Dickens und Shakespeare," p. 76.

220Johnson, II, 623.

221
   The Dickensian, XLV (1949), 81-90.

222
   Reprinted from Sotheran's "Price Current of Literature," nos. CLXXIV and
CLXXV, ed. J. H. Stonehouse (London, 1925).

223The Dickensian, XLIII (1947), 83-84.

issued to Dickens and finds Shakespeare's works occupying an important place.
Even so, Hill believes that there is insufficient evidence for claiming "as
one biographer says, . . . that his Museum reading was mostly dramatic works"
and doubts whether Dickens read works of Shakespeare other than those he had
seen performed. Yet he also maintains that before Dickens "knew Macready at
all, he had in Sketches by Boz . . . no less than eleven allusions to Shakespeare." The number is probably far too low. One is reminded of Cumberland
Clark's rather ludicrous estimate that "there are eighteen different references
and allusions to Shakespeare in Dickens' works."[224] The Stevens-Davis tables
list many more and even they are far from accurate since no criterion has been
established for determining what constitutes an oblique reference. The following
summation by Johnson reveals the extent of Dickens's love for the dramatist in
his reading: "As soon as he was eighteen, on February 7, 1830 (the very earliest
date possible), he applied for a reader's ticket at the British Museum. . . .
These days in the Museum, sometimes reading Addison, sometimes the works of
Shakespeare or his Life by Symonds . . . were a valuable supplement to his
brief formal education. In later years he would refer to them as the most useful
to himself that he had ever passed."[225] One cannot **refrain from considering here**
another parallel Clark omits: that both Shakespeare and Dickens must have, to
a large extent, educated themselves. (5) Dickens knew Shakespeare well enough
to quote him whenever the opportunity arose, not merely in his letters. A short
note in The Englishwoman's Domestic Magazine, X, 336, by E. P. reveals that, at
least according to a lady of Dickens's circle, his daily conversation was full

---

224
    Clark, p. 34.

225Johnson, I, 58-59.

of quotations from Shakespeare. Eleanor E. Christian, in "Recollections of

Charles Dickens. His Family and Friends," records the following:

> One day Millie and I were standing on the balcony of our house when
> Dickens came sauntering by. On seeing us he promptly struck an
> attitude, with one hand pressed to his heart, and the other thrown
> out aloft as he spouted dramatically--
> "'Tis my lady! 'Tis my love! Oh, that I were a dove upon that
> hand, that I might touch that cheek!"
> "Which of us /Christian asked him/ do you intend to be Juliet
> to your Romeo?"
> "Whichever you choose, my little dears!" he answered touching his
> hat airly and strolling on. . . . I was horribly afraid of him some-
> times, and told him so once, greatly to his amusement.
> "Why there's nothing formidable about me!"
> "Isn't there?" I exclaimed. "You look like a forest lion with a
> shaggy mane, on the prowl; and I always think of the words,
> > 'He roared so loud, and looked
> > so wondrous grim,
> > His very shadow dared not follow him.'"
> Dickens laughed aloud, and cried "What! do you play shadow to my
> lion? Nay, then, as Bottom the Weaver says, 'I must aggravate my
> voice, I will roar you as gently as any sucking dove!'"226

The shift from one Shakespearian allusion to another in a different play was

thus not uncommon with Dickens, even as here he easily turned from Romeo and

Juliet to A Midsummer Night's Dream. It seems, however, that she prompted

this change here. Her description of Dickens dancing is also worth quoting:

> Needless to say the measure we trod was probably as unlike a
> saraband as anything imaginable; but Charles edified the spectators by
> his Turveydrop deportment, and Malvolio airs of smirking conceit.
> Once we proceeded to tread this measure in an imposingly
> majestic style, when suddenly Dickens burst into an unearthly howl
> expressive of mortal agony. We all stopped, appalled. He subsided
> into groans and moans, accompanied by contortions that outdid the
> writhings of Laocoon. After a few seconds of grotesque facial and
> and muscular performance he turned to Mr. Smithson with an injured
> and upbraiding air, and faltered out: "When next you tread a measure

---

226
    Christian, p. 489.

in my vicinity, be humane enough to <u>measure</u> <u>your</u> <u>tread</u>, and don't stamp down with your fourteen-stone-avoirdupois-weight on that unlucky corn-field, my poor foot. I might be tempted to wreak a dire revenge, and repay you the same <u>measure</u> <u>for</u> <u>measure</u>."[227]

The episode is, perhaps, more suggestive of Dickens as a Malvolio than as a proper allusion to <u>Measure</u> <u>for</u> <u>Measure</u>, but the Shakespearian reference certainly reveals the impish delight with which Dickens referred to the dramatist. (6) Finally, Dickens's love for Gad's Hill, the scene of Falstaff's famous robbery, needs attention. Ever since he was a young boy, he had admired Gad's Hill Place and at length he was able to retire there. Johnson writes how Dickens took walks with his father: "They could pass into the shady depths of Cobham Wood and come out by Gad's Hill, where Falstaff robbed the travelers, and the Sir John Falstaff Inn stood to commemorate the fact. Here the boy would always gaze across the road at the ivied front and white portico of Gad's Hill Place. And here, while his father elegantly informed him again that if he were to work very, very hard he might someday come to live there, the boy would heave once more a deep low sigh of incredulity and longing."[228] How strange it was that Dickens's retirement to this locale was prompted by the very kind of escapade which may have haunted his mind from the time he **first played** Falstaff and then Shallow in a production of <u>The</u> <u>Merry</u> <u>Wives</u> <u>of</u> <u>Windsor</u> to raise money for the Shakespeare House curatorship! In those days he himself had felt "like Falstaff,"[229] and can there be much question that the protracted theme of the play, namely, the frustrations entailed in attempting adultery, affected the novelist's private life? For even as Falstaff was shamed into subservience after his ignominious

---

227
    Christian, pp. 484-485.

228Johnson, I, 19.

229See Johnson, II, 645.

attempt to commit adultery, so Dickens, after his successful venture to do
the same, decided to leave his wife and retire to, of all places, Falstaff's
territory.[230] There he set up an illuminated plaque with a proper quotation
from 1 Henry IV, and his favorite Shakespearian actor, Charles Fechter, provided
him with a Swiss chalet, where he composed his later works.

So far the external evidence for Dickens's interest in Shakespeare
as well as major scholarly and critical statements have been given. There remain
a number of other points minor yet in their way detailed which bear consideration;
they are the numerous articles in the back pages of The Dickensian, the publication
of the Dickens Fellowship, as well as Dickens Studies in the United States. The late
T. W. Hill's articles already cited are representative. A number of other notes have
also been mentioned in connection with the general scope of the influence and
literary relationship as well as in terms of such minute matters as the books
Dickens borrowed from the British Museum. To my mind, The Dickensian is not as
worthy of its illustrious namesake as it might be, though; some of its contributors
have stressed such slight matters as the observation that ever since Dickens created
Mrs. Gamp, the word Gamp has been used in England to refer to the antithesis of the
Savile Row well-furled umbrella. Then there was the proposed Dickens Variorum discussed
at a recent meeting of Dickensians and reported in The Dickensian; that meeting

---

[230]
But just as Shakespeare's mistress of the sonnets may not have been an errant
woman, so his Falstaff may not have been so bad after all. We should bear in mind
that severe temptation to commit adultery is not committing adultery. Whether
Dickens was fully aware of this distinction is, of course, another matter.

did not provide the best answer to Dickens scholarship since some of the Dickensians present thought that prolonged textual criticism and debates about cruces were out of the question. The amount of scholarly energy devoted to profound textual matters in Shakespearian drama was deplored, the members vowing that they would never allow their Dickens to fall into the hands of the dissectors. I do not wish to disparage well-meaning lovers of Dickens, but much work still remains to be done. (When I first wrote these words, I indicated that the time should be ripe for The Dickens Biannual; hardly were they written when an American periodical budded forth: Dickens Studies.)

One aspect of the Shakespeare-Dickens relationship discussed in The Dickensian at length is the comic one. Thus T. M. Phillips, in his paper "Dickens and the Comic Spirit," writes: "In such comic creations as Falstaff, Bottom, or Malvolio, Shakespeare laughs and makes us laugh, but never dreams of warming our hearts." Dickens succeeds in so doing, he says. "We laugh whenever a person gives us the impression of being a mere thing. We laugh at Sancho Panza being tumbled into a bedquilt, and tossed about like a football; we laugh at Falstaff being stuffed into a washing-basket, and similarly at Parson Adams in the same pickle. Dickens joins in the laugh with Cervantes, Shakespeare and Sterne, at that delightful hour in his career as a tale writer, in which he cuts short the rogueries of Silas Wegg by shoving him over the shoulders of Sloppy into his ultimate home of rest in the muck-cart."[231] With Dickens, the human and thereby humane quality is also evident, though; there is not merely slap-stick. Micawber is a very funny man, but we tend to pity him too. So often a Shakespearian comic is amusing only in being satiric. That biting edge of wit is characteristic of the

---

[231] The Dickensian, XII (1916), 101, 131. Cf. Anonymous, "Shakespeare and Dickens": "In the greatest gift of genius--humour--you place Dickens beyond Shakespeare. 'He is the only English writer of whom it can be truly said that in any one line in which Shakespeare was not only great, but at his greatest, this other was greater than he'" (p. 146). To some extent, Dickens's humor may have foreshadowed comic-strip artistry, but only superficially.

dramatist. Dickens, as Santayana has pointed out, is, if satiric at all, poking fun at the whole human race, and thus he succeeds in warming the heart as well as raising a belly-laugh. In this sense, he relates to Kafka, whose grotesque humor at times transcends his satire.

In another note, Helen Roberts relates the "light-hearted and roguish camaraderie of Charley Bates and the Artful Dodger" in Oliver Twist to Dickens's conception of friendship;[232] this very notion may have been derived from Shakespeare's Neo-Platonic views of friendship, not only as revealed in The Two Gentlemen of Verona, but in terms of the similar comic interplay of characters in Twelfth Night, such as with Sir Andrew Aguecheek and Sir Toby Belch. Dickens's delight in Falstaff no doubt prompted similar friendly feelings toward such creations of his as the Artful Dodger. The note of humor is here struck again, for what other quality serves as a link of friendship better than the sense of humor? Thus Johnson refers to "Dickens's delight in his own impish insight into the grotesque,"[233] claims that "no writer so intimately fuses the familiar and the strange as Dickens does"[234] and speaks of the novelist's "infectious drollery of vision."[235] It is precisely this "droll" aspect of his humor which makes it so lasting; it represents a dry form of funniness, a core of mirth behind the straight face. But it is also "humourousness" in the old-fashioned sense of bodily imbalance; Johnson's adjective infectious connotes the biological. In terms of sheer wit, Shakespeare wins out, however. And so Adolf Ball, in Dickens und seine Hauptwerke: Eine Kritische Studie, aptly speaks of "Dickens' Humor . . . in dem

---

[232]"The Idea of Friendship as Revealed in the Works of Dickens," The Dickensian, IV (1908), 40.

[233] Johnson, I, 162.

[234] Johnson, I, 22.

[235] Johnson, I, 162.

Boz nur von Shakespeare, dem König des echten Humors, übertroffen wird."[236]

In a note on "Daniel Quilp,"[237] J. Murray Minck relates the dwarfish villain of The Old Curiosity Shop to the monster in The Tempest (probably Shakespeare's most original character): "He gives us a Caliban in modern attire; rusty black clothes, soiled linen, and a tall hat." Indeed, there is a peculiarly symbolic aspect of Caliban in terms of the Shakespeare-Dickens relationship in that he is the most Dickensian (in the non-chronological sense) of Shakespeare's characters. George Sampson, in remarks from The Concise Cambridge History of English Literature previously referred to, finds that there is something quite Dickensian about Shakespeare's "mechanicals," but the adjective Dickensian, if it is to be used at all in this connection, would apply just as well to Shakespeare's less "mechanical" individuals. If in the history plays we rarely find a figure who stands out in comic relief except for Falstaff, still in The Tempest Caliban has the function of existing on his own, entirely unconventionally. As part man and part fish, he relates to Arnold's forsaken merman or to the demon from the deep hinted at in Goethe's "Erlkönig." In his very proneness to dramatize himself, he strongly suggests something more typical of the Dickensian character than of the more usual Shakespearian type. Therefore, Minck's remark that Quilp is "a Caliban in modern attire" is historically accurate, although we might also speak with just as much justification of the monster as a pre-Quilpine character. For, in the larger perspective of literary values, such a judgment would be eminently fair--some of the early eighteenth-century pre-

---

[236]
Braunschweig, 1885, p. 4. Cf. the anonymous Dickensian article "Shakespeare and Dickens," where Dickens is considered superior to Shakespeare in his sense of humor.

[237]
The Dickensian, XIII (1917), 73-75.

romantics did not intend to be "pre-romantic," and yet the designation is convenient for studying them and, in the long run, not opposed to their intentions.

It is possible, also, to relate many other freaks in the Dickens character gallery to the fish-man of The Tempest: Mrs. Mowcher in David Copperfield, the Marchioness of The Old Curiosity Shop, and even Fagin (unnatural spook of the underworld that he is) fit the bill. But the principal similarity between Shakespeare's and Dickens's character creations is not so much their eccentricity as their appeal to the average comic sensibility. It is the same kind of humorous appeal that may be found in the writings of Smollett and Fielding. Frank Wilson, in "Dickens in seinen Beziehungen zu den Humoristen Fielding and Smollett," has discovered a number of parallels that warrant our consideration; citing Forster as claiming that Dickens liked Smollett best ("Forster, der Smollett Dickens' 'favourite' nennt"), he offers on his own accord a few resemblances to eighteenth-century novelists, such as the following to Fielding: Tom Jones (II.x.2), ". . . in plain English, it was now midnight" (cf. II.xi.9) with Pickwick Papers (XIX, 235), ". . . In plain commonplace matter-of-fact, then, it was a fine morning," and Martin Chuzzlewit (VI, 87), "it was morning, and the beautiful Aurora. . . ."[238] Not that I should want to disparage the influence of the eighteenth-century novel, or Fielding in particular, upon Dickens, and yet it does strike me critically that Wilson is making too much of these slight correspondences. The quotation from Tom Jones which he relates to Pickwick Papers is not so different from a similar circumlocution of Polonius's in Hamlet, and the reference to the dawn in such rhetorical terms has its source in the Greek epic, in Homer that is, and later

---

[238]
    Doctoral diss., Leipzig, 1899, pp. 8, 43.

in the French aubade, which had a considerable influence upon English dawn songs
particularly during the Renaissance. It thus impressed Shakespeare and is best
known in Romeo's dawn-speech ("Arise fair sun . . .") from the most popular romantic
tragedy in English.

In another Dickensian article, W. A. C. Chevalier finds a parallel between
Shakespeare and Dickens in terms of their business-like manner of conducting their
affairs. He concludes: "It is a well-known fact by all who knew Charles Dickens, that
he was a good man of business, that he refuted in his character and practice the
conventional idea of an author as a careless man of affairs. But I wonder how many
have noticed that in this respect Dickens was a parallel of Shakespeare, and moreover
that John Shakespeare the father of the poet and John Dickens the father of the novelist
were also parallels."[239] Coincidental though they may be, these references are very
much related to those provided by Cumberland Clark. With regard to their respective
social statuses, the problem of whether Dickens really thought of Shakespeare as the
author of the plays ascribed to him is worth passing notice. On the grounds of their
mutual self-education alone, we may say that it is unlikely that the novelist would have
questioned the traditional authorship of the plays on any such flimsy foundation as the
notion that a Stratfordian would not have been cultivated enough to compose such drama.
T. W. Baldwin et al. have shown in considerable detail that the school at Stratford commands
respect. Moreover, to reverse the customary tactics of the defense, how would someone
so totally connected with the court like the Earl of Oxford, or with society
like Lord Francis Bacon, have been able to portray the almost naturalistic, domestic, rustic

---

[239]
"Shakespeare and Dickens as Men of Affairs," The Dickensian, III (1907), 44.
There is some question, however, about just how good a paymaster Dickens was, as my
Victorian professor and dissertation adviser has pointed out: Professor William E.
Buckler.

environment Shakespeare knew so well? Nevertheless, Baconian J. P. Baxter

confidently asserts, in a prologue to The Greatest of Literary Problems, that

Dickens was anti-Stratfordian, if not pro-Baconian. Fortunately, this charge,

which indicts Dickens as well as Shakespeare, has been debunked by J. Cuming Walters,

who asserts that there is no evidence whatever that Dickens questioned Shakespeare's

authorship.[240]

"In nothing did the 'practicality' or business capacity of Dickens show itself

more strongly than in stage management, in which he was an expert," Chevalier remarks.

"And in this also Dickens was a parallel of Shakespeare. The very term of reproach

applied to our great poet by his contemporary Greene, 'Johannes Factotum,' is a tribute

to Shakespeare's industry and practical ability."[241] We may bring this to a climax

by pointing to the similarity in their spiritual as well as material interests. So

T. W. Hill writes, in "A Dickensian's View of Shakespeare," as follows: "Finally the

intense religious feeling of both these large-hearted men is shewn by the almost

identical terms in their respective wills. Shakespeare's runs: 'I commend my soul into

the hands of God, my Creator, hoping, and assuredly believing, through the only merits

of Jesus Christ my Saviour, to be made partaker of life everlasting.' That of Dickens

reads: 'I commit my soul to the mercy of God through our Lord and Saviour Jesus Christ,

and I exhort my dear children humbly to try to guide themselves by the teaching of the

New Testament in its broad spirit.'"[242] The first quotation from Shakespeare has

---

[240] "Dickens and the Shakespeare Mystery," The Dickensian, XII (1916), 89-91.
What Dickens had actually said was: "It is a great comfort, to my thinking, that so
little is known concerning the poet. It is a fine mystery." (See Walters, p. 89.)
This statement does not, of course, mean that Dickens was anti-Stratfordian at all.

[241] Chevalier, p. 67.

[242] Hill, p. 97. By "the New Testament in its broad spirit," Dickens probably
meant that, above all, the spirit of tolerance and brotherly love should be held
uppermost.

been construed as revealing that the dramatist, whatever his religious up-
bringing, died an Anglican ("through the only merits of Jesus Christ my
Saviour" differs from the Roman Catholic formula), but such evidence is not
complete; it is more important that, like Dickens, he was a believing Christian.

Another Dickensian item of interest here is Vernon Rendall's letter to
the editor;[243] in spite of the fact that it starts out with a reference to
Baxter's Baconian treatise, the connection drawn between the authors shows how
pronounced the subject was during the time Dibelius and Clark composed their
articles: "It would be interesting to connect the names and work of two of the
greatest writers that this country can boast. Dickens's works--naturally from
his gifts as an actor--have frequent references to our greatest dramatist, and
it might be possible to show that Shakespeare had specially influenced him. The
combination by both, for instance, of woodbine and honeysuckle is certainly
curious, however it may be explained. I started the subject some time since in
'Notes and Queries' and noticed a reference to the point two days ago in Fitz-
Gerald's letters." Of the critical comparisons, J. A. Lovat Fraser's "Gashford
and his Prototype" is particularly enlightening for the Shakespeare references:

One of the most interesting of the characters of Dickens is Gashford,
in Barnaby Rudge. . . . The novelist weaves into his narrative the
story of the riots as Scott weaved the story of the Porteous riot into
The Heart of Midlothian. Lord George Gordon, the leader of the Protestants,
is one of the chief characters in the novel, and Gashford is his secretary.
. . . He bends his master to his wicked purposes as skilfully as Iago
guides Othello. . . .

Gashford, the secretary, is drawn in striking contrast to Gordon's body
servant, John Grueby. Gashford commends himself to his master, as Cimber
tried to commend himself to Julius Caesar in the play--

---

[243]"Dickens and Shakespeare" (letter to the editor), The Dickensian, XII
(1916), 75-76. I have been unsuccessful in tracing the article in Notes and
Queries as well as the references. But probably the horticultural imagery
considered here is of relatively slight import.

"With that which melteth fools, I mean sweet words,
Low crooked court'sies and base spaniel fawning."

Grueby is bluff and outspoken like Kent in King Lear--

"He cannot flatter, he,
An honest mind and plain, he must speak truth!"[244]

From all that has been said, one might well consider that the association of the two authors has become a virtual commonplace. This was true perhaps even in Victorian times; one thinks of Swinburne's delight in comparing the two authors. In the first volume of Parley's Penny Library or Treasury of Knowledge, Entertainment, and Delight, published in 1841, the following inscription is found:

To

the Living Shakespeare

Charles Dickens

the last and best creation of whose genius,

Master Humphrey's Clock,

is herein analytically reproduced . . . .[245]

Was it, then, a common judgment that Dickens earned the title of a Shakespeare II? Compare the following comment in The Best of all Good Company:

---

[244] The Dickensian, II (1906), 39.

[245] See C. H. Simmonds, "Peter Parley and Dickens," The Dickensian, XVIII (1922), 129-132.

A Day with Charles Dickens, ed. Blanchard Jerrold: "Observe the critic's
method. He supposes that Dickens is Shakspere--or has been put by his
admirers by the side of Shakspere--and then cries: 'Here's a pretty companion
for the greatest genius the world ever saw. Hamlet with Pickwick: Sam
Weller with Othello: Mrs. Gamp with Lady Macbeth!'"[246] Perhaps this
hypothetical critic was one following Ruskin, who remarks that "there is
no vulgarity in the emaciation of Don Quixote, the deformity of the Black
Dwarf, or the corpulence of Falstaff; but much in the same personal characters
as they are seen in Uriah Heep, Quilp, and Chadband."[247] And in recent
times Philip Collins has struck the same note: "This episode /in the first
part of A Tale of Two Cities, VI, 42-48_7 recalls Mr Dombey's salvation by
his faithful daughter Florence, which Mrs. Tillotson /Novels of the Eighteen-
Forties, p. 170_7 has already compared with the reunion between Lear and
Cordelia. The Dickensian treatment, especially in A Tale of Two Cities, even
more resembles Pericles--but I would not assert that Dickens was 'influenced'
by either play; if he was, Lear is much more likely. The comparison, I hardly
need add, is very damaging to Dickens."[248] Was, then, Dickens a Second
Shakespeare only at his own cost? The critical statements cited are typical
of the rather flagrant ones. Mainly such remarks tend to harp on Dickens's
loose syntax as inferior to Shakespeare's; yet if we went by Shakespeare's
own punctuation and not that of his more astute editors, even the matter of
style would need reconsideration. There must be as many examples of loose

---

[246]
London, 1871, p. 61. Cf. Gross, p. 94.

[247] Modern Painters in the Library Edition of the Works, ed. E. T. Cook
and Alexander Wedderburn (London, 1905), VII, 355.

[248] Dickens and Crime, p. 332. Collins also says, however, that Dickens
was "haunted" by Shakespeare in the development of his characters. For a
fuller discussion, see Chapter Six.

syntax in Shakespeare as there are in Dickens. The major critical difference would rather seem to be what Ruskin called "vulgarity": the point that Shakespeare's appeal was mainly to the social elite and Dickens's more to the common mind. If the members of the social classes in the respective works of these authors are any indication, the distinction is valid, though Dickens can also have an appeal for the uncommon mind. The pageantry of Shakespearian drama does attract the average citizen now, as it did in the dramatist's own day, but one wonders whether most people feel particularly edified today in contemplating the subject of tragedy as the fall of kings, whether the basis be Aristotelian or Elizabethan.

Finally, one should consider some of the more modern works on Dickens in order to assess his current reputation as related to the Shakespeare influence upon him. K. J. Fielding, in his review of Dickens and the Twentieth Century, considered earlier, writes that "in their way, these new authors are more Dickensian than the Dickensians. . . . The book confirms that several of its contributors naturally resort to the adjective 'Shakespearean.'"[249] This corroborates my own findings. But so far the use of the term has been rather vague. Trying to be more specific, Sylvère Monod, in Dickens Romancier: Etude sur la Création Littéraire dans les Romans de Charles Dickens,[250] asserts that the Shakespeare influence is of considerable import, but then, out of 845 different allusions, finds only 69 relating to Shakespeare. This is a gross underestimation. Furthermore, the Shakespeare allusions are considered as principally to Macbeth, Hamlet, and The Merchant of Venice; but the number of references to King Lear far exceeds those, say, to The Merchant of Venice.[251] The obvious general parallel between Shylock and Fagin

---

[249] The Dickensian, LIX (1963), 45.

[250] Paris, 1953, pp. 39-42 especially.

[251] See "'Fancy's Knell,'" p. 125; cf. Chapter Five.

no doubt led Monod astray. Though it is quite possible that Dickens was influenced by Shakespeare's Jew, this single influence can be overrated. And,
after all, Dickens did revise his views and portray a likable Semite, Riah in
Our Mutual Friend. (It is conceivable that this very shift was influenced, in
part at least, by Shylock's own required shift from Judaism to Christianity; with
both authors, the change comes through compulsion: Shylock has to pay a penalty
in becoming converted, and Dickens has to cope with criticism of Fagin as an
anti-Semitic portrait. Whether or not the influence of Shakespeare is evident
here, it certain appears that way in the recent stage adaptation of Oliver Twist
wherein Fagin decides to repent of his own accord.)[252]

Turning from Monod, whose numerous allusions to the Shakespeare influence
are too unsubstantiated to be discussed at length here, one comes upon two major
advocates of the Shakespeare-Dickens parallel. They are W. Walter Crotch and
Hesketh Pearson. Crotch, in The Soul of Dickens, presents a basis for the very
kind of examination I am conducting:

> I have said that Dickens and Shakespeare were alike in many things. I
> am not sure that a whole volume could not be written upon their resemblances.
> They were akin in that strange tenacity which, coupled with a keen eye to
> the business side of life, enabled Shakespeare to retire a rich man at
> the close of his days to his native town; just as Dickens, before he
> died, bought the house at Gad's Hill that had captured his boyish fancy.
>
> Shakespeare, who saw trees as men walking /_Birnam Wood in Macbeth _7. . . .
> And how many times has not Dickens made a chair live for us or even a
> door-knocker speak to our souls?[253]

It is the last reference which is most suggestive, for there Crotch takes what has
often been designated as "pathetic fallacy" (the Ruskinian critical term for
applying animate criteria to inanimate matter) and makes a case out for it. Even
as the dramatist imbued a forest with life, as it were, so Dickens vitalized

---

[252] Lionel Bart's Oliver!

[253] London, 1916, pp. 24, 28. The date of publication is of interest with
respect to the other works of scholarship (notably Dibelius's) on the parallel
at the same time.

his domestic surroundings, making a chair come alive and a door-knocker
(perhaps the Gothic griffin-type with the knocker part thrust in its mouth)
tingle the imagination. This is again a kind of magic, not the profound
appearance-reality type related to the witchcraft imagery in Macbeth, but a
verbal form of necromancy, a love of play for its own sake or a Spieltrieb.
As Crotch states, it is the "soul" of artistic creativity; he sees the two
authors as essentially alike in their ability to have their imagination rule
over matter. Thus he writes: "Shakespeare, indeed, quite clearly held the
belief--an old one in the world's history--that to man had been given power
over matter, and in the mouth of Prospero he has placed the enunciation of
a dogma."[254] It is, lastly, gratifying to know that Crotch was anticipating
this work of my own when he wrote, "Dickens and Shakespeare were alike in many
things. I am not sure that a whole volume could not be written upon their
resemblances."

Hesketh Pearson, like Crotch, also writes ardently of the Shakespeare-
Dickens relationship, although more critically:

> If Dickens indulged in more self-pity than Shakespeare, and much more
> than Scott, to mention the only two writers in English who are in his
> creative class, it is because he was an actor by temperament; he
> allowed his emotions to run away with him, and too easily saw himself
> as the central figure in a sentimental drama. The fact that the most
> popular play ever written is Hamlet, its stage popularity being due to
> the ambition of nearly every actor to play the leading part, is a sure
> sign, not only that self-pity is the commonest of human emotions, but
> that it finds a perfect outlet in self-dramatisation, which is the ob-
> verse of exhibitionism, which is another term for acting. Dickens was
> at his happiest on the stage. . . .

254
  Crotch, p. 28.

> Sam /Weller_7 was the making of the book, but most modern readers
> feel that he comes near to unmaking it. No famous comic character
> in fiction is less funny, except Touchstone, of whom there is
> mercifully nothing like so much. For us the greatest creation in
> the work is Sam's father, Tony Weller, whose description of his
> wife's death is almost worthy to stand beside Mistress Quickly's
> description of Falstaff.[255]

Thus our attention is drawn again to a possible influence of the description

of Falstaff's death upon Dickens. If such is evident with Pickwick Papers,

it is also possible in The Old Curiosity Shop, for both novels preceded the

references in Dickens's letters to Morgann's essay on Falstaff with the

commentary, already cited, on how the Knight succumbed.

A more intriguing recent approach than either Crotch's or Pearson's

is that of J. F. G. Heerma van Voss-Moeton, however, in an article called

"Tears in Literature: Particularly in Dickens."[256] One may be reminded, by verbal

contrast, of Margaret Webster's Shakespeare Without Tears:[257]

> First of all, I would like to have it understood that there is no
> reason to be ashamed of shedding tears. Shakespeare's men frequently
> burst into passionate tears and in the sixteenth century this was con-
> sidered quite normal. In the first meeting between Hamlet and Horatio,
> Hamlet does not recognize the latter because his eyes are dim with
> tears. Referring to this Granville Barker says: "I do not know when
> it first became 'the thing' for Englishmen not to cry."
>
> Again when Antonio takes leaves /sic_7 of Bassanio, he weeps /Merchant
> of Venice, II.viii.46_7. In Julius Caesar, Mark Antony speaks of
> "gracious drops," i.e. holy pious tears when the proper cry at the
> betrayal of Caesar / III.ii.198_7. In King Lear, Shakespeare speaks

---

[255] Pearson, pp. 241 and 37.

[256] The Dickensian, LVIII (1962), 182-187.

[257] Rev. ed., Cleveland, 1955.

of: the "holy water" in Cordelia's eyes /IV.iii.32/. Tears
in Shakespeare often point to the awakening of the soul. In
his indignation about the behaviour of his daughters Lear says:
"O let not women's weapons, waterdrops, stain my man's cheeks"
/II.iv.280/. . . . His soul has not yet awakened, i.e. he has
not proceeded beyond his own grief, but as soon as, in the storm
on the heath, he regards his poor faithful fool for the first
time with feelings of love, he can weep and his tears show him
the way to prayer, even prayer for his fellowmen /III.iv.27/.
In the tragedy of Macbeth where there is no repentance, there
are no tears; only horror and despair.

In Measure for Measure, Shakespeare depicts the angels as weeping
about man's follies / II.ii.122 /:

> "But man, proud man,
> Dress'd in a little brief authority,
> Most ignorant of what he's most assured,
> His glassy essence, like an angry ape,
> Plays such fantastic tricks before high heaven
> As make the angels weep. . . ."[258]

Dickens referred to the concept of angels weeping in his work, and he
probably derived the idea from Shakespeare. There are numerous instances
of tears flowing from the novelist's characters. A passage by Hans
Christian Andersen describing a play in which Dickens acted bears repeating:
"A prologue (in a mist) was recited by Dickens. Scenery in the second act
with snow falling through the air very beautiful. . . . The piece was
well played, the author performing the part of the happy lover, Dickens
that of the unhappy one, which is the main part. He showed himself to be
a quite remarkable actor, so free from all those mannerisms one finds in
England and France just in tragic parts. It was so true, so natural. . . .
The death-scene so moving I burst into tears at it." Here the image of
snow falling and the moving death-scene recalls the final scenes of The

---

258
    Van Voss-Moeton, p. 82. Cf. the tears of Homeric heroes in The Iliad.

Old Curiosity Shop; likewise, the theatrical setting with Dickens playing
the main role contributes to the reflection of King Lear in that novel.[259]
Still another paper of value in this connection is that entitled "Mr. W.
Shakespeare, Solicitor" in Household Words, which has been considered earlier.
Believing that Dickens had knowledge of the healing effects of hydropathy,
what would now more likely be called hydrotherapy, the anonymous author of this
article (as well as a book on hydropathic elements in Shakespeare) contends
that there is sufficient data to assume that the dramatist knew of the healing
qualities of water, whether consciously or not, and that such therapy was
evident in his time. He points to the water-cure ("sea-change") of The
Tempest, the dream of a cold water bath by the Duke of Clarence, King Lear's
cooling shower in the storm with his invocation to the watery powers that be
to drench him ("Pour on, I will endure"), and to such sensitive aquatic
references as "the cold brook candied with ice." But he fails to mention, at
least in this article, one which Dickens most probably read, that tears form
a vital part of hydropathy, perhaps being the most cathartic form of relief
man has in communion with Nature. Thus the "holy water" in Cordelia's eyes,
to which J. F. G. Heerma van Voss-Moeton has referred, reflects an additional
cure by water, one already intimated in her friend the Fool's reminder to the
weakening King that "court Holy-water in a dry house is better than this rain-
water out o' door" (III.ii.10). The implicit analogous relationship to the
spiritual effects of Christian baptism, especially here ab volo, is evident
in the ancient tradition of the purification rite as found also in heathen
fertility customs and utilized in our century by T. S. Eliot in the final

---

259
    See my "'Fancy's Knell,'" p. 125. Edgar Johnson, by describing The
Old Curiosity Shop in terms of a Märchen, prompts the Dickens-Andersen
relationship in literary study.

section of The Wasteland ("What the Thunder Said").

Such a concern with water, tears, and their spiritual effects represents
Shakespeare's capacity to deal with Nature, and likewise Dickens's. Thus K.
J. Fielding, in commenting on Pickwick Papers, acknowledges that "in the words
of the earlier critics of Shakespeare, it deals with Nature. . . . Dickens
gives a picture of manners and life. His swift changes from grave to gay can
be justified by Dr. Johnson's verdict on Shakespeare's intermingling of comic
and tragic scenes."[260]

A fitting ending to this discussion of Dickens's knowledge of the
dramatist might well be to return to the novelist, to some of his personal remarks
in speeches and interviews. Consider the following address he delivered at the
Birmingham and Midland Institute (27 September 1869):

> The one, serviceable, safe, certain, remunerative, attainable quality
> in every study and in every pursuit is the quality of attention. My
> own invention or imagination, such as it is, I can most truthfully
> assure you, would never have served me as it has, but for the habit
> of common-place, humble, patient, daily, toiling, drudging attention.
> Genius, vivacity, quickness of penetration, brilliancy in association
> of ideas—such mental qualities, like the qualities of the apparition
> of the externally armed head in Macbeth, will not be commanded; but
> attention, after due term of submissive service, always will.
>
> Well, ladies and gentlemen, I have done. . . . I could not say to
> myself when I began just now, in Shakespeare's line:
>
>> "I will be Bright and shine in gold,"
>
> but I could say to myself, and I did say to myself, "I will be as
> natural and as easy as I possibly can, because my heart has long been
> in my subject . . . ."[261]

260
    Fielding, pp. 22-23.

261From a manuscript in the collection of the John M. Olin Library of Cornell
University, pp. 13, 14. Cf. Titus Andronicus, II.i.19 (Shakespeare has "pearl
and gold"). The address is reprinted by K. J. Fielding in The Speeches of Charles
Dickens (Oxford, 1960), pp. 397-408, with minor changes in punctuation. For other
Shakespearian allusions in the speeches, see pp. 63-64, 74, 79, 93, 100, 187, 202,
216-219 especially.

Compare with these a few of the episodes Johnson tells of, such as Dickens's visit
with the chief executive of the United States: "The President rose, and said, 'Is
this Mr. Dickens?' 'Sir, it is.' 'I am astonished to see so young a man, Sir,' said
the President. Dickens smiled, and thought of returning the compliment, but the
President looked so worn and jaded 'that it stuck in my throat like Macbeth's amen.'"[262]
Johnson further writes that "the great dinner of Tuesday, February 1st [1843], was
the public climax of the novelist's reception at Boston. . . . The speaking began with
an eloquent introduction by Josiah Quincy, Jr. Quoting Falstaff, he said, 'If the
rascal have not [sic] given me medicines to make me love him, I'll be hanged: it
could not be else--I have drunk medicines."[263] Though Dickens did not say this himself,
he might have easily; Quincy was, in effect, speaking for him.

Finally, a reference to John T. Winterich's An American Friend of Dickens may
serve as a link to the pages following. Thomas F. Madigan, presumably speaking for
Winterich in the preface, refers to Dickens as "the greatest portrayer of character
in the English language since Shakespeare,"[264] a view which has been echoed throughout
the pages preceding. Included in the volume is a facsimile letter from Dickens to Dr.
Elisha Bartlett of 26 December 1850 wherein the author refers to himself impersonally:
"I suppose I may congratulate you on your appointment to a chair in the New York
University? It has a pleasant sound in my ears. . . . Have you read David Copperfield
. . . ? They tell me that he bestowed a great deal of time upon it, and took an un-
speakable interest and pleasure in its composition."[265] Consequently, Copperfield,
considered by its inventor to be his favorite, now deserves attention first of all.

---

[262]Johnson, I, 400.

[263] Johnson, I, 375.

[264]New York, 1933, p. i.

[265] Winterich, p. 11.

CHAPTER THREE:

THE INDEBTEDNESS TO SHAKESPEARE IN

DAVID COPPERFIELD

Wilkins Micawber, credited by J. B. Priestley as being the greatest English
comic character since Falstaff, makes one of his characteristic pronouncements
in the fifty-second chapter of David Copperfield: "As the philosophic Dane
observes, with that universal applicability which distinguishes the illustrious
ornament of the Elizabethan Era, worse remains behind." He is thereby alluding to
Prince Hamlet's contention "I must be cruel, only to be kind: / Thus bad begins
and worse remains behind" (III.iv.178). The two characters are very different indeed:
Micawber is expressing his optimism; Hamlet, an ironic sense of pessimism. Is Micawber
consciously parodying Hamlet? Or did perhaps Dickens intend him to do so for the
reader's benefit, but without his character's full awareness? These questions will be
considered later at some length. All that is necessary to say now is that the
reference constitutes a factual influence, that Hamlet's words, having universal
applicability, fit Micawber's modified use of them, and that Dickens uses this
quotation to persuade the reader that his character may indeed be related to Hamlet.
The quotation, furthermore, becomes illustrative of that very universal applicability
that supports my view concerning a basic Hamlet influence upon Dickens--not just
in David Copperfield, but in Great Expectations and other novels as well.

141

That the novelist, in the disguise of Micawber, recognized Hamlet as having such far-reaching appeal and creative adaptability may be an indication that he was conscious of his great indebtedness to Shakespeare in the novels. His statement that he found the dramatist, especially in Hamlet, such an "unspeakable source of delight" (letter to Forster, 22 March 1842) could be augmented, then, to say that the dramatist's works were for the novelist a truly analyzable source of thematic material. Micawber's allusion may therefore serve as a useful starting point for a more extended investigation of the Shakespearian elements, particularly those from Hamlet, in Dickens's favorite and most autobiographical novel. So I should like to begin with David Copperfield, considering the novel first in terms of plot structure and, second, with regard to character relationships. In covering the first part, I shall rely largely upon Dickens's chapter-headings as a means of determining the relation of chapter division to plot structure, thereby taking into account the organization deliberately indicated by the novelist. With Great Expectations, a more basic structural device is provided in the three stages of Pip's development, but Dickens also clearly indicates that there are larger divisions in David Copperfield by means of what may be called "structured descriptions."[266]

In support of my discussion of the plot, I am presenting two lists: the first representing a breakdown of the chapter-headings, the second providing characteristic Shakespearian quotations in the novel. When I commence finally with my study of

---

[266] Mainly thinking in terms of the formal characteristics, Richard Lettis and William E. Morris tell of "what is increasingly often described as Dickens's greatest novel." See Assessing Great Expectations, ed. Lettis and Morris (San Francisco, 1960), p. vii. Great Expectations is more theatrically effective, I agree, but when the structure of David Copperfield is more clearly defined, its power may allow it to compete more significantly for first place. James R. Kincaid has another study of this novel's structure to be compared with mine: "The Darkness of David Copperfield," Dickens Studies, I (1965), 65-75.

character relationships, I shall present a diagram to serve as an aid to
understanding personality developments and interrelationships in terms of
the Hamlet elements. With regard to the list of quotations from and allusions
to Shakespeare in the novel, we might note that a number of the more explicit
ones have already been pointed out by the late T. W. Hill in his glossarial lists
on Dickens's novels. A reference to an allusion discussed by Hill, however briefly,
has an asterisk before it. This procedure will then be continued with the commentary
on Great Expectations and Martin Chuzzlewit, though not in Chapter Six with The
Old Curiosity Shop since that is mainly a recapitulation of my master's thesis.
Hill has separate articles on each novel, and his comments are sometimes pertinent.
He made no attempt to be as comprehensive in his listing of Shakespearian
references as I have (though it is quite possible that even I may not have found all).
Certainly the number of oblique allusions to the dramatist's works that I have
noticed shows that the account given by either Stevens or Monod, or even that
furnished most recently by Earle Davis,[267] falls far short of the actual mark.
Stevens and those following him believe that there are just sixty-nine
references to the works of Shakespeare in all of the output of Dickens. My study

---

[267]
    Davis writes of "more than 170" references to Dickens in the novels. He
thus finds more than one hundred more references than Stevens did. See The
Flint and the Flame: The Artistry of Charles Dickens (Columbia, Mo., 1963), p.
313, n. 15. He adds that "Dickens refers to Shakespeare more than to any other
writer" and claims that the "favorite Shakespearian plays were those in which
Macready distinguished himself, Richard III and Macbeth" (p. 60). But my
studies have indicated clearly that Dickens refers much more often to Hamlet
and King Lear. (I suspect that Davis cites the two plays he does because of
the crippled Richard and the weird sisters, who would seem to be particularly
related to Dickensian eccentrics. Davis's work is still, however, of considerable
value.)

shows that there are approximately two-thirds that number in a single novel.

In my list of references, I have included a number which at first reading may appear to be too speculative for consideration. Such allusions are singled out with minus signs before their numbers. After the quotation I have entered both the chapter number, in roman numerals, and the page number, in arabic numerals (since editions differ), then have included a commentary within brackets. If the quotation from Shakespeare alluded to by Dickens is not obvious, I have provided that too. In certain cases a relatively long gloss was called for; in others a summary statement was deemed sufficient. Cross-references cited are often of considerable importance, for the full impact of the Shakespearian source may not emerge unless a particular reference is seen in relation to others.

I

In the plot structure of David Copperfield following, I have made a basic five-fold division that has not yet been pointed out by Dickens scholars. Whether it will be found useful or whether it truly relates to Dickens's intent in the setting up of his chapter-headings—these are problems to be answered in the course of my analysis (though perhaps I ought to add right away that if I did not imagine that the novelist himself intended a particular matter, I would not be considering it here). The novelist did not leave a detailed report of his intentions. To an extent, the serialization of the novels may serve as a basis for ascertaining the correct structure, though in terms of the finished novel such considerations would be somewhat irrelevant: they pertain more to the writing of the work than to the final product. Internal evidence does show, however, that a five-fold division was intended. If I cannot deny that other types of structural divisions can be set up justifiably, what I must maintain is that the groupings I suggest are present and that Dickens indicated breaks in his novel by repeated introductions of the novel's main form in miniature units. I discern five beginnings and, corresponding to them, five ends in the novel: each of the five parts constitutes a whole and employs the narrative method characteristic of the entire novel. Just as Shakespeare's play-within-the-play has its role as a major factor in the drama,[268] these five novelettes "act" their parts in providing substance for later developments or, in the case of the fifth, in extracting final resolutions and meanings from the other four. Now, within each of these five sections there is a sub-section set off from the larger unit, indeed to some extent defining the boundary of the larger grouping: this is the "structured description," a cluster of chapter-headings that comprises a smaller unit in itself. The criterion of the sub-section is the first and last chapter-headings seen together as forming a beginning and an end, a birth of activity and a cessation of activity leading to a rebirth. A glance at the outline provided should clarify this division without any difficulty. That, on the surface, only the headings themselves are involved should be no deterrent since their purpose is to categorize their content; hence what is intimated in the heading signifies a basic formal pattern in the text.

This is how Dickens goes about it. He commences in the first chapter with an account of David's birth; this chapter naturally also serves as the first part of the first little novel-within-the-novel. The first six chapters serve as one such structural unit in a most revealing way: as David gradually grows, the respective lengths of the chapter-headings grow in accord, viz.:

268
    Charles R. Forker, in "Shakespeare's Theatrical Symbolism and its Function in Hamlet," Shakespeare Quarterly, XIV (1963), 215-229, has the most recent account of the play's movement: "ULTIMATE REALITY--ACTUAL WORLD--PLAY WORLD--PLAY-WITHIN-THE-PLAY WORLD" (p. 216n).

I. I am Born.

II. I Observe.

III. I Have a Change.

IV. I Fall into Disgrace.

V. I am Sent Away from Home.

VI. I Enlarge my Circle of Acquaintances.

The word Enlarge in VI is seemingly the key for this "organic" structure, which abruptly ends with the seventh chapter; this is indicated for us not only by a shorter (and unrelated) length of the line, but in that the word I is no longer used. David has left home for Salem House, and there is a natural break in the meaning pattern as well as the chapter-heading pattern. One might compare the corresponding relationship of meaning to visual artifice in the structure of the Petrarchan sonnet. David's break from home at this point serves as a kind of death to the old life and a beginning of a new one. Consequently, we have in miniature a story-within-a-story from Chapter One through Chapter Six. One may call the division anything one likes, but the fact remains that it is there and seems indicative of Dickens's conscious intent.

The second major part (one might advisedly use Dickens's own term in Great Expectations, namely, stage) begins with Chapter Fifteen with a return to the start of the novel form, metaphorically. "Another Beginning" reads the chapter-heading. For David, this is symbolic of another start in life, a more abrupt one than that separating him from his home when he went to Salem House. After this chapter, a natural break does not come until Chapter Eighteen, where there is a "Retrospect." If there seems to be not enough justification for pointing this out here as a deliberate division in the novel, notice that very similar divisions later in the novel bear it out. In the third major part or

stage, Chapter Thirty-Two is entitled "The Beginning of a Long Journey," and
Chapter Forty-Three is entitled "Another Retrospect"; in the fourth part,
Chapter Fifty-One is entitled "The Beginning of a Longer Journey," and Chapter
Fifty-Three is entitled also "Another Retrospect" (as in the third part); in
the fifth stage, Chapter Fifty-Eight is entitled "Absence," and Chapter Sixty-
Four is entitled "A Last Retrospect." If the reader is still in doubt regarding
the recurrence and patterning of these forms, he need but refer to the following
diagram, where I have indicated how each larger section corresponds roughly to
a stage in David's development (perhaps analogous to that in Pip's): from
actual birth and youth to young manhood to adulthood to maturity to remarriage.
In each section, further subdivisions (other than the "structured descriptions")
relating to Steerforth underscore his import in the novel. To be sure, they
relate also to David; but they still truly represent a secondary "romantic" motif
in contrast to the otherwise more traditionally realistic treatment of David.

Does the plot structure suggested reveal any Shakespearian influence?
One might consider whether the five-part division relates at all to the characteristic five-act division of Shakespearian drama (though it is evident from the
Second Quarto of Hamlet, purportedly based on the dramatist's foul papers as
well as prompt-copy, that Shakespeare did not divide his plays into acts and
scenes, T. W. Baldwin in his important Shakspere's Five-Act Structure sees
the classical origin of the division as deriving from Terence's Andria with
its three-part protasis, epitasis, and catastrophe modified to meet Elizabethan
dramatic requirements). If Dickens intended the division I have suggested, and
the unquestionable breaks and parallel structure of the novel indicate as much,
then he surely saw the division in terms of five separate units. Did this have
a particularly theatrical meaning for him? Such a suggestion seems plausible.

In each of the following divisions, the basis for making a break is the "structured
description" or unit of chapter-headings based on a beginning-retrospect cluster. In
the first major part, the "structured description" is only partially based on such a
cluster, but there the initial grouping of chapter-headings is not delineating, for
another principle, namely that of "organic" clustering, is operative. In the fifth
major part, the chapter-heading "Absence" serves as a figurative "new beginning" inasmuch as such "journey" is evident clearly in parts three and four.

    I.   Birth and Youth (I-XIV)

        A) Structured Description: "I am Born"--(I-VI)
        B) Adjustment (VII-XIV)
            1. Introduction to Steerforth

    II. Young Manhood (XV-XXXI)

        A) Structured Description: "Another Beginning"--"Retrospect" (XV-XVIII)
        B) Vicissitudes (XIX-XXXI)
            1. Return to Steerforth (XIX-XXI)
            2. Life's Contrasts (XXII-XXVIII)
            3. Steerforth Revisited (XXIX-XXXI)

    III. Adulthood (XXXII-L)

        A) Structured Description: "The Beginning of a Long Journey"--
                                "Another Retrospect" (XXXII-XLIII)

        B) Marital Life (XLIV-L)
            1. Marries Dora (XLIV-XLV)
            2. News of Steerforth (XLVII-XLVIII)
            3. Domestic Issues (XLVIII-XLIX)
            4. Em'ly's Return (L)

    IV. Maturity (LI-LVII)

        A) Structured Description: "The Beginning of a Longer Journey"--
                               "Another Retrospect" (LI-LIII)
        B) Retribution (LII, LIV-LVII)
            1. Micawber's Vindication (LI, LIV, LVII)
            2. Steerforth's Death (LV-LVI)

    V. Remarriage (LVIII-LXIV)

        A) Structured Description: "Absence" ("in the beginning of the change
                        that gradually worked in me"--"A Last
                        Retrospect" (LVIII-LXIV)

A List of the Principal References to Shakespeare in <u>David Copperfield</u>:[269]

-*1. "I was privileged to see ghosts and spirits" (I, 1).

> $\lfloor$ Hamlet and Macbeth were both privileged to see apparitions
> too. So were other non-Shakespearian characters, of
> course, but the explicit references to Hamlet and the
> Ghost in this chapter point to a Hamlet allusion here. It
> is, furthermore, significant that Hamlet was in a very
> special sense given the privilege of seeing the ghost
> of the late King, a privilege denied, for example, to
> Gertrude in the bedroom scene. In a similar manner, Macbeth
> was privileged to see Banquo's ghost though his dinner
> guests were not. $\rfloor$

-2. "My father's eyes had closed upon the light of this world. . . .
the shadowy remembrance that I have of my first childish associations
with his white gravestone in the churchyard, and of the indefinable
compassion I used to feel for it" (I, 2).

> $\lfloor$ The death of Hamlet's father, the Prince's devotion
> to him, the later Graveyard Scene, and the theme of
> Death, which G. Wilson Knight finds central to <u>Hamlet</u>,
> are all suggested here. $\rfloor$

3. "A hamlet on the sea-coast" (I, 3).

> $\lfloor$ The possibility of a secondary reference to <u>Hamlet</u>, to
> Elsinore, and to the Danish sea-coast is evident. The
> echo may be more one of sound than of meaning. $\rfloor$

4. "He walked as softly as the Ghost in Hamlet, and more slowly";

"He spoke as slowly as he walked";

"He wouldn't have been rude . . . ,
he couldn't have been quick . . . ,
for any earthly consideration";

"The delivery of his oration" (I, 9-11).

> $\lfloor$ These are all references to Dr. Chillip as a kind of
> <u>Hamlet</u> Ghost. $\rfloor$

269
   See T. W. Hill, "Notes on <u>David Copperfield</u>," <u>The Dickensian</u>, XXXIX (1943), 79-
88, 123-131, 197-201; XL (1943), 11-14.

-5. "One of those supernatural beings whom it was popularly supposed I
was entitled to see" (I, 12).

> ⌈This reference relates back to number 1. In the context
> of the Hamlet references in the first chapter, it is hard
> to dismiss the possibility of at least a partial influence
> of Hamlet here too. See also number 6, the next reference.
> To be sure, "one of those supernatural beings" could refer
> to another kind of apparition in addition to its oblique
> reference to Shakespeare's tragedy. ⌋

6. "Betsey Trotwood Copperfield was for ever in the land of dreams and
shadows, the tremendous region whence I had so lately travelled; and
the light upon the window of our room shone out upon the earthly
bourne of all such travellers, and the mound above the ashes and
dust that once was he, without whom I had never been" (I, 12).

> ⌈The italics are mine. The influence of the to-be-or-not-to-be
> soliloquy is unmistakable. Thus John Jones refers to the
> passage "which Dickens no doubt has at the back of his mind
> because of his description of Doctor Chillip walking 'as softly
> as the Ghost in Hamlet,' three pages earlier." Op. cit., p.
> 143. ⌋

-7. "One Sunday night my mother reads to Peggotty and me in there, how
Lazarus was raised up from the dead. And I am so frightened that
they are afterwards obliged to take me out of bed, and show me the
quiet churchyard out of the bedroom window, with the dead all lying
in their graves at rest, below the solemn moon" (II, 14).

> ⌈This is another oblique allusion to the Hamlet Ghost and
> especially to its religious nature, its references to the
> Sacraments of the Church, and other New Testament allusions
> in the play. ⌋

-8. "'But if you marry a person, and the person dies, why then you may
marry another person, mayn't you, Peggotty?'
'You MAY,' says Peggotty, 'if you choose, my dear. That's a matter
of opinion'" (II, 16).

> ⌈In the larger context of the many Hamlet references, in
> Chapter One especially, this interchange reflects the great
> concern Hamlet shows at the beginning of the drama over
> his mother's hasty remarriage. The same question arises
> in Webster's The Duchess of Malfi. It is hard to believe
> that there is not some echo of Hamlet here, be it ever so
> slight. ⌋

-9. "'Did you give your son the name of Ham, because you lived in a sort of ark?' Mr. Peggotty seemed to think it a deep idea, but answered--'No sir. I never gave him no name'" (III, 31).

> *[If Mr. Peggotty did not give him his name and, in effect, denied that there was a Ham-ark relationship in this case, perhaps the name derived from Shakespeare's tragedy obliquely. If so, the echo would seem to be entirely linguistic, phonemic not semantic. The sound of the word Hamlet could very well have had a mnemonic effect upon Dickens. Compare "a hamlet on the sea-coast" (I, 3) and "nobody had the least idea of the etymology" (III, 32).]*

10. "But there have been times since, in my manhood, many times there have been, when I have thought, Is it possible, among the possibilities of hidden things, that in the sudden rashness of the child and her wild look so far off, there was any merciful attraction of her into danger, any tempting her towards him permitted on the part of her dead father, that her life might have a chance of ending that day. There has been a time since when I have wondered whether, if the life before her could have been revealed to me at a glance, I ought to have held it up to save her. There has been a time since--I do not say it lasted long, but it has been--when I have asked myself the question, would it have been better for little Em'ly to have had the waters close above her head that morning in my sight; and when I have answered Yes, it would have been" (III, 35).

> *[Here starts the Ophelia parallel. Notice especially "her wild look so far off," "her dead father," and "to have had the waters close above her head." These echoes, too obvious to demand explication, are reinforced by later numbers (35-38).]*

11. "Mr. Micawber would be transported with grief and mortification, even to the length (as I was once made aware by a scream from his wife) of making motions at himself with a razor" (XI, 154).

> *[This reference to a suicide attempt is to be seen here as an allusion to Hamlet's thoughts about suicide--though not necessarily or principally about the possibility of his committing suicide himself--in the larger context of Micawber's propensity for referring to Hamlet, as in the very next chapter, and of the novelist's familiarity with the to-be-or-not-to-be soliloquy, as in number 6. Micawber carries "that universal applicability" of the "philosophic Dane," as he puts it, a little too far sometimes. See number 42.]*

*12. "'My advice is, never do to-morrow what you can do to-day.
Procrastination is the thief of time. Collar him!' 'My
poor papa's maxim,' Mrs. Micawber observed. 'My dear,'
said Mr. Micawber, 'your papa was very well in his way,
and Heaven forbid that I should disparage him. Take him
for all in all'" (XII, 169).

⎾Hamlet, I.ii.184, 187:
 ──── "My father!--methinks I see my father."
 "He was a man, take him for all in all . . . ."

 III.i.86, 88 (to-be-or-not-to-be):
 ". . . enterprises of great pith and moment /
 . . . / . . . lose the name of action." ⏌

*13. Mr. Micawber: "a sickly mask of mirth."

⎾Hamlet, III.i.85 (to-be-or-not-to-be):
 ──── "sicklied o'er with the pale cast of thought."
 Notice how the line is part of Hamlet's discursus on
 procrastination, a key theme with Micawber, who is in
 his way another kind of pseudo-procrastinator. ⏌

*14. "The shade of a young butcher arises, like the apparition of an
armed head in Macbeth" (XVIII, 259).

⎾This allusion pertains to David only, constituting part
 of his reflections on his school days. Compare a similar
 Macbeth reference when David talks to Steerforth before the
 fire. ⏌

*15. "Better angel" (XVIII, 261).

⎾Sonnet CXLIV:
 "Two loves I have, of comfort and despair,
 Which like two spirits do suggest me still:
 The better angel is a man right fair,
 The worser spirit a woman colored ill" (1-4).
 Here apparently Dickens takes the central idea of the good
 angel, as opposed to the evil angel, and borrows that without
 incorporating sex differences. Dickens's allusion to the
 "better angel" is recurrent. ⏌

16. "I resolved to go to the play. It was Covent Garden Theatre
    that I chose; and there, from the back of a centre box, I saw
    Julius Caesar and the new Pantomime. To have all those noble
    Romans alive before me, and walking in and out for my enter-
    tainment, instead of being the stern taskmasters they had been
    at school, was a most novel and delightful effect. But the
    mingled reality and mystery of the whole show, the influence
    upon me of the poetry, the lights, the music, the company, the
    smooth stupendous changes of glittering and brilliant scenery,
    were so dazzling and opened up such illimitable regions of
    delight, that when I came out into the rainy street, at twelve
    o'clock at night, I felt as if I had come from the clouds, where
    I had been leading a romantic life for ages, to a bawling,
    splashing, link-lighted, umbrella-struggling, hackney-coach-
    jostling, patten-clinking, muddy, miserable world" (XIX, 278).

    ⌐Hamlet, too, contains such reflections on Julius Caesar,
     e.g.:
            "In the most high and palmy state of Rome,
             A little ere the mightiest Julius fell,
             The graves stood tenantless, and the sheeted dead
             Did squeak and gibber in the Roman streets"
                                    (I.i.113-116);
            "I did enact Julius Caesar: I was killed i' the
             Capitol; Brutus killed me" (III.ii.97-98).

     Compare allusions to Senecan drama or the stoics ("stern
     taskmasters"):
            "When Roscious was an actor in Rome" (II.ii.380);
            "Seneca cannot be too heavy" (II.ii.388). ⌐

17. "But, in the then condition of my mind, where the play was still
    running high, his former protection of me appeared so deserving
    of my gratitude, and my old love for him overflowed my breast so
    freshly and spontaneously, that I went up to him at once, with a
    fast-beating heart, and said--'Steerforth! won't you speak to me?'"
                                                        (XIX, 279).

    ⌐Again, the stoic comradeship in Julius Caesar is reflected
     in the Hamlet-Horatio relationship (especially in Shakespeare's
     reference to the friend as more of an "antique Roman than
     a Dane"); this in turn is now reflected in David Copperfield.
     That Dickens intended a Shakespearian association appears
     evident from David's expression of his feelings. ⌐

18. "Steerforth gave me lessons in fencing" (XXI, 292).

    ⌐The fencing match in Hamlet comes to mind. Steerforth's
     personality as related to Hamlet's gradually begins to
     emerge. ⌐

19. Steerforth: "What is 'seems' . . . ?" (XXI, 302).

> ⌊Hamlet, I.ii.76: "Seems, madam! nay, it is; I know
> not 'seems.'" ⌋

*20. "His ⌊Steerforth's⌋ face was always full of expression, but I
never saw it express such a dark kind of earnestness as when he
said these words, with his glance bent on the fire. 'So much for
that!' he said, making as if he tossed something light into the
air, with his hand.
'"Why, being gone, I am a man again,"
like Macbeth. And now for dinner! If I have not (Macbeth-like)
broken up the feast with most admired disorder'" (XXII, 314).

> ⌊Macbeth, III.iv.106-109:
> > Macbeth: "Why, so: being gone,
> > I am a man again."
> > Lady Macbeth: "You have displac'd the mirth, broke
> > the good meeting,
> > With most admir'd disorder." ⌋

*21. "'Shakespeare has observed, my dear Agnes, how strange it is that a
man should put an enemy into his mouth'" (XXV, 355).

> ⌊Othello, II.iii.291:
> > "O God, that men should put an enemy in their
> > mouths to steal away their brains!" ⌋

22. "'On warning you,' said Agnes, with a steady glance, 'against your
bad Angel.' 'My dear Agnes,' I began, 'if you mean Steerforth--'
'I do, Trotwood,' she returned" (XXV, 356).

> ⌊Sonnet CXLIV again; compare number 15. The title of
> Chapter XXV is "Good and Bad Angels." Dickens adapts
> Shakespeare's conception with a reversal: for Shakespeare,
> the bad angel is a woman and the better one a man; for
> Dickens, the bad angel is Steerforth and the better one
> is Agnes. ⌋

23. "Conscience made cowards of us both" (XXV, 361).

> ⌊Hamlet, III.i.83 (to-be-or-not-to-be): "Thus conscience
> does make cowards of us all." ⌋

24. "A very awful lady in a black velvet dress, and a great black velvet hat, whom I remember as looking like a near relation of Hamlet's--say his aunt" (XXV, 361).

"The gloom of Hamlet's aunt" (XXV, 363).

"To mend the matter, Hamlet's aunt had the family failing of indulging in soliloquy, and held forth in a desultory manner, by herself, on every topic that was introduced" (XXV, 363-364).

"'Oh! There is nothing,' observed Hamlet's aunt, 'so satisfactory to one! There is nothing that is so much one's beau-ideal of--of all that sort of thing, speaking generally. There are some low minds (not many, I am happy to believe, but there are some) that would prefer to do what I should call bow down before idols. Positive idols! Before services, intellect, and so on. But these are intangible points. Blood is not so. We see Blood in a nose, and we know it. We meet with it in a chin, and we say, "There it is! That's Blood!" It is an actual matter of fact. We point it out. It admits of no doubt'" (XXV, 364).

> [These descriptive passages on a make-believe aunt of Hamlet's are important in reiterating the Prince's epistemological dilemma, as Dickens saw it. Hamlet deliberates, does not perform the crucial act of revenge at the outset, because he wants to make sure of the truth; he thus tests the honesty of the Ghost and the supposed bad conscience of the King by the play-within-the-play. The results become the "grounds more relative" whereby he can act. Likewise, Hamlet's aunt, as described above, also wants facts, not theory. Her acceptance of blood as factual relates to the blood-revenge underlying Shakespeare's tragedy. The entire description is comparable to that of Micawber, who likewise soliloquizes (by quoting from the to-be-or-not-to-be soliloquy, for instance), deliberates, and has moments of melancholy when he thinks of blood (that is, by taking a straight razor to his throat). Thus Hamlet's aunt here complements Micawber. But whereas Micawber, though humorous, is ultimately to be taken seriously as a well-meaning human being, the aunt is more of a burlesque of the Prince, a possible characterization of his "feminine" or effete nature as characterized on the nineteenth-century stage by S. Bernhardt.]

25. "'People can't die, along the coast,' said Mr. Peggotty,
'except when the tide's pretty nigh out. They can't be born,
unless it's pretty nigh in--not properly born, till flood.
He's a going out with the tide. It's ebb at half-arter three,
slack water half an hour. If he lives till it turns, he'll
hold his own till past the flood, and go out with the next
tide'" (XXX, 432).

     / Henry V, II.iii.13: "Even at the turning o' the tide."
     Thus John Jones writes: "Not that it is necessarily a
     bad thing to plunder Shakespeare, of course. If
     Dickens got the idea of Barkis going out with the tide
     from Falstaff's dying 'just between twelve and one,
     ev'n at the turning o' the tide', the idea is still a
     good one," op. cit., p. 143n. /

-*26. "There wasn't room to swing a cat there" (XXV, 486).

     / Dickens may have picked up this adage from Shakespeare's
     use of it in Much Ado about Nothing, I.i.259. /

*27. "Also referred to Patience on Monument. (Qy. Why on monument?
J.M.)" (XXXVIII, 546).

     / Twelfth Night, II.iv.113-117:
               "She never told her love,
     But let concealment, like a worm i' the bud,
     Feed on her damask cheek: she pined in thought,
     And with a green and yellow melancholy
     She sat like patience on a monument,
     Smiling at grief." /

28. "They had a lurking suspicion even, that he died of secret love;
though I must say there was a picture of him in the house
with a damask nose, which concealment did not appear to have ever
preyed upon" (XLI, 579).

"'The canker is in the flower. . . . The worm is at his work"
(XLVIII, 677).

     / Twelfth Night, II,iv.113-117. Directly the same as
     number 27. Compare other allusions to Shakespeare's
     favorite image of the worm-in-the-flower, e.g., "Why should
     the worm intrude the maiden bud?" (Lucrece, 848) and "The
     canker galls the infants of the spring / Too oft before
     their buttons be disclosed" (Hamlet, I.iii.39). The allusion
     to green-sickness ("a green and yellow melancholy") is in-
     teresting with regard to Dickens's account of this elsewhere,
     for example in his letter to Forster, August 1846, with its
     account of "male green-sickness." /

*29. "'You have no idea what obstinate hair mine is, Copperfield. I
am quite a fretful porcupine'" (XLI, 576).

> /_Hamlet, I.v.19-20:
> "And each particular hair to stand on end,
> Like quills upon the fretful porpentine."
> The allusion is to Traddles looking as if he had just
> seen a ghost, a reference which lends itself to the
> quotation from Hamlet also dealing with a ghost._/

-30. "'Think, ma'am,' I rapturously began, 'oh! . . .'" (XLI, 581).

> /_Hamlet, I.ii.76 (as in number 19):
> "Seems, madam! nay, it is; I know not 'seems.'"
> The context makes the allusion perfectly clear. _/

-31. "'The rest is with you'" (XLI, 584).

> /_Hamlet, V.ii.369: "The rest is silence." _/

-32. "I was wonderfully relieved to find that my aunt and Dora's aunts
rubbed on, all things considered, much more smoothly than I could
have expected" (XLI, 587).

> /_Hamlet, III.i.65: "There's the rub." _/

33. "I have come legally to man's estate. I have attained the dignity
of twenty-one. But this is a sort of dignity that may be thrust upon
me" (XLIII, 610).

> /_Twelfth Night, II.v.158; III.iv.49:
> "Some are born great, some achieve greatness,
> and some have greatness thrust upon 'em."
> In view of the other quotations and adaptations in the novel
> from Twelfth Night and in view of the representative "tag"
> of Malvolio, influence appears to be definite. _/

-34. "But my mind could not go by it and leave it, as my body did; and it
usually awakened a long train of meditations. Coming before me on this
particular evening that I mention, mingled with the childish recollections and later fancies, the ghosts of half-formed hopes, the
broken shadows of disappointments dimly seen and understood, the
blending of experience and imagination, incidental to the occupation
with which my thoughts had been busy, it was more than commonly
suggestive. I fell into a brown study" (XLVI, 648-649).

> /_Are these "ghosts of half-formed hopes" the kind of
> apparitions David was privileged to envisage? See
> numbers 1 and 5. _/

35. "'She may have drowned herself, miss' . . . . Oh, Emily!
Unhappy beauty! What a picture before me of her sitting on
the far-off shore, among the children like herself when she
was innocent, listening to little voices such as might have
called her Mother . . . and to the great voice of the sea,
with its eternal 'Never more!'" (XLVI, 653).

      /Ophelia's plight in Hamlet was surely influential here
        as in number 10. Compare the speculation by the grave-
        diggers over whether she actually committed suicide or
        not. /

36. "'Maybe the first shock was too rough, and in the wildness of her
art-- That there blue water as she used to speak on. Could she
have thowt /sic/ o' that so many year, because it was to be her
grave?'" (XLVI, 660).

      /Relating again to the Ophelia influence, the passage also
      prepares the reader for Steerforth's death by drowning. /

-37. Martha: "'I know it's /the river is/ like me!' she exclaimed. 'I
know that I belong to it. I know that it's the natural
company of such as I am! It comes from country places,
where there was once no harm in it--and it creeps through
the dismal streets, defiled and miserable--and it goes away,
like my life, to a great sea, that is always troubled--and
I feel that I must go with it!'" (XLVII, 663).

        /Compare Ophelia's distracted language before her death
        by drowning. /

-38. "'She is in a state of frenzy,' I whispered to him" (XLVII, 664).

      /Compare Ophelia's madness. /

39. "I read Shakespeare to her--and fatigued her to the last degree. . . .
In particular, it was clear to me, that she thought Shakespeare a
terrible fellow" (XLVIII, 676-677).

      /The reference is very likely to The Rape of Lucrece. Compare
      a very similar reference in Martin Chuzzlewit (VI, 101-102).
      The length and elaborate rhetoric of Shakespeare's narrative
      poems are the source of the tedium. The use of the word
      terrible suggests Lucrece./

-40. "A very porcupine or hedgehog, bristling all over with determination"
(XLVIII, 677).

      /This is very likely an indirect influence of "fretful porpentine"
      as in number 29. /

-41. "Traddles, who was flushed with walking, and whose hair, under the combined
effects of exercise and excitement, stood on end as if he saw a cheerful
ghost" (XLIX, 685).

          /‾Traddles has been associated with ghosts ever since he was described
          drawing skeletons on his Salem-House slate. Compare the cheerfully
          created Hamlet ghosts in the novel: Dr. Chillip and Betsey Trotwood.
          The allusion is related to the play in that it is directly associated
          with the "fretful porcupine" references in numbers 29 and 40, which
          derive from the ghost scenes in Hamlet. Compare the Hamlet ghosts
          in Great Expectations. ‾/

42. Micawber: " This reception of a shattered fragment of the Temple once called
Man--if I may be permitted so to express myself" (XLIX, 688).

"Mr. Micawber was for the most part plunged into deep gloom" (XLIX, 690).

"His relapses into profound melancholy" (XLIX, 690).

"Mr. Micawber . . . had a mental wrestle with himself" (XLIX, 690).

"A man who is struggling with a complicated burden of perplexity and disquiet"
(XLIX, 691).

Micawber's "vacillations between an evident disposition to reveal something,
and a counter-disposition to reveal nothing" (XLIX, 691).

"'Each in his narrow cell for ever laid, / The rude forefathers of the hamlet
sleep,' '--With the plain inscription, / 'WILKINS MICAWBER'" (XLIX, 695).

Micawber: "If I may so Shakespearianly express myself, to dwindle, peak, and
pine . . . . This was bad enough; but, as the philosophic Dane observes, with
that universal applicability which distinguishes the illustrious ornament of
the Elizabethan Era, worse remains behind!" (LII, 733).

          /‾These references are all direct or indirect allusions to Hamlet,
          whom Micawber enjoys referring to most of all. Compare his remark
          about "a shattered fragment of the Temple once called Man" with
          the following prose passage from the tragedy: "What a piece of
          work is man! how noble in reason! how infinite in faculty! in form
          and moving how express and admirable! in action how like an angel!
          in apprehension how like a god! the beauty of the world! the paragon
          of animals! And yet, to me, what is this quintessence of dust? man
          delights not me" (II.ii.298-303). The next to the last reference
          above is a direct allusion to Thomas Gray, yet in the context of
          the many other Hamlet allusions in these pages, an indirect reference
          to the tragedy is surely here also, one of "the rude forefathers
          of (the) hamlet" being the Ghost--perhaps "rude" in more ways than one.‾/

43. "'Gentlemen,' returned Mr. Micawber, 'do with me as you will! I am a straw upon the surface of the deep, and am tossed in all directions by the elephants--I beg your pardon; I should have said the elements'" (XLIX, 690).

[The pre-Malapropism elephants, instead of elements, with the apologetic statement following shows the influence of Mistress Pistol's likewise humorous verbal confusions. Compare her reference to Falstaff "passing directly into Arthur's bosom, if ever a man went into the bosom of Arthur" (quoted from Morgann). She apparently means Abraham's Bosom, but the confusion is not an unhappy one, for Falstaff was a knight and might well have returned to the legendary "bosom" of King Arthur. Compare the better known influence of Mistress Pistol on Mrs. Gamp of Martin Chuzzlewit; the reference to Micawber being at the mercy of the elements may also reflect the storm scene in King Lear, as also influential in Chuzzlewit. Micawber's use of technical legal terminology, such as the Latin words in esse and in posse (XLIX, 688), reflects similar language used by Justice Shallow (as played by Dickens) in The Merry Wives of Windsor.]

44. "'The struggle is over!' said Mr. Micawber, violently gesticulating with his pocket-handkerchief, and fairly striking out from time to time with both arms, as if he were swimming under superhuman difficulties" (XLIX, 693).

[One of the most striking of Dickens's allusions to Hamlet in David Copperfield, this quotation is derived from Hamlet's to-be-or-not-to-be soliloquy, specifically the phrase "to take arms against a sea of troubles." He originally wished to emend Shakespeare's line by substituting for the first three words, the infinitive phrase "to make arms" (reported in his letter to Forster of 19 September 1847). Forster responded that "swimming through your troubles would not be 'opposing' them." Then Dickens creatively adapted his scholarly, albeit critically questionable, suggestion in David Copperfield, published a year or two after his letter to Forster.]

45. "The tables were cleared as if by art-magic" (LXIII, 851).

[An obvious allusion to the banquet-removal in The Tempest.]

Of these references, the following relate to Hamlet: 1, 2, 3, 4, 5, 6, 7, 8, 9, 10, 11, 12, 13, 18, 19, 23, 24, 29, 30, 31, 32, 34, 35, 36, 37, 38, 40, 41, 43, and 44. The allusions to Julius Caesar could be added, for though they may relate overtly to the Roman Tragedy, they none the less may relate indirectly to Hamlet in that the Danish Tragedy contains definite allusions

to Julius Caesar (see 16 and 17). In a few places, Macbeth begins to rival
Hamlet for first place in the line of influence, especially in the fire-watching
episode (see 20); but even there Steerforth's introspection for the moment is more
Hamlet-like than Macbeth-like in spite of the fact that immediately afterwards
he refers to Banquo's Ghost. Occasional references to Twelfth Night, Othello,
Henry V, The Merry Wives, The Tempest, a sonnet, and possibly Lucrece are noteworthy
but can hardly be conceived of as relating structurally to the form of the novel.

A few of the allusions are oblique, as I have indicated earlier, and may
seem obscure until their signification and significance have been established; I
hope to have done this to some extent in my commentaries and shall continue to
elaborate on these matters in the following pages. Since I have already briefly
considered the plot structure, albeit without specific reference to the forty-five
points of influence, I shall now pass on to the character structure, attempting
thereby to shed more light on the plot structure still (basically the distinction
between plot and character structures is an articifical thing anyway, for whatever
is said about character is inevitably connected with plot).

III

As I indicated earlier, the reference in the first chapter to a "hamlet on
the sea-coast" can be considered only in the most indirect sense as relating to
Shakespeare's drama. That it cannot be totally ignored is evident for the following
reasons: (1) there are also several more definite references to the tragedy in the
same chapter, so that the associative process might help to support the assumption
of unconscious influence; (2) the play Hamlet does, in fact, have its setting on a
sea-coast, and we can hardly forget the sea environment especially as relating to
Fortinbras, to Hamlet's sea trip including his adventure with pirates (marauders

of the sea), and finally to Ophelia's death by drowning; (3) the possibility
of a sound echo is clearly plausible here. (Though a modern critic like
I. A. Richards might refer to it as an instance of "mnemonic irrelevance" if
he saw it in a critical essay, the creative act does utilize such "free
associationism" to advantage.) One might discover a similar sound echo in
the name Ham. For even though the more plausible etymology is Biblical, it is
not very conceivable that Dickens could have incorporated so much of the play into
his novel without also connoting an echo in probably the most obvious place.
Moreover, Ham, in being more like a brother to Emily than a lover (a point
exploited in the story), takes on some of Laertes's characteristics. Although
Polonius's son is more impetuous and articulate than Ham, he dies with Hamlet in
a manner which is somewhat akin to Ham's death with Steerforth (a Hamlet-type
as I shall shortly show). Thus the word Ham is a possible echo of Hamlet, but
it may then be an echo of the title of the play, not necessarily of the leading
character. At least one may consider the Hamlet-Ham relationship to be a minor
influence of Shakespeare's tragedy upon the character structure of the novel.

Who would be next? I propose Wilkins Micawber. This would not mean
that David's impecunious friend is to be thought a likeness of the Danish Prince
whom he is fond of quoting. In some ways, he seems like Polonius; his frequent
repetition of "in short" relates him to the aged counselor's also humorous
remark "I will be brief." He can be equally pompous and theatrical for the sake
of being rhetorical. But certain factors seem to militate against the Polonius-
association. For one thing, Micawber is such an imprudent, thriftless person;
Polonius, though imprudent in hiding behind the arras and crying aloud during the
Hamlet-Gertrude interchange, is still very much of a man of affairs when he instructs Laertes on how to behave abroad. True, one might argue that Micawber is
also that way, grotesquely, and perhaps Polonius and Micawber are good in pro-

claiming what kind of advice should be taken but are not so good in setting the
best example of how such advice should be carried out. Thus Micawber remarks, in
one of his oratorical moments, "Procrastination is the thief of time. Collar him!"
If he had tried to collar the thief in the way he advised, he would not have fallen
so deeply into debt.

Another reason why Micawber probably may not relate particularly to
Polonius, in spite of their superficial similarity, is that his short connective
phrases or interpolated expressions can be traced back to Fielding, who indulged
in similar bathos and humorous character portrayal. Surely Micawber's pontificating
resembles in a very general way the philosophic Square and Thwackum of Tom Jones.
And there may be a definite influence of that novel on David Copperfield. Thus
Earle Davis writes:

> Artistic ideals influenced his plans from the first. David Copperfield was
> to be no journeyman piece of work; it speedily became something special. He
> eventually said of it, "Of all my books, I like this the best." As the
> story took shape in his fancy, he turned to the greatest model in biographical
> fiction available to him, Fielding's Tom Jones. He asked himself: What did
> Fielding mean by the "comic epic"? How were his effects achieved? What
> exactly was he trying to do?
>   There is adequate evidence that Fielding directly influenced his
> creative consciousness. When Dickens' eighth child was born in 1849 he had
> planned to call him "Oliver Goldsmith" . . . . At the last minute Dickens
> changed his mind and called the child "Henry Fielding," a change "which he
> had made in a kind of homage to the style of work he was now so bent on
> beginning."[270]

Davis might have added that just as Dickens named a child after the eighteenth-

---

[270]The Flint and the Flame, p. 158. Davis goes on to say that "Dickens was
not particularly impressed with most of the satiric mannerisms by which Fielding
made fun of poetic epics. A division into eighteen books with an introductory
chapter parodying the 'invocation' for each one--this was outside his interest"
(p. 159). However, Dickens's use of what I have termed "structured descriptions"
in some of his clusters of chapter-headings may significantly relate to such
divisions and invocations, though on a smaller scale.

centu.y novelist he so much admired, so he also named one after William Macready, the Shakespearian actor he thought so highly of.

None the less, Micawber does quote Prince Hamlet a number of times, and so does Polonius. Neither Micawber nor Polonius quotes him accurately. If this does not suggest that Micawber is a Polonius figure, it does at least imply that he, like Polonius, takes a particular interest in Hamlet, whom he follows about, as it were. Perhaps Micawber, in remembering the Prince so often, is imitating him, is trying in some respects to be Hamlet-like himself. Such a proposition may seem absurd at first, but it may make more sense if we consider his personality and role more closely. First of all, Micawber does possess a certain dignity, regardless of Dickens's humor or intent; part of his stature is defined for us by his self-possession. He may be absent-minded, his thoughts may recoil upon themselves, and he is overly fond of using hackneyed vocabulary interspersed with grandiose embellishments; but all of this could be meant to simulate comically Hamlet's mind wandering from the subject at hand (Hamlet punctuates his early inaction with soliloquies which Micawber's long oratorical speeches may parallel in their own setting as they may parody Hamlet's style, which has been considered manneristic). Furthermore, Micawber's theatrical air and self-dramatization may be seen as relating, however grotesquely, to Hamlet's decision to play-act, to "put an antic disposition on." Hamlet is bent on having justice take its course with his step-father; Micawber likewise desires that justice be meted out to someone he has come to know as a scoundrel: Uriah Heep. Both men thus become the accusers and finally the avengers. Hamlet dies tragically in the act whereas Micawber appears to be himself in his triumph and then at peace with the world, takes himself and his family to South America, quite in keeping with Dickens's possible intent of parody. Can one say finally that because a number of scholars have found some evidence to indicate that

Hamlet was an obese person,[271] Micawber's corpulency is also Hamlet-like? To a degree, one might.

To be sure, there is no pattern of consistency in Micawber's reflections on Shakespeare's hero. And when he refers to Gray's Elegy Written in a Country Churchyard by quoting the lines "Each in his narrow cell for ever laid, / The rude forefathers of the hamlet sleep" (XLIX, 695), he hardly is making a deliberate association with King Hamlet's Ghost as another "rude forefather of . . . Hamlet." He is not, that is, if one accepts his statement that the lines refer to "the well-known strain of the Immortal exciseman nurtured beyond the Tweed" as the sole explanation, and there surely is no compelling reason to warrant ascribing the reference to any writer besides Gray.[272] However, if we consider the lines in the context of Chapter XLIX, we can legitimately speculate here that Micawber sees himself as a Hamlet out for destroying villainy and that this final verse is a deliberate reference to Hamlet, one cloaked in the words of Gray. Note the many quotations I have cited in number 42 in the list of annotated references. The verse serves to conclude and sum up a situation in which Micawber--actually for the first time--has found a real issue he can fight and rises from his usual comical, wordy display of ineffectual emotion to the role of accuser and avenger. He and Mr. Dick are an interesting pair in this chapter, and the many handshakes of Dick may be seen as an ingenious parallel to the promptings of the Hamlet Ghost. (Basically, however, Dick is one of Dickens's fool figures and, as such, derives more from Shakespeare's jesters, especially in King Lear.) Notice that number 44, one of the

---

[271]The locus classicus is E. Vale Blake's "The Impediment of Adipose," Popular Science Monthly, XVII (1880), 60-71. (E. E. Stoll claimed the opposite.)

[272]Likewise, T. S. Eliot's Prufrock instructs the reader not to see a Hamlet figure ("No! I am not Prince Hamlet, nor was meant to be"), though there is an influence of Laforgue's Hamlet adaptation without question. Dickens, of course, does not deny that the passage from Gray may also relate to Shakespeare's play; so one is warranted in seeing a possible influence of the tragedy here without contradicting the novelist's expressed intentions.

most vital of Micawber's Hamlet adaptations, is in this chapter. In the light
of these points and on the basis of Micawber's fondness for quoting Hamlet, a
propensity which puts him closer to the Prince than Polonius with his inconsequential
paraphrases, he might be called a Hamlet manqué.

A. O. J. Cockshut, in The Imagination of Charles Dickens, writes: "Everyone
can appreciate Mr. Micawber, but what can the critic say about him?" My answer thus
would be "plenty." Cockshut says that "all criticism naturally tends to con-
centrate on the topics about which the most interesting things can be said. No
doubt these topics tend to coincide, in a rough and ready way, with the greatest
literary achievements. But there are exceptions. To read of Mr. Micawber is, as
Chesterton said, like receiving a blow in the face. It is a deeply-felt experience,
but it is not susceptible of analytic description. It follows that any detailed
critical discussion of David Copperfield will tend to be unbalanced because it is
impossible to give appropriate space to Micawber."[273] Compare Earle Davis: "There
are the traditional worshippers who see Dickens as a 'Romantic artist.' They have
garlanded his memory with books which range from stubborn admiration to idealistic
idolatry. They begin with John Forster, reach a climax with Gilbert Keith
Chesterton. . . . Their most characteristic representative is probably Chesterton,
some of whose reasons for admiring Dickens may disconcert the modern reader. Chesterton remarks, for example: '. . . Dickens was a very great man, and there are many
ways of testing and stating this fact. But one permissible way is to say this, that
he was an ignorant man, ill-read in the past, and often confused about the present.
. . . '"[274] Chesterton was really trying to say that Dickens had genuine afflatus,

---

[273] New York, 1962, p. 114.

[274] The Flint and the Flame, pp. 2-3. The Chesterton quotation is from
Appreciations and Criticisms of the Works of Charles Dickens (London, 1911), p. xv.

that not everything about him is subject to intellectualization, and that too "rationalistic" an approach may be heretical. But Chesterton's critical powers become blunted with a kind of literary fideism at times; he goes too far in implying that Dickens was not a knowledgeable person (for, indeed, the contributions to Household Words, All the Year Round, Bentley's Miscellany, and The Daily News prove quite the contrary), or that Micawber is unanalyzable.

The central figure of David Copperfield is, to be sure, David himself, and hence he should be something of a Hamlet-figure if a real Hamlet motif is present in the novel. That he starts out under the auspices of such a character is evident, I think, from the allusions to Shakespeare's tragedy, the Ghost in particular, in the first chapter. But that the novelist's original approach to David is remindful of Hamlet need not mean that it remains of paramount interest in the novel as a whole. A closer analysis of his role must therefore be made.

At David's birth, his father is dead. Hamlet's early confrontation with the Ghost of his dead father (or conceivably with another kind of spirit that, as Horatio says, "usurp'st" the night by appearing in the guise of the father) relates, though in a contrasting way, to the visits of both Chillip, the physician who brings David into the world, and Betsey Trotwood, the great-aunt, both waiting for their "victim" and alternating as a Dickensian incarnation of the Hamlet Ghost. They return significantly later in the novel.[275] Chillip is then as diffident as ever, acting as if he would blow away at any moment, even as a ghostly

---

[275] David, of course, turns to Betsey after running away from Murdstone-and-Grinby's in Chapter XII. She refers to David's mother then in a manner that relates to the Hamlet parallel: "She marries a second time—goes and marries a Murderer—or a man with a name like it—and stands in this child's light! And the natural consequence is, as anybody but a baby might have foreseen, that he prowls and wanders. He's as like Cain before he was grown up, as he can be" (XIII, 192). Hamlet is also a Cain-like figure, an outcast from his family. Chillip reappears in Chapter LIX.

visitant is obliged to disappear at the crow of the cock; Betsey later
loses her fortune owing to the villain Heep, even as her counterpart, King
Hamlet, lost his life at the hands of his envious brother. The Ghost-image of
Betsey is then restated in the image of "Hamlet's aunt," a theatrical device
of Dickens's that resembles a comic "walk-on" in a stage production. In the
light of such a female association of the Hamlet Ghost with Betsey and then
with the "aunt," one might speculate about whether Dickens was jocosely
anticipating the role Sarah Bernhardt took as a female Hamlet on the late
nineteenth-century stage. There is something in Shakespeare's tragedy that
lends itself to just such a sex-reversal: Hamlet's sensitiveness has at times
earned for him the epithet effete. One might compare here Betsey's strong
insistence that the child to be born ought to be a girl so that the baby could
be named after her. Her attitude produces one of the strongest effects at the
beginning of the novel and is significantly followed through later on when the
hero does turn to her and comes to adopt her name: Trotwood. Likewise,
Steerforth refers to David as Daisy, not a very masculine name. There seems to
be nothing markedly feminine about David, though, and his two marriages would
argue strongly to the contrary. But inasmuch as he may take after Shakespeare's
Prince, he displays certain so-called feminine characteristics, such as perhaps
his tendency to think a great deal about himself (a form of introspection not
so common in an out-going young male), his self-pity, and his unusual empathy
and consideration of others.

There is, then, definitely a stronger case to be made for David's being
a reflection, though a dim one, of Shakespeare's Prince than there is for
Micawber. In addition, we notice that the family situation develops similarly in
both play and novel: in both cases, the son is at the mercy of a villainous step-
father and a weak mother. Even as Hamlet is studying at Wittenberg when crucial

events take place, and returns home only to be sent away again shortly, so David
is likewise kept in the dark about his mother's remarriage and is also sent away
once more. Later Hamlet is to go to London and so is David; in both cases, the
trip is arranged for the purpose of getting rid of him, a scheme which backfires.
At this point, however, the parallel course of events, largely alien in substance,
more or less ceases. From time to time a Hamlet-like description of David later
in the novel may be cited (such as in Chapter Thirty-Four, where the "brown study"
of the hero is reminiscent of a Hamlet soliloquy, especially that beginning with
"O that this too too solid _[sullied?_] flesh would melt").[276] But, as Dickens's
hero turns more and more into the conventional middle-class character of Victorian
fiction, he becomes less and less analogous to Shakespeare's noble Prince. The
hero's "undisciplined heart," to which he so often refers,[277] is perhaps comparable

---

[276] I.ii.129. The Folio has "solid flesh," but this is, I believe, a compositor's
misreading of the form sallied found in both Quarto 1 and Quarto 2. Sallied is
most likely an Elizabethan variant spelling of sullied; possibly the strokes in
the original u were misread as part of an a (indeed Shakespeare's handwriting confirms the fact that his stroke lettering was individualistic). John Dover Wilson
and then Fredson Bowers have tried to substantiate the reading based on the quartos.
Though they have been challenged, a casual glance at the concordance shows that
Shakespeare regularly used the notion of polluted flesh throughout his drama and
just as regularly used the notion of solidity in connection with land. Later in
Act One, the Ghost says to Hamlet, "O wicked wit and gifts, that have the power /
So to seduce!--won to his shameful lust / The will of my most seeming-virtuous queen;
O Hamlet, what a falling-off was there!" (I.v.44-47). Now, the Folio version contains
the unusual compositor's error wonne to to this shameful, which seems to be a
possible careless echoing of this too too sullied, if one can assume that the
compositor was aware of the original "sallied" in either quarto or manuscript.
Note also the rhetorical repetition of the O. There are two more reasons for
believing sullied to be right: (1) Is not the phrase "solid flesh . . . melt"
really redundant since something would have to be solid in the first place in order
to melt? (2) There is a later reference to Ophelia's "unpolluted flesh" (V.i.228).

[277] See Gwendolyn B. Needham, "The Undisciplined Heart of David Copperfield,"
Nineteenth-Century Fiction, IX (1954), 81-107.

to Hamlet's need for soul-searching, even as Tennyson's Hamlet-figures in
"Ulysses," "In Memoriam," and "Maud" reflect a similar need. David is incapable of achieving stability in life until toward the very end when he is
finally wed to Agnes Wickfield, a woman whose influence had already been
important in warning him against Steerforth. Dora may be regarded as a kind
of Ophelia. But, otherwise, Hamlet and David are pretty far apart. In
conclusion, one may say that there is similarity in the respective childhood
situations mainly. Thereafter, the Hamlet motif is picked up by Steerforth.

The strongest Hamlet potential is discernible in the nature of James
Steerforth. Already at Salem House David is a child-Horatio to Steerforth.
Hamlet found Horatio to be a philosophic Stoic; likewise Steerforth finds
David then to be more meditatively philosophic or self-contained than he is.
It is especially significant that the original friendship the two have at school
(just as Hamlet and Horatio form their friendship at the University of Wittenberg presumably) is reinforced when they meet again after attending a performance
of Julius Caesar. David, the more stoical of the two, thinks highly of the play
and the production; Steerforth, who, like Hamlet, thinks that there is more in
life than may be summed up in stoic philosophy perhaps, is dissatisfied. Finally,
Steerforth's relationship to Emily in some respects offers a rather close parallel
to Hamlet's connection with Ophelia. In order to substantiate these statements,
it is necessary to examine the Hamlet-Steerforth analogy in some detail.

From the time in Salem House, where the arrogant, though fascinating,
Steerforth acts as a protective friend to David, the new boy, he is gradually
growing into the leading role. He is more dashing, witty, brave, and intriguing
as a character than David. Whereas David remains relatively subdued and docile,
perceptive but not quick to assume the initiative, Steerforth is more princely

in his fastidiousness and claim to leadership. The schoolmaster is afraid of his steady, fixed gaze and lordly manners. He possesses a daemonic quality which is precisely what makes him so captivating in spite of his arrogance. Thus Doris Langley-Levy writes in "The Fascination of Steerforth" that he "with the most nonchalant air in the world, induces the youthful David to surrender his pocket-money for a 'spread,' and we begin to feel his magnetism immediately. David is stricken with awe to see how his new acquaintance is hero-worshipped, and to learn that even the brutal Creakle never does violence to this schoolboy demi-god."[278] One may be reminded that Hamlet was likewise idolized by the multitudes. But, in my estimation, the most Hamlet-like part of Steerforth's role is the attraction he held for the two women, his mother and Emily, an attraction serving both women ill and, at least in the mother, coupled with a sense of guilt. His own attitude toward them, a mixture of love and cruelty, may also remind us of Hamlet's although, of course, the reasons are quite different. The basic similarity between the two is on an aesthetic level: searching for some foundation outside of the ordinary, Hamlet seeks proof of the Ghost's message, and Steerforth seeks proof that life is worth living; whereas Steerforth finds a great deal attractive but nothing commanding his loyalty, Hamlet finds enough proof and yet revolts against his role as avenger while convinced of its moral necessity; Steerforth, at last facing death, becomes unified in himself in a show of wild, defiant courage, while Hamlet at last is aroused to action by a direct assault on his life and likewise displays courage and the ability to triumph in death. Their fascination lies in their determination to find their own way which does

---

[278]The Dickensian, XVIII (1922), 193.

not express itself through energy and accomplishments but rather in their attitude, their potential, their disregard for the conventional and expected. One senses that their private inner life is rich, daring, exclusive, that they are of a finer mettle than the rest. If Hamlet is obese physically (the point is in dispute), he certainly is not in spirit. And Steerforth is handsome. Their appeal therefore is to the reader's aesthetic sense. It is the beauty and mystery of individuality pitched against the group and against fate which provides the fascination.

William H. Marshall, in "The Image of Steerforth and the Structure of David Copperfield," writes that

> throughout the image of James Steerforth in the mind of David is crucial. . . . Stephen Leacock . . . , who found the substance of the novel "in the people who circulate in David's life" rather than in David himself, considered Steerforth "a blot on the story . . . in the artistic sense, in that he doesn't come out as Dickens meant him to"; intended to be "a dissolute gentleman," Steerforth emerges as "a contemptible cad." The judgment thus becomes moral: "Dickens's own impression, no doubt, was that Steerforth was a charming fellow. Most readers find him repulsive." The suggestion is that Dickens simply did not understand Steerforth, but within the structure of the novel it is David who does not properly evaluate the quality of Steerforth.[279]

To my mind, Marshall is mistaken in accepting Leacock's remark that Steerforth is "a contemptible cad." Fortunately, he qualifies the assertion somewhat in adding that "although David's 'lurking distrust of Steerforth' (Ch. XXVI) can be regarded as the novelist's instrument for anticipation—which from one point of view is clearly valid—still it is significant that David is aware of this only before he falls suddenly and violently in love with Dora Spenlow."[280] The suggestion is

---

[279] Tennessee Studies in Literature, V (1960), 58.

[280] Marshall, p. 62. The shift in allegiance may appear to be an inconsistency, but the novel is marked by such twisting development. Thus E. K. Brown writes, in "David Copperfield," The Yale Review, XXXVII (1948), 650-666: "The neatness of such a plot as Dickens elaborated in 'Great Expectations' would have been a solecism in the expression of the primary idea of 'Copperfield.' A plot not only may but should ramble and twist when it is to render a character and career which began in deep misfortune, remained all too long enslaved to forces of greater effect," and so forth (p. 661).

that, David's affection having shifted, his particular feelings about his
former friend have cooled and made it possible for him to see Steerforth objectively. But that says little actually about the value of Steerforth as such
and as a figure in the novel. To the very end, he is a Tennysonian figure, a
man of destiny poised against the backdrop of blusterous weather and turbulent
ocean in his determination to exert his sense of freedom. But the pity and fear
he evokes is essentially related to his daemonic nature. As his body is washed
ashore, may one not be reminded of Tennyson's picturesque yet awesome **poetry**, of
the sad destruction of the **waves**: "Break, break, break" . . . ? Whether or not
we find him defiant in the vein of Don Juan, or just waywardly pathetic, he
retains our interest, if not our sympathy, in spite of his irresponsible actions.
Likewise, the fact that David has turned his affectionate attention from his friend
to Dora does not mean that Dickens himself has lost interest in Steerforth; for,
indeed, Steerforth's death turns out to be one of terrible fascination, one even
reminiscent of Hamlet's in the daring that the doomed man at the mercy of fate
shows in the face of adversity. (I use the term terrible not so much to recall
Aristotle's tragic catharsis, for Steerforth's death cannot be called tragic in
the proper sense, but to suggest the sense of terrifying disaster, aesthetically
arresting, such as is found in some of Matthew Arnold's poetry, notably in "Sohrab
and Rustum.") His ambivalent character, if you please, expresses the basic
Victorian antinomy between a faith in the freedom of the will as a moral
necessity and the devastation of moral bankrupcy following upon unscrupulous
exploitation of the individual.

Even as Hamlet is Shakespeare's most exquisite creation, so Steerforth
is Dickens's. Thus Doris Langley-Levy comments that David's hero is the
novelist's "finest-cut cameo, the most faultless study."[281] Both heroes have

---

[281]"The Fascination of Steerforth," p. 191. In contrast to Steerforth, Micawber
is Dickens's "**most entertaining** character" (her italics). Though there is a
certain "exquisite" quality about Steerforth which sets him apart from Copperfield,
he is not on the level of the latter, of course: the main focus is on David.

a striking attachment to the mother, and both are insuperable egoists. Finally, if Hamlet is mainly a hero and Steerforth mainly a villain, we should not forget that in the case of both there may be an outside influence working upon them for which they may not be wholly responsible, that such a force may be more powerful than their individual moral wilfullness. To such a consideration I now wish to devote a few pages.

IV

A careful survey of the plot structure further reveals how interrelated the chapters on Steerforth are with the ones on David's gradual development: they serve to show how Steerforth's "amoral" development works in counterpoint to David's moral maturation. (There are intimations of this already with the names: Steerforth suggests a romantic "steering forth" and indeed he does steer forth to sea at the end only to be drowned; David is the traditional Hebraistic word of divine purpose as symbolized in the Judaic "star of David." One may be reminded of Faulkner's comment on the name Joe Christmas: ". . . how a man's name, which is supposed to be just the sound of who he is, can be somehow an augur of what he will do, if other men can only read the meaning in time.")[282] In each of the first four stages into which I have divided the novel on the basis of the "structured descriptions" Dickens has deliberately provided for us, references to Steerforth serve as a subdominant motif and are developed in section B on the chart. In almost every instance, his appearance in the novel serves a particular theatrical purpose. Thus David's first meeting with James indicates the initial stage in his growing-up process; then his re-encounter with the hero of his

---

[282]
Light in August (New York, 1950), p. 29.

childhood after a performance of Julius Caesar marks a renewal of the old comradeship. Again in the second part, the chapters concerning David's visit paid to Mrs. Steerforth and the subsequent acquaintance with Rosa Dartle and Miss Mowcher are revealing in their descriptions of the familiar as well as bizarre features of Steerforth's friendships. There is the visit that Steerforth and David pay to Mr. Peggotty and his group by the sea. In the second part, the climax is reached (another theatrical moment) when Steerforth absconds with Emily; this makes one wonder if Steerforth, the would-be gentleman (we recall the old proposition, reiterated in King Lear, III.iv.143, that the "Prince of Darkness is a gentleman"), is not to be out-matched by Mr. Peggotty, the bonafide man of distinction, be he ever so modest, if Dickens ever drew one.[283] In the third part, we follow Mr. Peggotty on his search for his niece, finally have news of Steerforth through Littmer, and at last Emily is found. The reunion of Mr. Peggotty and Little Emily is one of the most touching scenes the novelist has written. It is not until the fourth part, however, that the mighty "Tempest" chapter (LV) brings our knowledge of Steerforth to a close. As he lies on the shore, with David gazing sadly at his drowned body, the reader may wonder if Steerforth perhaps has not grown up, has not really used his potential; for lying as he does, "with his head upon his arm, as I had often seen him lie at school," he has become once again the Olympian schoolboy. And his end is thus somehow all the more an occasion for sentiment.

Now, there is one specific moment in the plot when Steerforth's nature shows itself most poignantly. It is the scene by the fire in Chapter XXII. Here

---

[283] E. Ashby Norris, "Mr. Peggotty, Gentleman," The Dickensian, V (1909), 241, may be consulted.

Steerforth's daemon comes to the fore, and the basic antinomy stands revealed, one which underlies his attempt to assume a highly controversial role and be a daredevil. We have intimations of this side of his disposition earlier, here and there in passing, such as in Chapter VII, where it is reported that "Steerforth laughed in church," thus summoning up not only the gargoylish spirits of Gothic Art but the God-defying demons of the nether regions. Another boy is punished for it, and Steerforth does not interfere. There is no reason given for his puzzling behavior; it is simply another commentary on his enigmatic spirit; it reveals his daemonic nature. It is here that I should like to offer a new bit of evidence regarding the structure of Hamlet, a piece of interpretation that has, as we shall see, an oblique relation to David Copperfield. Then I shall return again to Steerforth.

I refer to the possibility that Shakespeare's drama reveals a case of diabolic possession, in the historical, scholastic, and technical sense of the term; that explicit reference is made to such a possibility in the drama and that Hamlet may undergo such a stage of devilish temptation, in the literal sense, when he wishes to send Claudius to hell; finally, that Dickens had some notion of this in portraying Steerforth's character, especially as it is set forth to us in the fire-watching episode. Let us briefly consider each of these points in turn.

At the outset of the tragedy, the first scene of the first act, the Ghost appears for the first time. Marcellus and Bernardo, the guards, are conversing; the former enjoins Hamlet's friend to address the spectre: "Thou art a scholar; speak to it, Horatio" (I.1.42). The traditional interpretation of this passage is as follows: "Alluding to the use of Latin in exorcisms. Cf. Much Ado, ii.i.264: 'I would to God some scholar would conjure her!' Reed quotes Beaumont and Fletcher,

Night Walkers, ii.1: 'Let's call the butler up, for he speaks Latin, / And that
will daunt the devil.' In like manner the honest butler in Addison's Drummer
recommends the steward to speak Latin to the ghost."[284] More recently, Alfred
Harbage has written: "The others wish Horatio to speak to it because he is a
scholar (42)--that is, proficient in Latin, the language used in exorcising evil
spirits. Evil is thus immediately associated with this spirit."[285] Thus I
have proved the point that explicit reference to diabolical possession by an
evil spirit is made in the drama. To claim that Hamlet is under this influence
in the scene where Claudius is trying to pray is harder to prove, but the
possibility, when seen in the light of·the earlier reference to exorcism, may be
considered a plausibility. Consider the evidence: Hamlet is uttering a totally
unchristian sentiment, one completely out of keeping with his more sensitive
meditations earlier; there is little basis for considering him simply mad at
the time unless one were to accept a pre-Freudian motivation with which Shakespeare
was unfamiliar; the entire damnation speech almost smells of brimstone:

> But in our circumstance and course of thought,
> 'T is heavy with him; and am I then reveng'd,
> To take him in the purging of his soul,
> When he is fit and season'd for his passage?
> No!
> Up, sword, and know thou a more horrid hent:
> When he is drunk asleep, or in his rage,
> Or in the incestuous pleasure of his bed;
> At gaming, swearing, or about some act
> That has no relish of salvation in 't;
> Then trip him, that his heels may kick at heaven,
> And that his soul may be as damn'd and black
> As hell, whereto it goes.   (III.iii.83-95)

---

[284]Hamlet, ed. William J. Rolfe (New York, 1878), p. 172, n. 42.

[285]William Shakespeare: A Reader's Guide, p. 303. Referring later to Horatio's
defiant attitude toward the Ghost, Harbage adds: "Although not an exorcism, his
speech has ritualistic features" (p. 304). Yet exorcism is still on the reader's
mind connotatively.

Dr. Samuel Johnson considered the full speech "too horrible to be read or to be uttered."[286] Sister Miriam Joseph Rauh has stated that it is at this point that Hamlet "taints his mind," thereby failing to follow the injunction of the Ghost and promoting a Christian tragedy.[287] Harbage, however, disagrees: "Since the Ghost has previously revealed itself to others as well as Hamlet, we cannot conclude that it is a figment of Hamlet's imagination merely because Gertrude cannot see it; however, whether or not it be regarded as such a figment on the present occasion, its reference to Hamlet's almost blunted purpose (112) casts doubt on Hamlet's explanation of why he refrained from slaying Claudius in the scene immediately preceding."[288] He also writes that the reasons Hamlet gives "for failing to take advantage of the present opportunity /to slay the King at prayer_7 are logical, horribly logical. It seems gratuitous to doubt them, and yet we are bound to do so--"[289] Yet--why? Harbage tries to interpose a "psychological" reason, but such a conjectural justification fails to account fully for my reaction. Surely we can say that Hamlet's utterance is an excuse hiding a deeper reason (a "resolution sicklied o'er with the pale cast of thought"), but that is to side-step the issue. Consequently, it is better to accept Hamlet's statement, horrible as his words are, than to doubt it.

Now, the one thing that has escaped commentators so far is that the Prince's

---

[286] "Preface to Shakespeare" (1765) in _Johnson on Shakespeare: Essays and Notes Selected and Set Forth with an Introduction by Walter Raleigh_ (London, 1908), p. 193.

[287] See her paper "_Hamlet_, a Christian Tragedy," _Studies in Philology_, LIX (1962), 119-140.

[288] _William Shakespeare: A Reader's Guide_, p. 328. Italics Harbage's.

[289] Ibid., p. 326. Italics mine.

words themselves need not be taken as derived from his natural self. They do
not seem natural with Hamlet, no more natural than the words he thereafter uses
in addressing his mother, and we need not take them to be natural even though
the Prince utters them. This is fully understandable if we accept the time-
honored Roman Catholic belief that the devil (or an evil force in his power) has
the ability to infuse itself into another person in such a manner that his
speech becomes affected through its influence. Thus Hamlet's words would not be
naturally from his heart, but rather influenced by a preternatural force, the
"metaphysical" agency to which Lady Macbeth so villainously refers (I.v.27).
Such an interpretation would not have been disconcerting to the non-Catholic so
long as he believed in the power of evil; it little matters whether one takes the
spirit of the devil literally or figuratively in this instance. But according to
exorcists, if the force remains without (outside the individual), the man is
obsessed; if it is inside, the man is possessed. Now, it is possible that Hamlet,
though under the influence of diabolical forces when he makes his "damnation"
speech ("too horrible to be read or to be uttered"), was not actually possessed
by the forces. This would seem to be likely since he regains his composure later
in the play, although he may still be under the influence of such forces when he
has his verbal bout with his mother and thereupon slays the King's counselor.
At any rate, his trip to England certainly functions as a sea-change for him; he
is able to act decisively and promptly on the high seas and can then return to
Denmark to bide his time ("the interim is mine"). If there is any instance of
diabolical influence evident in the play, then it would appear that such influence
takes the form of obsession rather than possession, that Hamlet is obsessed at
the moment when he makes his infamous speech. Such is not so unlikely when one

considers that Claudius has been trying very hard to pray, we can assume; if
he had been devilishly inspired in his actions, killing the father of Hamlet and
marrying the queen, and was attempting to expunge his past crimes when the Prince came
upon the scene, is it not possible that the devil, seeing his prey slip from him,
took hold of the young man to prevent him from following the Ghost's command? Is
it not plausible that Claudius's plea for angelic assistance ("Help, angels!")
did not go unheeded and that there was angelic or divine intervention at that time,
thus saving the King's life as it was about to be taken by an avenger? Is not this
very scene an example of the efficacy of Christian prayer, a memento that there is,
as the New Testament proclaims, great joy in Heaven over one sinner who repents?
The possibility of diabolic obsession or possession should not be overlooked; by
resorting to it, we can explain a chain of events otherwise difficult to grasp.
Such diabolical influence upon the Prince in no way detracts from or adds to his own
(possible) guilt, though it is conceivable that a person under such a spell might
not be truly responsible for his actions, just as a person who is temporarily judged
insane would not be. A modern audience might find it easier to think of Hamlet's
remarks in terms of temporary mental or emotional illness rather than in the sense
advocated by the Scholastics and pre-Renaissance tradition, but the criterion of
comfortableness is not always one for deciding what is there in the play.

Let us now return to Chapter XXII of David Copperfield and the Fire Episode.
If we carefully examine this scene and consider what is running through Steerforth's
mind, we should be able to piece together several apparently disconnected parts of
the puzzle before us. Steerforth is watching the fire, contemplating whether or not
the proposed action is advisable even to his rather unscrupulous mind. We could
simply say that he has a bad conscience, but there seems to be more to it than that.
When he considers what is good or bad, he is thinking in terms of his own gain or
loss; for he is well aware of what is morally good and evil. His "utilitarian" sense

of values makes him wonder whether what is useful to him need be morally bad from
a more sophisticated viewpoint. (One may think, in passing, of Mill's essay on the
rights of the individual, On Liberty, or of Raskolnikov's speculations about the
right of the extraordinary individual in Dostoievski's Crime and Punishment.) If
the reader may be fascinated by Steerforth as Doris Langley-Levy says, then one
should likewise take into account that Steerforth himself is fascinated--by evil.
Like Macbeth, whom he quotes significantly at the time, he knows what is wrong,
weighs the consequences and his fate, and goes ahead and does it anyway. He sees
his own conscience in the fire as ghostly images briefly flickering; but these
ghosts are fleeting too (like that of Banquo in the passage he quotes from Macbeth),
and he determines to rely upon his "unconquerable will," to use Milton's description
of Satan.

To be sure, the major influence here is that of Macbeth, and the Hamlet
resemblance is evident mainly in one aspect: the sense of brooding indecision concerning a violent action and its consequences. The fire, too, suggests something,
if not necessarily related to religion, at least ritualistic. That it suggests
hell-fire fits in well with Steerforth's evil decision, of course. It is thus
possible that Steerforth, like Hamlet again, was obsessed by a diabolical agency;
if so, the fact that he put his wicked thoughts into execution suggests that he
became not just obsessed, but actually possessed. He eventually is so caught
up in his misadventures that he is unable to purge the evil in him except through
death.

Earlier I have considered how Steerforth's daemonic nature relates to
Goethe's conception of the term (derived ultimately from Greek pneumatology); if
so, it is hardly the same as the demonic personality ascribed to evil beings.

And that is just the point. Steerforth is not intrinsically an evil person; he is no demon. On the contrary, a demon has entered inside him, as it were, and has taken control of his will, foisting itself upon his mind and actions. If he were himself fully responsible for his sins, he would be demonic; if, on the other hand, he is under the control of a devil, he is not so. Indeed, his tutelary spirit, his daemon, is no doubt wrestling with the evil genius possessing him. Should this view seem difficult to accept, we need only turn to Goethe's Faust, where the hero, akin to Hamlet with his thoughts of self-destruction, his introspection and soul-searching, seduces Gretchen under the influence of Mephistopheles. This demon announces in no uncertain terms that he is the devil, and Faust makes a pact with him. Dickens was well acquainted with Goethe's drama (he mentions Faust in his letters), and so a tie with it here, obliquely another tie to Hamlet (a likely parallel since Goethe was himself so captivated by Shakespeare's play), is by no means unwarranted.

We may now close our case for the Hamlet parallels in David Copperfield, although no doubt more could be said. A separate case might be made for Little Emily as related to Ophelia, a parallel that has already been considered in the commentary to the list of quotations from the novel. A judgment of Earle Davis's deserves a comment in conclusion: "It is far-fetched to suggest that David Copperfield was Dickens' Odyssey or that Little Dorrit was his Hamlet; it is more nearly exact to say that Our Mutual Friend was his Inferno."[291] Surely, as I hope to have proved, David Copperfield was hardly his Odyssey at all, whether far-fetched or not; on the other hand, even as Tennyson referred to "Maud" as his "little Hamlet," so this

---

[291] The Flint and the Flame, p. 264. I suspect that Davis is playing up, whether consciously or not, to the commonplace that the word dickens is a euphemism for devil. I can earnestly say that the relevance of the euphemism did not enter my mind, however, until after I had considered the possibility of diabolic influence in both play and novel.

Dickens novel might enjoy a similar designation (after all, **since** Tennyson used
the term without even once referring to Shakespeare, Dickens stands a much better
chance).

A DOUBLE PATTERN IN THE CHARACTER STRUCTURE OF DAVID COPPERFIELD[*]

Hamlet-A
(undesignated hypothetical
Gestaltist type)

David

Ghost-A

Chillip   Trotwood
(Ghost-A_1)   (Ghost-A_2)

Confidant   Cruel Step-   Weak Mother
                    father

Mr. Murdstone

Hamlet-B   Hamlet-A Leaves Home

Steerforth
                                        School

Intelligent, Daemonic Appealing
   Witty   to
                          Women
                                                          To London

        Wins   To   To   To
        Power Mother Rosa Emily

        Alienation
        from Mother

     Ghost-B   Girl
    (Fire Image)   Abandoned

        Demise

----

   *The purpose of this chart is to suggest, as unobtrusively as possible, a direction
or psychological adjustment of the conative theory of affection to a consideration of
the Hamlet motif in the novel; the aim is not to prescribe a neatness, but to describe
a form of awareness that exists between the Hamlet-conscious reader (as well as author)
and the construct. Inasmuch as this relates to pure artifact and thereby deviates from
the novelist's possible intent, it is valueless; but surely Dickens himself saw form
emerging in his novel and could have conceived of just such a proposed arrangement.
Parallels between Hamlet and Micawber were originally added but have been removed so
as not to complicate the interweaving character relationships.

CHAPTER FOUR:

THE INDEBTEDNESS TO SHAKESPEARE

IN GREAT EXPECTATIONS

In David Copperfield, the Hamlet influence divided itself among several

characters and assumed various degrees of modification. An examination of Shakespeare's

influence upon Great Expectations will reveal a similar important affinity between

Dickens and a number of Shakespeare's plays, notably Hamlet. Since there is a certain

play-acting atmosphere throughout with all the theatrical personages who display

themselves with such gusto, we might even go so far as to maintain that Shakespeare's

dramatic and histrionic genius can be felt influencing Great Expectations more than

David Copperfield.[292]

As before, we may best commence with a list of Shakespearian allusions;

---

[292]
At the time of writing, Dickens's childhood readings have been given special
attention as an influence upon the novels. Harry Stone, in "Dark Corners of the Mind:
Dickens' Childhood Reading," The Horn Book Magazine, XXXIX (1963), 306-321, concludes: When
Dickens "approached the end of Copperfield, he wrote, typically, of being 'turned inside
out.' 'I seem,' he continued, 'to be sending some part of myself into the Shadowy World.
. . . Captain Murderer [from a childhood story] contributes to the savagely hungry
Magwitch." Yet even Stone exploits a Shakespearian allusion when he says that "Dickens
caused many additional childhood 'literary' experiences to suffer a sea-change into
something rich and strange," an allusion to The Tempest, I.ii.486-487.

those commented upon by the late T. W. Hill[293] are, once again, starred.

I

A List of the Principal Shakespearian References in Great Expectations:

1. "Something like a religious cross of the Ghost in Hamlet with Richard the Third" (IV, 23).

*2. "Mark Antony's oration over the body of Caesar" (VII, 41).

⌐The allusion is, of course, to the most famous piece of
rhetoric in Julius Caesar (III.ii.73-106). As in David
Copperfield, allusions to the Roman Play may relate to
Hamlet, which, as I have pointed out, contains its own
allusions to the same drama. Compare such apparently
casual references as Mrs. Micawber's desire that her
husband should become the "Caesar" of his fortunes. Whereas
a performance of Caesar highlights the structure of
Copperfield, bringing David and Steerforth together once
more, the reference here anticipates (as does the Barnwell
tragedy later) the Hamlet performance of Wopsle's. ⌐

*3. "Mere Mooncalfs" (VII, 49).

⌐Hill's gloss: "A mooncalf is a dolt, a congenital idiot,
from the medical meaning of the term for a monstrous birth,
supposed by the ancients to be due to the malign influence
of the moon. In Shakespeare's The Tempest, Stephano accosts
the monster Caliban, who says he used to be 'the man-i'-the-
moon when time was,' thus:
    'How now mooncalf, how does thine ague?'"
Compare Dickens's use of the term mooncalf in a letter to Mary
Boyle, 28 December 1860. ⌐

*4. "Mr. Wopsle finished off with a most terrifically snarling passage from Richard the Third" (X, 73).

⌐Hill comments that Act I, Scene iii, containing the unfriendly
conversation between Richard Duke of Gloucester and Queen
Margaret, is full of snarling passages about relationships,
especially in lines 175-182. ⌐

293
    "Notes to Great Expectations," The Dickensian, LIII (1957), 119-126, 184-
186; LIV (1958), 53-60, 123-125, 185; LV (1959), 57-59.

5. "Much as Cleopatra or any other sovereign lady on the Rampage" (XIII, 94).

> ⌐The allusion is surely to Shakespeare's Cleopatra.
> Compare the "infinite variety" of Mrs. Skewton as Dickens's
> Cleopatra in Dombey and Son. That Dickens deliberately
> transforms Shakespeare's queen of Egypt in that novel.
> points strongly to his having the same representation in
> mind here. ⌐

6. "Mr. Wopsle had in his hand the affecting tragedy of George Barnwell.
    . . . I never assisted at any other representation of George Barnwell.
    . . . What stung me, was the identification of the whole affair with my
    unoffending self. When Barnwell began to go wrong, I declare I felt
    positively apologetic. . . . At once ferocious and maudlin, I was made
    to murder my uncle with no extenuating circumstances whatever. . . . it
    became sheer monomania in my master's daughter to care a button for me;
    and all I can say for my gasping and procrastinating conduct on the fatal
    morning is, that it was worthy of the general feebleness of my character.
    . . . Even after . . . Wopsle had closed the book, Pumblechook sat staring
    at me, and shaking his head, and saying, 'Take warning, boy, take warning!'
    as if it were a well-known fact that I contemplated murdering a near
    relation" (XV, 112).

> ⌐Compare the Hamlet parallels: the hero murders his uncle,
> his sweetheart develops a literal monomania, and "pro-
> crastinating conduct" is strongly related to "the general
> feebleness of . . . character." Pip's identification with
> the hero is akin to, and an anticipation of, his similar
> identification with Hamlet after witnessing Wopsle's pro-
> duction. ⌐

*7. "Bosworth Field" (XV, 113).

> ⌐Hill: "A reference to the final scene in Shakespeare's
> King Richard the Third"; compare number 4. ⌐

*8. "The greatest agonies at Glastonbury" (XV, 113).

> ⌐Hill: "Many commentators have tried to trace the source of
> this allusion but so far without success. It appears likely
> that Dickens may have been thinking of the death-scene in
> King John by Shakespeare, in which act v, scene 7 is laid
> in the orchard of Swinstead Abbey, and that he made a slip
> in calling it Glastonbury. Certainly great actors of the
> past have taken full advantage of the tragic possibilities
> of the scene, among others Garrick, J. P. Kemble, Macready,
> Phelps, Charles Kean and Beerbohm Tree. Dickens saw Macready
> act this part in 1842 and went behind the scenes after the
> performance to congratulate his friend. In 1836 Macready

recorded in his diary: 'My dying scene was the best.' One can
imagine Macready's writhings and contortions as he spoke these
lines:

> '. . . all my bowels crumble up in dust;
> I am a scribbled form, drawn with a pen
> Upon a parchment; and against this fire
> Do I shrink up. . . .
> Within me is a lull; and there the poison
> Is, as a friend.'" ⌐

*9. "The coroner, in Mr. Wopsle's hands, became Timon of Athens; the beadle,
Coriolanus" (XVIII, 127).

⌐Hill: "Wopsle's coroner was endowed with all the dignity and
nobility of character of Timon before he became a misanthrope";
"the beadle showed the same scorn for the citizens that Coriolanus
did in Shakespeare's play. It recalls Dickens's hatred of official-
dom for which Bumble was so notable in Oliver Twist." The unusual
Dickensian reference to Coriolanus is of special interest in that
one theme of that Roman Play is snobbery, an echo of which may be
traced in Pip's attitude toward Joe and his former rustic companions
after his attaining financial eminence. ⌐

*10. "'Bear in mind then, that Brag is a good dog, but that Holdfast is a better.
Bear that in mind, will you? . . . Now, I return to this young fellow. And
the communication I have got to make is, that he has Great Expectations'"
(XVIII, 132).

⌐Hill: "Brag as the name for a dog is very old and is found as far
back as the fifteenth century. The present proverb, used by
Jaggers, is included in Dyke's English Proverbs, 1748, and this
is foreshadowed by Shakespeare in King Henry the Fifth:
> 'For oaths are straws, men's faiths are wafer-cakes,
>   And hold-fast is the only dog, my duck'" (II.iii.53-54).
The reference then to "Great Expectations" symbolizes, in a small
way, the relationship of the Shakespearian allusions to the novel
as a whole. ⌐

11. "My guardian was in his room, washing his hands. . . . I embrace this
opportunity of remarking that he washed his clients off. . . . He would
wash his hands. . . . We found him with his head butted into this closet,
. . . washing his hands" (XXVI, 201-202).

⌐This is probably an allusion to Lady Macbeth's compulsive washing
of hands, a well-known event in Shakespeare's Scottish Play. Notice
the proximity of a direct allusion to Macbeth in number 12. In a
real sense, Jaggers, like Lady Macbeth, is abetting criminal action.
Compare Dickens's further reference to the "hand-washing" image as
in Oliver Twist, where the Macbeth parallel is especially clear. ⌐

*12. "Rather tall, of a lithe nimble figure, extremely pale, with large faded eyes, and a quantity of streaming hair. I cannot say whether any diseased affection of the heart caused her lips to be parted as if she were panting, and her face to bear a curious expression of suddenness and flutter; but I know that I had been to see Macbeth at the theatre, a night or two before, and that her face looked to me as if it were all disturbed by fiery air, like faces I had seen rise out of the Witches' caldron" (XXVI, 203).

13. "I had got on so fast of late, that I had even started a boy in boots--top boots--in bondage and slavery to whom I might be said to pass my days. . . . With . . . horrible requirements he haunted my existence" (XXVII, 209-210); "this avenging phantom" (XXVII, 210); "the Avenger--if I may connect that expression with one who never attended on me if he could possibly help it" (XXVIII, 217); "as confidence was out of the question with the Avenger in the hall, which could merely be regarded in the light of an ante-chamber to the keyhole, I sent him to the Play" (XXX, 238); "the canary-breasted Avenger" (XXXIV, 263).

⌊This is another Dickensian Hamlet adaptation, one akin to the description of "Hamlet's Aunt" in David Copperfield. Notice how it is again associated with the Ghost motif ("horrible requirements"--"haunted my existence"). The reference to the Avenger's clothes recalls the clothing Goethe made famous in his description of Werther in Die Leiden des Jungen Werthers; this association is of some relevance since Goethe's theories about Hamlet were probably the most famous of any in the nineteenth century (there are echoes of it in the Household Words article on the tragedy, "Something that Shakespeare Wrote"). Since Goethe found the Prince to be too sensitive for revenge, Dickens may have adapted that theory here in his own way by making the Avenger boyish, possibly shy or diffident (though the inattentiveness may be ascribed to Pip's airs, it probably has a literal meaning), even cowardly in the manner of slyly obtaining information and being "canary-breasted"--with its connotations of being "yellow" in the sense of being pusillanimous. ⌋

14. "I took what Joe gave me, and found it to be the crumpled playbill of a small metropolitan theatre, announcing the first appearance, in that very week, of 'the celebrated Provincial Amateur of Roscian renown, whose unique performance in the highest tragic walk of our National Bard has lately occasioned so great a sensation in local dramatic circles.'
    'Were you at his performance, Joe?' I inquired.
    'I were,' said Joe, with emphasis and solemnity.
    'Was there a great sensation?'
    'Why, said Joe, 'yes, there certainly were a peck of orange-peel. Partickler when he see the ghost. Though I put it to yourself, sir, whether it were calc'lated to keep a man up to his work with a good

hart, to be continiwally cutting in betwixt him and the Ghost with 'Amen!'
A man may have had a misfortun' and been in the Church,' said Joe, lowering
his voice to an argumentative and feeling tone, 'but that is no reason why
you should put him out at such a time. Which I meantersay, if the ghost of
a man's own father cannot be allowed to claim his attention, what can, Sir?
Still more, when his mourning 'at is unfortunately made so small as that the
weight of the black feathers brings it off, try to keep it on how you may.'
A ghost-seeing effect in Joe's own countenance informed me that Herbert had
entered the room. So, I presented Joe to Herbert, who held out his hand; but
Joe backed from it, and held on by the bird's nest.

'Your servant, Sir,' said Joe, 'which I hope as you and Pip'--here his eye
fell on the Avenger. . . " (XXVII. 211-212).

/ The reference to the "unique performance in the highest tragic
walk of our National Bard" can hardly be anything else but a
reference to Hamlet, particularly with the reference to "the
ghost of a man's own father" following. Compare the Wopsle
Hamlet performance later. /

15. "On our arrival in Denmark, we found the king and queen of that country in two
arm-chairs on a kitchen-table, holding a Court. The whole of the Danish nobility
were in attendance; consisting of a noble boy in the wash-leather boots of a
gigantic ancestor, a venerable Peer with a dirty face, who seemed to have risen
from the people late in life, and the Danish chivalry with a comb in its hair and
a pair of white silk legs, and presenting on the whole a feminine appearance. My
gifted townsman stood gloomily apart, with folded arms, and I could have wished
that his curls and forehead had been more probable.

Several curious little circumstances transpired as the action proceeded.
The late king of the country not only appeared to have been troubled with a cough
at the time of his decease, but to have taken it with him to the tomb, and to have
brought it back. The royal phantom also carried a ghostly manuscript round its
truncheon, to which it had the appearance of occasionally referring, and that, too,
with an air of anxiety and a tendency to lose the place of reference which were
suggestive of a state of mortality. It was this, I conceive, which led to the
Shade's being advised by the gallery to 'turn over!'--a recommendation which it
took extremely ill. It was likewise to be noted of this majestic spirit that
whereas it always appeared with an air of having been out a long time and walked
an immense distance, it perceptibly came from a closely-contiguous wall. This
occasioned its terrors to be received derisively. The Queen of Denmark, a very
buxom lady, though no doubt historically brazen, was considered by the public to
have too much brass about her; her chin being attached to her diadem by a broad
band of that metal (as if she had a gorgeous toothache), her waist being en-
circled by another, and each of her arms by another, so that she was openly
mentioned as 'the kettledrum.' The noble boy in the ancestral boots, was inconsistent; representing himself, as it were in one breath, as an able seaman, a
strolling actor, a grave-digger, a clergyman, and a person of the utmost
importance at a Court fencing-match, on the authority of whose practised eye
and nice discrimination the finest strokes were judged. This gradually led to
a want of toleration for him, and even--on his being directed in holy orders,
and declining to perform the funeral service--to the general indignation taking
the form of nuts. Lastly, Ophelia was a prey to such slow musical madness, that

when, in course of time, she had taken off her white muslin scarf, folded it up, and buried it, a sulky man who had been long cooling his impatient nose against an iron bar in the front row of the gallery, growled, 'Now the baby's put to bed, let's have supper!' Which, to say the least of it, was out of keeping.

Upon my unfortunate townsman all these incidents accumulated with playful effect. Whenever that undecided Prince had to ask a question or state a doubt, the public helped him out with it. As for example; on the question whether 'twas nobler in the mind to suffer, some roared yes, and some no, and some inclining to both opinions said 'toss up for it'; and quite a Debating Society arose. When he asked what should such fellows as he do crawling between earth and heaven, he was encouraged with loud cries of 'Hear, hear!' When he appeared with his stockings disordered (its disorder expressed, according to usage, by one very neat fold in the top, which I suppose to be always got up with a flat iron), a conversation took place in the gallery respecting the paleness of his leg, and whether it was occasioned by the turn the ghost had given him. On his taking the recorders--very like a black flute that had just been played in the orchestra and handed out at the door--he was called upon unanimously for Rule Britannia. When he recommended the player not to saw the air thus, the sulky man said, 'And don't you do it, neither; you're a deal worse than him!' And I grieve to add that peals of laughter greeted Mr. Wopsle on every one of these occasions.

But his greatest trials were in the churchyards: which had the appearance of a primeval forest, with a kind of small ecclesiastical wash-house on one side, and a turnpike gate on the other. Mr. Wopsle, in a comprehensive black cloak, being descried entering at the turnpike, the gravedigger was admonished in a friendly way, 'Look out! Here's the undertaker a coming, to see how you're getting on with your work!' I believe it is well known in a constitutional country that Mr. Wopsle could not possibly have returned the skull, after moralizing over it, without dusting his fingers on a white napkin taken from his breast; but even that innocent and indispensable action did not pass without the comment 'Wai-ter!' The arrival of the body for interment (in an empty black box with the lid tumbling open), was the signal for a general joy which was much enhanced by the discovery, among the bearers, of an individual obnoxious to identification. The joy attended Mr. Wopsle through his struggle with Laertes on the brink of the orchestra and the grave, and slackened no more until he had tumbled the king off the kitchen-table, and had died by inches from the ankles upwards.

We had made some pale efforts in the beginning to applaud Mr. Wopsle; but they were too hopeless to be persisted in. Therefore we had sat, feeling keenly for him, but laughing, nevertheless, from ear to ear. I laughed in spite of myself all the time, the whole thing was so droll; and yet I had a latent impression that there was something decidedly fine in Mr. Wopsle's elocution--not for old associations' sake, I am afraid, but because it was very slow, very dreary, very up-hill and down-hill, and very unlike any way in which any man in any natural circumstance of life or death ever expressed himself about anything. When the tragedy was over, and he had been called for and hooted,

I said to Herbert, 'Let us go at once, or perhaps we shall meet him'"
(XXXI, 244-246).

"'When he come to the grave,' said our conductor, 'he showed his
cloak beautiful. But, judging from the wing, it looked to me that when he
see the ghost in the queen's apartment, he might have made more of his
stockings'" (XXXI, 247).

"'But I'll tell you one thing, Mr. Waldengarver,' said the man who
was on his knees, 'in which you're out in your reading. Now mind! I don't
care who says contrary; I tell you so. You're out in your reading of Hamlet
when you get your legs in profile. The last Hamlet as I dressed, made the
same mistakes in his reading at rehearsal, till I got him to put a large
red wafer on each of his shins. . ." (XXXI, 248).

"Mr. Wopsle shut his eyes, and opened them again; performing both
ceremonies very slowly. 'You must have observed, gentlemen,' said he, 'an
ignorant and a blatant ass, with a rasping throat and a countenance expressive
of low malignity, who went through--I will not say sustained--the rôle
(if I may use a French expression) of Claudius King of Denmark'" (XXI, 249).

"Miserably I went to bed after all, and miserably thought of Estella,
and miserably dreamed that my expectations were all cancelled, and that I had
to give my hand in marriage to Herbert's Clara, or play Hamlet to Miss
Havisham's Ghost, before twenty thousand people, without knowing twenty
words of it" (XXXI, 249).

        /This chapter is famous for its description of the performance of
        Hamlet with Mr. Wopsle taking the leading part. It is so
        striking that Dickens surely intended it to relate significantly
        to the structure, thus confirming or endorsing the existence
        of a Hamlet motif in the novel. Thus at the end Pip dreams of
        having to "play Hamlet to Miss Havisham's Ghost," a phrase
        surely recalling through verbal association "King Hamlet's Ghost."
        The earlier references to legs relate to a similar anatomical
        account in Martin Chuzzlewit and in the article "Legs" in
        Household Words; in both of these analogous descriptions Shakespeare
        is introduced. Glancing at the chapter as a whole, one should
        recognize that Dickens was not parodying the dramatist but rather
        a certain kind of audience watching the tragedy. /

II

Although the "cross of the Ghost in Hamlet with Richard the Third," the first

item in the list of annotated references, might be taken to indicate that there is a

linking of two motifs in the novel, that of Hamlet and Richard III, any such hybrid would play havoc with the basic structure. To be sure, another reference to Wopsle underscores the Richard III parallel, the "most terrifically snarling passage" mentioned in number 4, but all both these allusions combined suggest is that Mr. Wopsle enjoys referring to the history play. Perhaps there is something grotesque in his character, something which sets him up as a Dickensian Richard III, one later combined or crossed with a Dickensian Hamlet during the stage production of the play. The main Shakespearian motif in the plot structure, however, is that of Hamlet. Wth this in mind, a diagram may be useful to consider. There is no need here to consider the chapter structure in terms of larger divisions, such as the five-part structure in David Copperfield; for in the later novel the basic divisions have already been made for us: the first two stages of Pip's expectations followed by the denouement, a description of how these anticipated results were, to use G. Robert Stange's term, "well lost."[294]

CHARACTER AND PLOT STRUCTURE OF GREAT EXPECTATIONS

I. The First Stage of Pip's Expectations

Hamlet Encounters a Ghost Desirous of Revenge

Witches of Mac-beth (number 12)	Pip Meets Magwitch (Ghost A) Desirous of Revenge on Compeyson and Society	Pip Meets Miss Havisham (Ghost B) Desirous of Revenge on Men	Betsey as Ghost in Copperfield; "Hamlet's aunt"
	Horatio and Hamlet Confide in Each Other	Ophelia and Hamlet Estranged	
	Pocket and Pip Tussle in Anticipation of their later Friendship	Estella and Pip Estranged	

---

[294] "Expectations Well Lost: Dickens' Fable for his Time," College English, XVI (1954), 9-17.

Polonius as
Sententious
Choric Figure

Pumblechook
as
Sententious
Choric Figure

The Play-Within-the-Play:
The Murder of Gonzago

The Play-Within-the-Novel (A):
The Barnwell Tragedy

II. The Second Stage of Pip's Expectations

Hamlet, the Pseudo-Actor

Pip as Pseudo-Hamlet   Pip as "Handel"
to Miss Havisham's   David Copperfield
David Copperfield   Ghost   as "Daisy"
as Hamlet to
Betsey's Ghost

The Play-Within-the Play:
The Murder of Gonzago

The Play-Within-the-Novel (B):
Wopsle's Hamlet Performance

Reappearance of the Ghost

Return of Magwitch

III. The Third ("Well Lost") Stage of Pip's Expectations

The Revenge Accomplished:
Claudius Brought to Justice

Justice Accomplished: Micawber's
Compeyson Attacked by Magwitch   Vindication

Hamlet Loses Ophelia
(Both Die Separately)
David loses Dora

Pip Loses Estella
(Estella Marries;
they part as friends)

There are no separate titles for chapters as there are in David Copperfield; this eliminates the temptation of reinterpreting the plot structure in terms of chapter-headings. But the fact that Dickens did divide up his chapters into three groupings in his later Hamlet-novel[295] provides further evidence that he perhaps intended a similar grouping in his earlier Hamlet-novel.

What can be said about the organization of Great Expectations from the "Hamletian" structure in it? Is it the structure of the novel? Surely that provided by the novelist in the three "stages" is primarily operative, and the one I offer is dependent on that, though it may work also in counterpoint with it. Taking the tripartite division already given, John H. Hagan, Jr., remarks that "the central plot is still a variation on an old picaresque motif--just as Tom Jones, for example, discovers the worthiness of his origins and thereby wins the lovely Sophia, so Pip discovers the ignominious origins of his wealth and loses the lovely Estella--but the artistry with which Dickens constructs his story and clearly and consistently, with full truth to life, marks out every stage of his hero's development, completely raises Great Expectations into a new class."[296] Hagan subdivides the parts as follows:

> Part I. Boyhood. Chaps. 1-6, 7-11, 12-17, 18-19;
>
> Part II. Youth. Chaps. 20-27, 28-35, 36-39;
>
> Part III. Maturity. Chaps. 40-46, 47-51, 52-56, 57-59.

---

[295]The term Hamlet-novel is a technical one (hence the hyphenation) and has been applied to works as divergent from Shakespeare's drama as a Hauptmann novel; it is used here in the same sense in which Tennyson called "Maud" his "little Hamlet" as well as "slightly akin to Hamlet."

[296]"Structural Patterns in Dickens's Great Expectations," English Literary History, XXI (1954), 54.

He finds the basic unifying patterns to be like this: chapters 20-27, 28-35, and 36-39
represent the center of the novel (Pip in London, Pip's return to his native village,
and Pip's coming of age). He points to such careful balancings as the following:
chapters 1-6, 40-46, deal with Pip and Magwitch; chapters 7-11, 47-51, deal with the
relationship between Estella and Miss Havisham, and their effect upon Pip. The
characters form three basic groupings: Jo and Biddy; Magwitch, Miss Havisham, Matthew
Pocket, Jaggers; Pumblechook, Wopsle, Sarah Pocket, Mrs. Matthew Pocket, Camilla and
Herbert Pocket. Pip and Estella stand outside these categories and transcend them.
The key to each group is the way its members relate themselves to the theme of "great
expectations" as wealth or social prestige: the first group is constituted by the two
persons to whom the whole question of great expectations is totally alien; the middle
group is composed of those who have had high hopes at one time; the final group
comprises those who have no such expectations of their own and would like to have some.
One might examine the nuances of Pip's relationship to each of these three groups
in some detail, but that is not the purpose here; my concern is rather with a
structure which is also fitting and may be analyzed and broken down into even more
interesting components.

To begin, there is the initial encounter between Pip and Magwitch, a meeting
that surely presents a <u>Hamlet</u> parallel insofar as the Convict and the Ghost play
comparable parts. At the very commencement of the drama, the revenant announces
to Prince Hamlet that it has come from the confines of Purgatory but that it is
not allowed to tell of its "prison-house" secrets: it does not ask for Hamlet's
prayers, as might be expected from a Catholic ghost, but rather exhorts him to seek
revenge. If the Prince can bring Claudius to justice, then presumably he will
also attain the throne which is rightfully his and thereby his princely

expectations will be realized.

Pip's surprise upon encountering a convict in a graveyard and on the marshes is similar to the astonishment of Hamlet and his friends when they witness the Ghost in the murky climate of Denmark (perhaps an incidental parallel to fog-ridden England): "Angels and ministers of grace defend us!" (I.iv.39). The implication is that this ghost is one from which we would indeed need to be defended by supernatural agency; in this respect, it is an immediate parallel to the vile criminal Magwitch, whose very name connotes an evil being or witch. True, Magwitch is pure flesh and blood, no apparition; however, he appears from behind a tombstone "like a ghost from among the graves" as Professor Stange puts it, and he acts very oddly, turning Pip upside down (to empty his pockets). In this way, he is certainly akin to the familiar sprite or goblin of native superstition, most of all to the wraith which is said to be abroad on All Hallows Eve. Now, the Hamlet Ghost is a sophisticated type of apparition; the Convict-Ghost in the novel is a terrestrial spirit that may appeal more to a layman who can appreciate the theatrical effect of such a meeting without his having to pronounce judgment on what it means psychologically. None the less, Magwitch, like King Hamlet's Ghost, wants to be avenged, and he enlists the service of Pip, an impressionable young person like Hamlet. He commands Pip to procure food for him, and the hero does so unflinchingly, stealing a pork pie and other edibles from the larder of Mrs. Joe. He thereby begins to become "tainted" by criminality. Pip also presents the Convict with a file whereby he can free himself from a kind of imprisonment similar to that which the Ghost encounters (the Convict has iron shackles whereas the Hamlet Ghost has those of purgatorial restraint and austerity). The time of day for both encounters is "the very witching time of night, / When churchyards yawn and hell itself breathes out / Contagion to this world" (III.ii.363-365); with Shakespeare, it is almost literally so whereas, with Dickens, it is so figuratively (the "witching hour" is the hour for Magwitch). Christmas is probably not too many days away in Hamlet,[297] and this relates to the Christmas Eve celebrations in Great Expectations, where Wopsle reminds Pip of "the Ghost in Hamlet" (IV, 23).[298]

The very mention of "a religious cross" in connection with this allusion suggests the moment where Horatio, in confronting the Ghost, announces, "I'll cross it, though it blast me" (I.i.127), although the introduction of a reference to Richard III at the same time serves to distort the reference in a way characteristic of Great Expectations, where evil sometimes assumes a more extravagant form than in Hamlet. It would be well to pause briefly and examine Horatio's words. The gloss in the Rolfe edition is as follows: "Cross it. According to Blakeway, whoever crossed the spot on which a spectre was seen became subject to its malignant influence [thus: 'though it blast me']. Among the reasons for supposing the young Earl of Derby (who died in 1594) to have been bewitched, Lodge states that a figure of a tall man appeared in his chamber 'who twice crossed him swiftly,' and when the earl came to the place

---

[297] Two months previously the slain king had been alive, for Hamlet remarks, "But two months dead! nay, not so much, not two" (I.ii.138), and the Ghost says that he was "Sleeping within my orchard. / My custom always in the afternoon, / Upon my secure hour thy uncle stole, / With juice of cursed hebenon in a vial, / And in the porches of my ears did pour / The leperous distilment" (I.v.59-64). If King Hamlet had been sleeping outside in his garden or orchard but two months or so before the very cold weather emphasized as the time of the play, then it stands to reason that the assassination took place in the late summer or fall (the word orchard suggests the fall season since that is the time when fruit ripen on the trees); so the time of the play would probably be December.

[298] See the first reference in the list of annotated allusions. The context favors Wopsle's theatricality over the Convict-Ghost parallel, but I suggest that one overtone is contrapuntal to the other.

where he saw the apparition 'he fell sick.'"[299] Alfred Harbage writes, "The
wordplay of Horatio's I'll cross it (i.e. 'oppose it' and 'confront it with the
sign of the cross') is visually paralleled: the unusual stage direction He
spreads his arms indicates that Horatio puts himself in the posture of opposition,
and also that his body assumes the form of a cross. Although not an exorcism,
his speech has ritualistic features, with its three If clauses punctuated by
short lines: Speak to me . . . Speak to me . . . O speak" (I.i.129-135).[300]
But Horatio's body can assume a cross-like form only if he spreads his arms in
such a manner that they would be perpendicular to his torso; it may be more
likely, less contrived, to imagine that by spreading his arms he lifts them
straight up or at least diagonally from his body. I am thus inclined to accept
the more old-fashioned interpretation, which was that Horatio ventured to cross
the path of the Ghost in order to check its progress. To claim that Horatio makes
an emblematic sign of the cross is to go beyond what the text warrants, although
one might imagine that Shakespeare expected some producers to do just that;
moreover, we ought to remember that the traditional Roman Catholic sign of faith
in Christ's crucifixion is usually reserved for things holy, and so far in this
play there is no indication that there is anything pious at all about this
apparition. Further, Horatio is, in Hamlet's own words, "more an antique Roman
than a Dane," which means that he is stoical, not Roman Catholic as such.

None the less, now that I have disposed of such an intriguing religious
interpretation as unlikely, I wish to reinstate it on different terms. For, even
though Shakespeare hardly intended a sign of the cross here, the actor Charles
Fechter notably thought that he did and thereby used this very sacramental in his

---

299
   New York, 1878, p. 175n.
300Harbage, p. 304.

production of the play. A brief glance at the summary of his production in the standard Variorum Edition will confirm the fact that his use of the sign of the cross was so striking that it was set down by the scholars and critics of his day as appropriate, especially since Fechter was a Roman Catholic.[301] The very same interpretation has been recently restored by Sister Miriam Joseph Rauh:

> [Horatio] notes in detail the resemblance of the apparition to the dead king. He realizes, however, that he has "not a real but a phantasmal body" and is consequently, as Marcellus discovers by striking at it vainly with his sword, "as the air invulnerable" (145). Therefore when the apparition returns, Horatio bids it, "Stay illusion" (127). Considering now that it must be either an evil spirit or a good one, he takes a recommended precaution against the worse of these two remaining possibilities, making the sign of the cross as he courageously steps forward saying, "I'll cross it, though it blast me" (127). Yet with an open mind as to its nature whether evil or good, Horatio asks the apparition three questions which were thought to be reasons why a spirit might return from the dead.[302]

The point is, then, that Dickens, in having such admiration for Fechter, utilized the interpretation that "I'll cross it" refers to Horatio making the sign of the cross and then modified it to suit his purposes. Conceivably there was some doubt in his mind concerning whether or not Shakespeare intended a reference to the sacramental in spite of his firm liking for Fechter's performance; indeed he may have resolved the dilemma by suggesting that the word cross implies not only possibly the sign of the cross or standing in the path of the Ghost to check its progress, but also a hybrid, a cross-fertilization, as it were, of various meanings. It would be absurd

---

301
    Thus Kate Field ("Fechter as Hamlet," Atlantic Monthly [1870]) is quoted in the New Variorum Edition, ed. H. H. Furness (Philadelphia, 1877), II, 253-255, as follows: "'I'll cross it though it blast me.' Heretofore Horatios have senselessly crossed the Ghost's path, as if such a step would stay its progress. Not so with Fechter, whose Horatio makes the sign of the cross, at which the Ghost stops, as a Catholic ghost should" (p. 253).

302
    "Discerning the Ghost in Hamlet," p. 495.

to carry such conjectures too far, of course, but it is just as wearisome to indict Dickens as a superficial writer without depth and let interpretation go at that. It could well be that Horatio's "I'll cross it," which has been ambiguous in Hamlet scholarship from Victorian times down to the present, was initially conceived of as being so by Charles Dickens. His application of Horatio's words to a speech of Wopsle's is not just an example of creative transformation (similar to his use of "to take ⌈make⌉ arms against a sea of troubles," considered earlier, as first an emendation and then as relegated to a speech of Micawber's), but an example of a critical or scholarly train of thought. The implications of "a religious cross of the Ghost in Hamlet with Richard the Third" are, then, as follows: (1) There is the direct contextual meaning, the humorous note of Wopsle yoking together the two unrelated Shakespearian figures; (2) Dickens was apparently well aware of Fechter's personal, Catholic interpretation of "I'll cross it" in connection with the Hamlet Ghost, and his reference is an echo of the passage; (3) he very likely questioned the authenticity of Fechter's interpretation and thereby felt free to convert the ritualistic effect of "crossing" to his own purposes; (4) in so doing, he preserved the original Shakespearian meaning by showing how a "religious cross" (whether a "sign of" or not) is somewhat unwarranted in a Revenge Play like Hamlet. Indeed, he possibly felt that it was not only inappropriate in such a Senecan context, but downright outré. Yet one should keep in mind throughout that the fact that Dickens may have been well aware of how ambiguous the phrase "I'll cross it" had become does not mean that Shakespeare ever deliberately intended any ambiguity; nor did Dickens intend his modification to be taken ambiguously. True, interpretation may be complex enough, but that is no guarantee that either author was "hedging." To my mind, the very act of artistic creativity rules out intentional ambiguity or double-talk.[303]

If Magwitch is the first "ghost" for Pip's Hamlet, however, he is not the only Dickensian "apparition" in the novel. Just as, in David Copperfield, Chillip, and Betsey Trotwood alternate as Hamlet-ghosts at the beginning, so in Great Expectations Magwitch and Miss Havisham alternate in a somewhat similar, but more significant manner. Miss Havisham is described in the novel as a kind of apparition; consider, in addition, Pip's reference to her as "my fairy god-mother" (XIX). Somewhat akin to William Faulkner's Emily,[304] Miss Havisham is the embodiment of a kind of ghost in more ways than one: first, she appears more dead than alive, a kind of living corpse haunted by memories of a wedding ceremony that never came to be; second, like Magwitch, she bids Pip do things for her because she too desires revenge, though a totally different kind from Magwitch's (her plan is to wreak vengeance upon the entire male sex--including Pip at first, to be sure--by means of her beautiful protégé, Estella, as cold of heart as she is attractive to look upon, one who acts as an Ophelia for Pip's Hamlet); third, Miss Havisham actually turns into a ghost when Pip dreams that he is obliged to "play Hamlet to Miss Havisham's Ghost."

Estella is a thoroughly interesting young siren, quite a contrast to Little Emily of David Copperfield. Edgar Johnson and others taking after him have strongly maintained that the very name Estella derives from a combination of phonemes and letters in the name of Dickens's mistress, Ellen Lawless Ternan;[305]

---

[303]Doubtless, a creative writer may portray ambiguity within the mind of an individual he creates if he so chooses; but such a choice may be doubtful at that, and, at any rate, his conception of such evil or deficiency cannot itself be ambiguous to be successful.

[304]This parallel occurred to me soon after reading Faulkner's "A Rose for Emily"; Earle Davis, however, has recently commented as follows on the comparison: "The relationship between Faulkner's Emily and Dickens' Miss Havisham could become apparent only after the advent of Faulkner" (The Flint and the Flame, pp. 310-311).

[305]Johnson writes, "It is inevitable that we should associate Pip's helpless enslavement to Estella with Dickens's desperate passion for Ellen Lawless Ternan. The very name 'Estella' seems a kind of lawless anagram upon some of the syllables and initials of Ellen's name" (II, 991)--underscoring mine.

for, they argue, Pip was unable to be happy with Estella, which would correspond
to Ellen's not very happy relationship with Dickens.[306] This may be true, but I
am nevertheless inclined to believe that Estella is an echo of Ophelia, perhaps
a combination of both influences. (A double influence is, to be sure, possible
without the effect of ambiguity.) The number of letters and syllables, as well
as the stress, is the same in both names, the closing vowels are the same, the
"-el" phoneme is similar, and the last four letters in both words are convincingly
analogous. Elizabeth Hope Gordon, in her study on the naming of Dickens's characters,
previously mentioned, surely would have approved of the possibility of such
influence.[307] Moreover, the Hamlet (revenge) theme of the novel with its Ghost
references and Wopsle's presentation of the play itself support also the assumption
of an Ophelia influence. Dickens had a consummated love relationship with Ellen
Ternan whereas the nearest that young Pip ever got to Estella was to touch his lips
to her cheek as a reward for having done well in a scuffle with young Pocket.
In view of this, the parallel seems much closer to Hamlet and Ophelia. Even Hamlet's
world-weary suggestion that Ophelia enter a nunnery suggests the chastity of their
relationship, one comparable to that between Pip and Estella; it may even have

---

306
     J. B. Priestley writes, "She confessed afterwards that the situation in
which she found herself during these years was one she deeply disliked, and she
probably helped to keep the secret not so much out of concern for Dickens's public
reputation as out of a feeling of shame, and with it a desire to forget this
chapter of her life" (pp. 91-92).

307
     The sounds of the two names Ophelia and Estella are similar in that they
both contain vowels which lend themselves to sonorous effects; as such, they are
reminiscent of Tennyson's fascination with vowel sounds, particularly as exemplified
in the names of some of his poetic female figures, such as Oenone, Adeline, and
Oriana.

been influenced in the famous final scene wherein hero and heroine determine to part as friends.[308] Even as Ophelia is for a time a would-be princess for Prince Hamlet, so Estella is referred to as "Princess" (XXIX, 223). True, Estella is turned into a paragon of frigidity by Miss Havisham; so possibly Hamlet's simulated coldness and cruelty to Ophelia presents a contrast to Pip's situation. However, we might remember from the letters that Dickens himself did not believe a true Hamlet should be especially cruel to Ophelia, that being precisely one of the reasons why he approved of Fechter's gentlemanly role.[309] Yet the similarity between the two couples (Hamlet and Ophelia, Pip and Estella) can be argued for without reference to Estella's coldness.

If the male-female relationship is comparable enough in both play and novel, so is the relationship between hero and confidant. Recalling how the friendship of Hamlet and Horatio is already underscored by the alliteration of the names, one sees now how such "euphuism" is carried over in a two-fold manner with the association of "Handel" Pip to Herbert Pocket, his best male friend. Much more important is that the two young men share each other's experience and arrive at similar Weltanschauungen. Herbert introduces his friend to society much as Horatio serves as a kind of social companion and at times stoical conscience for Hamlet.

---

[308]
    This is taken over, very likely, from a Renaissance convention, one based on the Neo-Platonic conception of friendliness. Cf. the well-known sonnet of Drayton's beginning "Since there's no help, come, let us kiss and part" (Idea, number 61).

[309]
    Cf. John Forster's essay of 11 October 1835, "Macready as Hamlet," reprinted in Dramatic Essays: John Forster, G. H. Lewes (London, 1896), p. 10.

There are other influences that suggest themselves. In the "first stage" of Pip's expectations, only an incident in the home life before the London adventures deserves further notice. Wopsle's interest in histrionics illustrates a very significant Shakespeare influence, indeed the most direct of all the Hamlet influences on the novelist. At the beginning of the reading of the George Barnwell tragedy chapter, we get a real inkling of the Hamlet influence to come. Since Pip "assists" at the reading and thereby identifies himself directly with the hero of the play, the importance of the event should not be minimized. It is similar to Hamlet even in an uncle being murdered. It may be seen as a variation of the play-within-a-play, similar to The Murder of Gonzago in Hamlet; as such, it serves as an anticipation of coming events. The analogy is admittedly a minor one, and yet it is there. If one still questions the coincidence of the stage troupe in Hamlet happening to have such a Hamlet-like play in its repertoire,[310] he ought to reflect on the situation in Great Expectations where the mere reading of the George Barnwell tragedy serves as an anticipation of the later Hamlet production. Dickens surely intended this. Pumblechook's admonitions to Pip following the reading slightly recall Polonius's sententiousness. Indeed, Pip's disrespectful reference to "that ass, Pumblechook" (XII, 91) recalls Hamlet's mockery of Polonius as one of those "tedious old fools!" (II.ii.218). Pip does recognize his rudeness and lack of consideration in time when he admits "for all that, I remember feeling convinced that I had been mistaken

---

[310] Hamlet does insert speeches in The Murder of Gonzago, but the basic similarity is there from the start. Thus Professor Samuel C. Chew, in his review of J. Dover Wilson's What Happens in "Hamlet," New York Herald Tribune Books, 9 February 1936, writes, "He does not account for the coincidence that the visiting players have in their repertory 'The Murder of Gonzago'" (p. 5).

in him, and that he was a sensible practical good-hearted prime fellow" (XIX, 148-149), but his last meeting with Pumblechook is utterly derisive.

The so-called "second stage" of Pip's expectations is separated from the first in the diagram by the description of the reading of the George Barnwell tragedy. We might also bring in Wopsle's reading of the murder story in the paper when Jaggers appears; he sees then how difficult it is to be sure of a person's guilt (Hamlet's dilemma!). This division in the novel may be recognized as corresponding to the division of Shakespeare's tragedy into two parts: that which precedes and that which follows the play-within-the-play. The analogy has far-reaching implications, for even as the Gonzago tragedy confirms as well as implements the real tragedy, so the Barnwell tragedy foreshadows and prompts the more impressive production of Hamlet in Great Expectations. It has become popular now to regard that tragedy as a play actually about playing, a drama concerned with action, inaction, and thereby the very nature of acting itself.[311] According to such views, the play-within-the-play serves mainly to point out this very basic premise (even as, say, Coleridge's "Kubla Khan" has recently been called a poem about how to write a poem and thereby contains its own miniature poem within itself).[312] If, then, the assumption is an accurate one, that is if the theory matches the design, it may carry over into Great Expectations where there is, not a novel-within-a-novel to be sure, but (1) a play-within-a-novel that relates to (2) another play-within-a-novel, just as the

---

[311] Cf. Jean S. Calhoun, "'Hamlet' and the Circumference of Action," Renaissance News, XV (1962), 281-298.

[312] See George Watson, "The Meaning of 'Kubla Khan,'" The Review of English Literature, II (1961), 21-29. (Professor Watson advises me that he is in the process of revising this essay, however, so its conclusions may be somewhat modified in its later form.)

play-within-the-play in Hamlet relates to (2) this play-within-a-novel. In other words, we have another example of Dickens adapting Shakespeare's devices to fit his own ends. Realizing the import of the play-within-the-play to the structure of Hamlet, he decided to incorporate this device within his novel.

In the "second stage" of his expectations, Pip begins to try to measure up to what is expected of him. Like Hamlet, he finds himself dissimulating; whereas the Prince feigns madness in order to distract attention from his real pursuit, Pip plays a social game in order to prove that he can be a gentleman and thereby, as he imagines, can win Estella. To be sure, the relationship is more one of contrast than of similarity, although since the Prince is the natural heir, his actions are, at least to some extent, naturally motivated by his right to succeed to the throne: in that sense, he too has "Great Expectations," and he too loses them, though in a more tragic way than does Pip.

III

There is now a point of great subtlety that needs consideration regarding the important line on Pip's apparently unconscious motivation to "play Hamlet to Miss Havisham's Ghost." One knows that Miss Havisham is a mad woman, what would medically be termed a paranoic; one also knows that Hamlet simulates madness and that a considerable number of scholars have concerned themselves with the question of whether or not he is, not just pretending to be deranged, but actually what he pretends to be. Thus the interesting question poses itself of whether there was a possible influence of the "madness" theme in Hamlet upon the "madness" of Miss Havisham as a Dickensian Hamlet Ghost. For inasmuch as Miss Havisham is such a spirit to Pip, whether unconsciously or not, she is indeed such a being in the structure of the novel; so the parallel is an entirely fair one to make.

One knows that Dickens was very much interested in the theme of derangement as seen in King Lear. So it is clearly possible that he was influenced by the problem of madness in Hamlet also. Now, scholarship (aside from the lunatic fringe) has confidently claimed in recent years that there is no evidence of real insanity in the character of the Prince; indeed, the common opinion is that we would not have the affection we have for Hamlet if he were deranged. The many references to the Hamlet Ghost in the novels suggest that if Dickens saw any madness at all in the tragedy, he found it more likely in the Ghost (as well as, of course, Ophelia) than in the Prince. True, the critical article on the play in Household Words mentioned earlier makes something of madness in the tragedy (thus: "it is made difficult to follow by the circumstance that two of the principal characters are mad, a third is foolish, and a fourth is a ghost"), but Dickens himself was no doubt acquainted with the authentic story of the Danish Prince which Shakespeare used and which was reported in a series of historically-oriented articles in the same periodical: "Touching the Lord Hamlet" and "Re-touching the Lord Hamlet."[313] If, then, Dickens was influenced by the "madness" theme in the tragedy when he developed his characterization of the paranoic "Ghost," Miss Havisham, he may have been influenced strictly by a mad apparition.

Let one see how well this tallies with the play itself. In recent years there has been much concern over what Shakespeare intended with the Hamlet Ghost: Was it supposed to be "ambiguous," pagan, or purgatorial? In terms of the sacramental references, it appears to be a Catholic spirit; yet to demand revenge

---

[313] Household Words, XVI (17 October 1857), 372-376; Household Words, XVI (5 December 1857), 545-548. Both articles deal with the literary sources of the story as found in the writings of Saxo Grammaticus's Historia Danica and François de Belleforest's Histoires Tragiques.

is clearly unchristian. Thus Sister Miriam Joseph Rauh, intent as she is to show that the Ghost has a basis in the writings of the Old Testament and therefore would not have been abrogated by Christ, who came not to deny but to fulfill, concedes the following: "West remarks aptly: '. . . Grant, too, Battenhouse's point that vindictiveness is not a suitable inclination in a purgatorial soul; we still feel that the ghost is Christian and from a Christian purgatory.'"[314] West means that, in spite of the fact that the Hamlet Ghost is being vindictive in demanding revenge, the feeling that the apparition is Christian and purgatorial does not leave the spectator-reader. He concludes that the Ghost is "ambiguous" (perhaps unresolved would be the best translation of what he means here). Alfred Harbage, however, takes a somewhat different stand; he claims that the apparition is "highly moral, even citing past marital fidelity . . . and fervidly religious, mentioning with horror the denial at death of the last rites of the church . . . and yet it is immorally and irreligiously demanding vengeance, thus compounding the sins for which it is at present suffering in purgatory."[315] The implications, then, are that the Ghost is indeed purgatorial and sinning (adding to its sins).

Is such an interpretation consistent with Roman Catholic teaching? The answer, at first blush, is negative. But then we have reason to believe that Shakespeare was not so staunchly influenced by strict Catholic doctrine; there is more evidence, at least in terms of his baptism and burial, that he was a member of the Church of England.[316] So he would not have been bound by Catholic

---

[314] "Discerning the Ghost in Hamlet," p. 502.

[315] Harbage, pp. 312-313.

[316] For more on Shakespeare's religion, see Robert F. Fleissner, "The Misused Sacrament in King John," The Shakespeare Newsletter, X (1960), 28.

d o g m a which states that it is impossible for a purgatorial soul to sin.
On the other hand, however, one can reconcile Shakespeare's idea with Catholic
teachings if one draws a sharp distinction between life and art, for certainly
such a spirit as a sinning purgatorial ghost is possible simply as a theatrical
device, at least as much so as half-man-half-fish Caliban is. Moreover,
strictly speaking one can argue that the Ghost is not really in but rather from
purgatorial confines (thus it refers to its "prison-house" in such a way as if
to imply that it was temporarily absent from the place of incarceration). Perhaps
the fairest interpretation is that the Ghost acts in a rather inebriated manner
for a supposedly pious spirit, that it is by no means a "normal purgatorial
ghost" but, if one pleases, a demented one. For what sane ghost, one may ask,
would add to its sins the way that this one does?

Dickens, in the recesses of his mind at least, had a similar idea; it is
rooted in common sense and would hardly escape the average mentality, let alone
such a creative mind as the novelist had. Let us glance at a scholarly comment:
"The Ghost is, for the most part, a dreadful bore, because he will babble so
much and to so little purpose; a weakness that his son inherited from him! His
message to Hamlet could have been conveyed in a dozen or so dramatic lines.
But we must not forget that Shakespeare may have been swayed by the desire to
give some declamatory actor a chance of distinction. Perhaps himself?"[317]

317
W. Teignmouth Shore, Shakespeare's Self (London, 1920), p. 146, partially
reprinted in Hamlet: Enter Critic, ed. Claire Sacks and Edgar Whan (New York, 1960),
pp. 201-208. Cf. the reference to the specter being a "talkative ghost" in the
Household Words article, "Something that Shakespeare Wrote."

Now, if the Ghost "will babble so much and to so little purpose" as Shore says
here, this would amount to another symptom of derangement.

It is not too far-fetched to conceive of a deranged ghost, for the
Elizabethans were universally interested in mad beings, liked to visit asylums
for the insane to watch the antics of the inmates, and they attended plays
dealing with the theme of madness in one way or another (such as Middleton and
Rowley's The Changeling, Middleton's A Mad World, My Masters, and Ford's The
Mad Lover). The Elizabethan connotation of the word mad in reference to the
Ghost would not have been necessarily derogatory because the word conveyed,
often enough, the meaning of exuberance rather than the more clinical one.
Furthermore, a member of the audience would not easily have identified himself
with such a spirit. Then as now, the average theatre-goer doubtlessly felt that
people who said that they saw ghosts were letting their imagination run away
with them. With a masterstroke, Shakespeare objectified this hallucinatory
performance by making the specter mad and thereby a parody, as it were, upon its
own existence. Far from making fun of himself, the dramatist was laughing at
the foibles of the human imagination; that he did so with ease is evident from
the tradition which says that he took the part of the Ghost on the stage.

Such a view is very helpful when we come to analyzing Dickens's
reactions to the play. Surely the novelist's Hamlet Ghost conceptions, from
Chillip and Betsey Trotwood to Miss Havisham, are also in their way mad enough
and thus such parodies as described above.

In connection with this effect of parody transformed into Dickensian
character, Pip's references to his servant, "The Avenger," ought to be glanced
at. That references to this individual pertain to the tragedy is clear from

the fact that they are introduced just before and just after Joe's description
of a production of the play. The shift from a description of King Hamlet's Ghost
in a production of the tragedy to the "ghost-seeing effect in Joe's own
countenance" and finally to "the Avenger" (XXVII, 211-212) provides the parallel
and analogy well enough. Moreover, it points emphatically to the forthcoming
production of Wopsle's followed by Pip's dream that he is playing the role of the
Prince to Miss Havisham's Ghost. Thus even as there is a "ghost-seeing effect
in Joe's own countenance," so there is such an effect in Pip's mind. Joe
temporarily comes under the influence, anticipating Pip's much stronger commitment.
His relationship to Pip at times is remindful of that between Ham and David in
Copperfield. Joe has just seen the play, has presumably identified himself with
the hero ("if the ghost of a man's own father cannot be allowed to claim his
attention, what can, Sir?"), and then he reacts momentarily as if he too sees a
ghost. The episode is relatively unimportant with regard to the overall structure
of the novel, but none the less genuinely Dickensian and of interest in the context
of this study. "The Avenger," in short, is a reflection of the Ghost as both
mad and a parody upon its own existence; rather than simply being a scapegoat for
Pip's snobbery (which is perhaps the more common view, but not the one closest
to Dickens's intent), this "Avenger" is really not out for revenge at all but is
merely a friendly, sometimes impish, haunting spirit. The other allusions to
the play in the "Avenger" references also point to this association.

IV

There are intimations of the religious issue in Dickens's description
of the Wopsle performance, such as the following: "The noble boy in the ancestral
boots, was inconsistent; representing himself, as it were in one breath, as an

able seaman, a strolling actor, a gravedigger, a clergyman. . . . This gradually
led to a want of toleration for him, and even--on his being directed in holy orders,
and declining to perform the funeral service--to the general indignation" (XXXI,
245). Further references to the graveyard scene, to the undertaker's profession,
and to soliloquizing about life and death strongly support the contention that
Dickens was aware of the religious element in the tragedy, as he naturally would
have been from having taken a special interest in Charles Fechter's Roman Catholic
production of it. One can then recall religious overtones in Great Expectations:
there is the season of the year, Christmas (this may have little to do with religion
in the novel, but one should not forget that Wopsle does say grace and that,
after all, Christmas feasting is basically a festivity in honor of the birth of
the Christ child); Pip goes to church with Joe and holds his prayerbook upside-
down, a plausible symbolic indication that his expectations eventually will tumble,
that he will fail to attain them in the end.[318] But the most important point
in Hamlet that may have been religiously influential here is the Ghost's injunction "Taint not thy mind" (I.v.85). Dickens may have been sufficiently
motivated by this admonition to adapt it in his novel in a significantly structural
manner so that even as the Prince's downfall may be ascribed to his having failed
to follow what the Ghost advised, so Pip's downfall, the loss of his great
expectations, results from a similar set of circumstances.

A number of prominent scholars have made much of the effect of "tainting"
in Great Expectations. Edgar Johnson thus writes of "the blacksmith and 'the

---

[318] An interesting comparable cross-reference here is Steerforth's laughing
in church, perhaps likewise an intimation of his destiny, his desire to flaunt
conventional morality. (Though it is true that some sermons by their very nature
contain humorous quips, a "laughing" reaction is not a proper one surely.)

214

taint of prison and crime' which have so mortified Pip, and of which he comes to feel a remorseful humiliation at ever having been ashamed."[319] G. Robert Stange likewise refers to "the patterns of culpability"[320] in the novel and describes how Pip soils his thoughts: "After visiting Newgate Pip, still complacent and self-deceived, thinks how strange it was that he should be encompassed by the taint of prison and crime. He tries to beat the prison dust off his feet and to exhale its air from his lungs; he is going to meet Estella, who must not be contaminated by the smell of crime,"[321] or so he thinks. Stange concludes that "the final moral vision of Great Expectations has to do with the nature of sin and guilt."

Now one should examine what Dickens himself said in the novel:

> I /¯Pip_7 consumed the whole time in thinking how strange it was that I
> should be encompassed by all this taint of prison and crimes; that, in
> my childhood out on our lonely marshes on a winter evening I should have
> first encountered it; that, it should have reappeared on two occasions,
> starting out like a stain that was faded but not gone; that, it should
> in this new way pervade my fortune and advancement. . . . So contaminated
> did I feel, remembering who was coming, that the coach came quickly after
> all, and I was not yet free from the soiling consciousness of Mr. Wemmick's
> observatory, when I saw her face at the coach window and her hand waving
> to me. (XXXII, 255--italics mine)

That is the strongest statement of Pip's awareness of being tainted. But in a previous chapter, he has already felt it encroaching upon him:

> I was to leave our village at five in the morning, carrying my little
> hand-portmanteau, and I had told Joe that I wished to walk away all alone. I

---

[319]Charles Dickens, II, 988-989.

[320]Stange, p. 17.

[321]Stange, p. 16.

was afraid--sore afraid--that this purpose originated in my sense of the contrast there would be between me and Joe, if we went to the coach together. I had pretended with myself that there was nothing of _this_ _taint_ in the arrangement; but when I went up to my little room on this last night, I felt compelled to admit that it might be done so, and had an impulse upon me to go down again and entreat Joe to walk with me in the morning. I did not. (XIX, 152--italics mine)

Whatever the inherent cause of Pip's feeling may be, whether it represents a social maladjustment or is symbolic, in a larger sense, of isolation or personal inadequacy,[322] the consciousness of being tainted is unmistakable. One thinks of the tragedy of the Danish Prince, of the Ghost's admonition, and of the imagery relating to decay and corruption in the drama. It appears as if the Prince could hardly have done anything else than taint his mind when there was "something rotten" in Denmark.[323] But why should Pip have had such a reaction to life in Victorian England?

Why, indeed? Julian Moynahan, in "The Hero's Guilt: The Case of Great Expectations," sums up the question as follows: "Snobbery is not a crime. Why should Pip feel like a criminal?"[324] To revert to Hamlet, one might ask also what should have made the Prince feel despondent about his mother's remarriage before he learns of his father's murder, aside from the moral corruption of which he is cognizant from the start. Or why did Hamlet allow himself to be influenced by the rotten state in which he found himself? Goethe's explanation, that the Prince's nature was too sensitive for the task imposed upon him (what has been anglicized

---

[322] It may be symbolic even of the effects of Original Sin.

[323] The most comprehensive work on the decay theme in the drama is Richard D. Altick, "Hamlet and the Odor of Mortality," Shakespeare Quarterly, V (1954), 167-176.

[324] Essays in Criticism, X (1960), 60.

as Hamlet's analogy to "an oaktree planted in a costly vase"),[325] is one
solution. Is it the correct one? Is Pip's nature also overly sensitive?

Forced to find a basis for the feeling of guilt, for this taint that
Pip feels, Moynahan relies on a literary hybrid: "In Great Expectations
criminality is displaced from the hero on to a melodramatic villain. But on
closer inspection that villain becomes part of a complex unity--we might call
it Pip-Orlick--in which all aspects of the problem of guilt become inter-
penetrant and co-operative."[326] His conclusion is that "regardless of the
fact that Pip's association with crimes and criminals is purely adventitious
and that he evidently bears no responsibility for any act or intention of
criminal violence, he must be condemned on the principle of guilt by association."[327]
In a similar manner, J. Hillis Miller writes of "the secret 'taint of prison
and crime.'"[328] Stange relates it all to Dickens himself: "A few years after
he wrote Great Expectations Dickens remarked to a friend that he felt always
as if he were wanted by the police--'irretrievably tainted.'"[329] Was the
novelist's guilt complex showing up in his novel? Possibly, but it seems much
more likely that, in terms of the Hamlet influence, Pip's fear of being tainted
was inspired by the Ghost's advice to the Prince.

Here is the evidence. Pip's "taint" derives from his association with
criminal forces and stolen money, and the convict is associated with ghostliness

---

[325]Variorum Edition, II, 273 (from Wilhelm Meiste., ed. Carlyle, V).

[326]Moynahan, p. 70.

[327]Moynahan, p. 62.

[328]
Miller, p. 271.

[329]
Stange, p. 17.

in Pip's mind. As mentioned earlier, Stange speaks of Magwitch rising up before
Pip in the cemetery from behind a tombstone "like a ghost from among the graves."
After Magwitch's final return, Pip's thoughts are disclosed: "I doubt if a
ghost could have been more terrible to me, up in those lonely rooms in the long
evenings and long nights, with the wind and the rain always rushing by. A
ghost could not have been taken and hanged on my account, and the consideration that
he could be, and the dread that he would be, were no small addition to my "horrors"
(XL, 327). But how does the Hamlet influence relate precisely to Pip's situation?

Consider the Ghost's remark in full: "But howsoever thou pursuest this act,
/ Taint not thy mind; nor let thy soul contrive / Against thy mother aught" (I.v.85-
86). The standard twentieth-century interpretation is that the Prince is hereby
warned not to allow his mind to become polluted with unsavory or unchristian
thoughts regarding how he should act toward his mother, knowing that she has wed
his father's and her former husband's murderer. But such a reading has come about
largely, I submit, because the semicolon in the Folio ("mind; nor") was replaced
by a comma in later collected editions. True, Elizabethan punctuation was not
always stable, and the pause with a semicolon need not always have been greater
than that with a comma. But the likelihood that a rhetorical shift was intended at
this point is strong.[330] (One might also consider the possibility that the
punctuation was only the compositor's, but Professor Fredson Bowers writes me that
there is no evidence of such contamination here.) Thus, in cautioning the Prince

---

[330] Cf. J. Dover Wilson: "The light pointing of the Second Quarto with its single
exclamation, and its couple of semi-colons, gives us a meditation, spoken swift as
thought, but with two striking pauses. And these pauses, these two semi-colons are
the clue to the speaker's mood." What Happens in "Hamlet" (Cambridge, 1951), p. 41.
(Professor Wilson, however, is not always consistent in his theories of punctuation.)
In relating "Taint not thy mind" to the mother rather than the father, Wilson claims
that the Ghost's command is "ominous," for the Prince's mind is already as polluted
as his flesh, i.e., "his blood is tainted, his very flesh corrupted, by what his
mother has done; since he is bone of her bone and flesh of her flesh" (p. 42); "That
royal couch! The thought of it . . . had begun to 'taint' Hamlet's mind before he
sees the Ghost" (p. 46). Yet cf. Measure for Measure, IV.iv.5: "Pray heaven his
wisdom be not tainted!"

to avoid contaminating his mind, the Ghost was reminding his son that he
could not accomplish his deed as just punishment if he allowed thoughts of
personal vengeance to interfere.[331]

Leaving aside the question of whether Hamlet actually pollutes his
mind as he is warned not to (I do not know the answer to this),[332] one can
assuredly state that there is no real evidence that Pip has committed a sin
in any grievous manner; his mind seems tainted, not his soul. His appetitive
faculty or will is not involved. Estella's capacity of affection, however,
is so stunted that she becomes the one in greater spiritual peril. Thus
whereas Pip loses his great expectations, his riches, she loses something far
more valuable: she loses him.

---

[331]
Taint is too strong a verb to relate to Gertrude as well as, or instead
of, Claudius. There is not enough evidence that Gertrude is guilty of adultery;
her weakness (cf. "frailty, thy name is woman") is possibly more related to moral
omission than commission. To consider "Taint not thy mind" as relating to Hamlet's
feelings about Gertrude and not to the method of pursuing the act of retributive
justice may well be to taint the meaning of the passage, to obscure Shakespeare's
intended meaning.

[332]
Sister Miriam Joseph Rauh contends, in her second article aforementioned,
that the Prince taints his mind at the precise moment when he wishes Claudius
damned. This may be so, but it is no proven fact. One might also argue the
point that Hamlet's wishing Claudius in hell is but an excuse for his not killing
the King at that time. One wonders which would have been more mind-tainting:
killing the King (an acknowledged sacrilege) or just wishing the King damned. Is
Hamlet not simply acknowledging that he does not want to strike a man whose back
is turned? (This was my contention in an unpublished controversy with Paul N.
Siegel for the Modern Language Association, one corroborated by Professor Peter
Alexander in his New York University public lecture on "The Psychoanalyst on
Shakespeare," 1963.) He is doing that, yes, but there is also reason enough to
think that the Prince is possessed or at least obsessed by an evil force when
he utters his terrible words. But that is no definite indication that he is
deliberately tainting his mind; on the contrary, it suggests that he is not
entirely in control of his mind at this point, not because he is mad (which he
is only pretending to be) but because an outside force is exerting control over
it. If his mind is tainted, it is hardly his responsibility then if he is unable
to exercise his freedom of will to the fullest extent.

CHAPTER FIVE:

THE INDEBTEDNESS TO SHAKESPEARE IN

MARTIN CHUZZLEWIT

In this chapter I am going to consider one of Dickens's fullest but at the same time most puzzling novels structurally. Martin Chuzzlewit, the work to be discussed, appears to split down the middle when Mark Tapley and Martin, the Younger Chuzzlewit, travel to America. Yet this defect may not seem so pronounced when we consider how Shakespeare's Winter's Tale likewise breaks in two, as has been said, and still is all the more effective perhaps for this division. At least, there is no reason why such a "break" need always be seen as destructive of the unity of a work of art; it may in certain cases add a measure of proportionality.

First, another list of annotated references will be presented; second, the meaning of a somewhat technical term designated the nil-factor will be considered linguistically; third, in the light of Dickens's use of this linguistic constituent, not only in Chuzzlewit but in the other novels, the particular meaning it had for him will be examined in relation to the influence of King Lear upon him; fourth, the other influences of that tragedy in the novel will be summarized. But my coup de grâce will be the hitherto unrevealed influence of the storm scene in Lear upon one here.

219

I

A List of the Principal Shakespearian References in Martin Chuzzlewit:[333]

1. "If it should ever be urged by grudging and malicious persons, that a Chuzzlewit, in any period of the family history, displayed an overweening amount of family pride. . ." (I, 1).

       /Since Aristotelian times, overweening pride or _hybris_ has been considered to be the basis for the _hamartia_, the tragic flaw or fault. Like a later reference to "Mr. Pecksniff as **Chorus**" (XLIII, 673), indeed "the Chorus in a Greek Tragedy" (XLIII, 673), this allusion serves to buttress the relationship between the novel and tragic drama. _/

2. "'John, there is scarcely a sin in the world that is in my eyes such a crying one as ingratitude'" (II, 23).

       /References to the theme of ingratitude permeate _King_ _Lear_, e.g., "Ingratitude, thou marble-hearted fiend" (I.iv.260). _/

3. "'Madness!' returned young Westlock. 'Certainly, it's madness. Who but a madman would suppose. . . , eh, Tom? Who but a madman would suppose it is the game of such a man as he, to have his name in everybody's mouth, connected with the thousand useless odds and ends you do (and which, of course, he taught you), eh, Tom? Who but a madman . . ., eh, Tom? . . . to be more wild and monstrous still, if that be possible, as well might one suppose . . . that Pecksniff traded in your nature, and that your nature was, to be timid and distrustful of yourself, and trustful of all other men, but most of all, of him who least deserves it. There would be madness, Tom!" (II, 25).

       /Here, as elsewhere, the very idea of madness suggests _Lear_. This is particularly reasonable with the reference to Tom, for one is apt to think of "Poor Tom," the mad impersonation taken by Edgar in the tragedy. _/

-4. Chapter III: A description of the "Blue Dragon" Inn and an ensuing description of dragonology.

       /Compare Shakespearian references to the dragon, particularly in _Lear_, I.i. 121, I.ii.132. _7

333
    See T. W. Hill, "Notes on _Martin_ _Chuzzlewit_," The _Dickensian_, XLII (1945), 141-148, 196-203; XLIII (1946), 28-35.

5. "He rather looked as if any quantity of butter might have been made out of him, by churning the milk of human kindness, as it spouted upwards from his heart" (III, 39).

> ⎾This is taken and adapted quite obviously from Macbeth, I.v.14-16: "Yet do I fear thy nature; / It is too full o' the milk of human kindness / To catch the nearest way." ⏌

6. Old Martin Chuzzlewit: "'The curse of my existence, and the realization of my own mad desire, is that by the golden standard which I bear about me, I am doomed to try the metal of all other men, and find it false and hollow'" (III, 40).

> ⎾This may be an oblique reference to the love-test at the beginning of King Lear. Afterwards the King discovers hypocrisy in his daughters, all save Cordelia who is obstinate, if not untrue; his awareness of this evil drives him gradually out of his wits. The humorous reference to the "golden standard" relates to Lear's false sense of hybris or pride that leads to the tragedy. For the King, in being unable to understand his youngest daughter, reveals that his own self-esteem is but dross, not the real golden standard that he would like to see in himself. ⏌

7. Old Martin Chuzzlewit: "'Oh self, self, self! At every turn nothing but self!' . . . 'Another will made and destroyed,' he said, 'nothing determined on, nothing done, and I might have died to-night!' . . . 'What lawsuits grow out of the graves of rich men every day: sowing perjury, hatred, and lies among near kindred, where there should be nothing but love!'"

"Universal self! Was there nothing of its shadow in these reflections, and in the history of Martin Chuzzlewit, on his own showing?" (III, 44).

> ⎾Here is the first major interplay of the nil-factor with the elements of the plot in the novel. As with number 6 above, the reference is very likely to Lear, to the pride of the King, his awareness of egotism in others and unfortunate lack of awareness of the same quality in himself. The repetition of the word nothing, considered in terms of the manifestation of the nil-factor throughout the novel, makes an allusion to the tragedy very likely. The context of the dying man and his will is relevant as is the phrase "nothing but love," which seems to echo Cordelia's love-response to the King ("Nothing"). That the play on the word subsequently reflects back on the King himself is evident both in the play and in Dickens's comment above ("Was there nothing . . .?"). ⏌

8. "Sir, if there is a man on earth whom a gentleman would feel proud and honoured to be mistaken for, that man is my friend Slyme. For he is, without exception, the highest-minded, the most independent-spirited, most original, spiritual, classical, talented, the most thoroughly Shakespearian, if not Miltonic, and at the same time the most disgustingly-unappreciated dog I know" (IV, 48).

"His sharp features being much pinched and nipped by long waiting in the cold, and his straggling red whiskers and frowzy hair being more than usually dishevelled from the same cause, he certainly looked rather un-wholesome and uncomfortable than Shakespearian or Miltonic" (IV, 49).

⌊The direct reference to Shakespeare tips the reader off and suggests that he be on the outlook for more extended allusions. ⌋

9. "'If I am gone to that what's-his-name from which no thingumbob comes back'" (IV, 48).

⌊A clear reference to Hamlet, III.i.79-80: "The undiscover'd country from whose bourn / No traveller returns" (the to-be-or-not-to-be soliloquy). Dickens has a clearer reference to the same passage in Copperfield (I, 12). ⌋

*10. "'As Hamlet says, Hercules may lay about him with his club in every possible direction, but he can't prevent the cats from making a most intolerable row on the roofs of the houses, or the dogs from being shot in the hot weather if they run about the streets unmuzzled'" (IV, 50).

⌊Hill: "A capital instance of the humorous way in which Dickens could deal with a quotation and turn it to his own purpose. The exact wording of the line from Hamlet is as follows: "Let Hercules himself do what he may, / The cat will mew, and dog will have his day" (V.i.281-282). ⌋

-11. "As to red noses (she observed) she had yet to learn that a red nose was any disgrace, inasmuch as people neither made nor coloured their own noses, but had that feature provided for them without being first consulted; though even upon that branch of the subject she had great doubts whether certain noses were redder than other noses, or indeed half as red as some" (IV, 58).

"It was morning; and the beautiful Aurora, of whom so much hath been written, said, and sung, did, with her rosy fingers, nip and tweak Miss Pecksniff's nose. It was the frolicsome custom of the Goddess, in her intercourse with the fair Cherry, so to do; or in more prosaic phrase, the tip of that feature in the sweet girl's countenance, was always very red at breakfast-time" (VI, 87).

/‾Since Shakespeare provided jokes on Bardolph's red nose
again and again, especially in The Merry Wives (in a production of which Dickens acted) and Henry V during the report
of Falstaff's death (which Dickens knew well too), it is
doubtful that he was not influenced by Shakespeare here as
well as by Fielding and the mock-heroic style. ‾/

-12. "He had much ado to see anything but his own knees" (V, 79); "much
ado" (XL, 635).

/‾The play on Much Ado about Nothing is very clear and serves
as a signal to the reader, one indicating that much ado about
the nil-factor (nothing, often in relation to something,
anything, and everything) will be forthcoming. Note the
Shakespearian reference in the very next sentence. See
number 25. ‾/

*13. "But it is an ill wind that blows nobody any good" (V, 79).

/‾Hill: "This originated apparently with Thomas Tusser (1523-1580):
'It is an ill wind that turns none to good,' and was adapted by
Shakespeare to its modern form: 'Not the ill wind which blows
no man to good'" (II King Henry IV, V.iii.90); compare "Ill blows
the wind that profits nobody" (III King Henry VI, II.v.55). ‾/

-14. "'What do you get for that, now?'
'Nothing,' answered Tom.
'Well,' returned his friend, 'you are a very strange fellow!'
To which remark there succeeded a brief silence.
'When I say nothing,' observed Mr. Pinch, cheerfully, 'I am wrong, and
don't say what I mean, because I get a great deal of pleasure from it, and
the means of passing some of the happiest hours I know /‾it being playing
the organ‾/. It led to something'" (V, 81).

/‾The love-test in Lear was influential again here, especially with
"it led to something" as a play on the King's "Nothing will come
of nothing." ‾/

-15. "He didn't know anything at all about it" (V, 83); "'such trifles as
girls love are here. Nothing more'" (V, 84); "a something to think of"
(V, 85); "Mr. Pinch . . . ate of everything" (V, 85).

/‾Here the interplay of anything, nothing, something, and everything
is striking (compare number 12). Such bunchings occur
throughout the novel at intervals. Consider: "'before I say
anything'"; "'What in the second place?' 'What in the second
place! . . . why, everything in the second place'"; "'anything
else but odds and ends that are of no use or service to anybody'"
(see number 54); "'I'll say anything'" (II, 23). ‾/

-16. Pecksniff "slept and dreamed at last. Thus in the quiet hours of the
night, one house shuts in as many incoherent and incongruous fancies as
a madman's head" (V, 87).

⌐The Pecksniff-Lear identification begins to emerge slowly
but never gets to the point where it really supersedes the
more striking Chuzzlewit-Lear relationship. Thus the playing
on "a madman's head" echoes number 3 with its similar talk
on "madness," relating to King Lear. ⌐

-17. "'There is nothing very selfish in that love, I think?'" (VI, 97); "he
said nothing to her" (VI, 98); "'to say nothing of her,' remarked Tom
Pinch, in a low voice. "'Exactly so,' rejoined Martin . . . . 'To say
nothing of her'" (VI, 100).

⌐The association of saying nothing (with reference to a lady)
appears to be a variation on the general theme of "more ado
about nothing" especially as echoed in Lear. ⌐

18. "'I'll fetch a book directly. What will you like? Shakespeare?'" (VI,
101).

"Mr. Pinch lost no time in moving away; and in a minute or two returned
with one of the precious volumes from the shelf beside his bed. Martin
had in the meantime made himself as comfortable as circumstances would
permit, by constructing before the fire a temporary sofa of three chairs
with Mercy's stool for a pillow, and lying down at full-length upon it.
   'Don't be too loud, please,' he said to Pinch.
   'No, no,' said Tom.
   'You're sure you're not cold?'
   'Not at all!'
   'I am quite ready, then.'
   Mr. Pinch accordingly, after turning over the leaves of his book
with as much care as if they were living and highly cherished creatures,
made his own selection, and began to read" (VI, 102).

⌐The phrase "What will you like? Shakespeare?" seems to echo
the dramatist's sub-title for Twelfth Night; which Dickens
knew, namely What You Will; it also echoes As You Like It.
The work of Shakespeare's referred to is a "poem" of many more
than "fifty lines" (VI, 102) and therefore has to be one of
the long narrative poems, either The Rape of Lucrece or Venus
and Adonis. In terms of Dickens's interests in criminology as
exemplified in Martin Chuzzlewit, the former poem would be more
apropos, though no conclusive evidence points to it. The long
rhetorical passages in Lucrece would also argue in favor of its
being referred to, especially since Martin is put to sleep by
the "sing-song" quality of the lines. What is more interesting
than the reference to a Shakespearian poem, with regard to the
influence of Lear, is the reflection of "Poor Tom's a-cold"
(III.iv.147 et passim) in "You're sure you're not cold?" Note
also that the name Pinch is itself Shakespearian and that
allusions to Tom as something of a fool(even like Edgar dressed
as Tom of Bedlam in Lear and exhibiting a comic antic disposition)
reverberate throughout the novel. Compare Barnaby Rudge and
Dick Swiveller as other fool-adaptations. ⌐

-19. "'Foxe's Book of Martyrs'" (VII, 105).

> ⌐This Elizabethan reference may point obliquely to
> Shakespeare again, since Foxe's standard work may
> well have had considerable impact upon Shakespeare
> (e.g., in Richard II). The book certainly provides
> a keynote and sets a mood with regard to Dickens's
> interest in martyrology as reflected especially in
> Barnaby Rudge and in the demise of a typical hero
> or heroine of his, such as Carton or Little Nell. ⌐

20. "'Was there ever . . . such an independent spirit as is possessed by
that extraordinary creature? Was there ever such a Roman as our
friend Chiv? Was there ever a man of such a purely classical turn
of thought, and of such a toga-like simplicity of nature?" (VII, 112).

> ⌐Inasmuch as Chiv is described as "most thoroughly
> Shakespearian" (IV, 48), the reference above is no
> doubt to the dramatist's Roman plays, perhaps including
> Hamlet with its references to Stoic friendship. ⌐

-21.   "'I won't ask you yet, my dears,' said Mr. Pecknsiff, looking
in at the door, 'how you like London. Shall I?'
'We haven't seen much of it, pa!' cried Mercy.
'Nothing, I hope,' said Cherry. (Both very miserably.)
'Indeed,' said Mr. Pecksniff, 'that's true. . .'" (VIII, 130).

> ⌐Another possible echo of Cordelia's response in the
> love-test in Lear is exemplified here. ⌐

22. "Does any one doubt the old saw, that the Devil (being a layman) quotes
Scripture for his own ends?" (XI, 178).

> ⌐The Merchant of Venice, I.iii.99. ⌐

-23. A description of Old Chuffey: "Such as he was, he came slowly creeping
on towards the table, until at last he crept into the vacant chair,
from which, as his dim faculties became conscious of the presence of
strangers, and those strangers ladies, he rose again, apparently
intending to make a bow. But he sat down once again, without having
made it, and breathing on his shrivelled hands to warm them, remained
with his poor blue nose immoveable about his plate, looking at
nothing, with eyes that saw nothing, and a face that meant nothing.
Take him in that state, and he was an embodiment of nothing. Nothing
else" (XI, 182-183).

> ⌐The nil-factor here is so striking that an influence
> of Shakespeare's use of it seems unquestionable. ⌐

24. "Tom entered as the words were spoken, with a radiant smile upon his face; and rubbing his hands, more from a sense of delight than because he was cold (for he had been running fast), sat down in his warm corner again, and was as happy as only Tom Pinch could be" (XII, 207).

    ⌐There appears to be another echo of "Tom's a-cold" here. See number 18. ⌐

-25. "He started off for London without more ado" (XIII, 224).

    ⌐This is another oblique link with Shakespeare: a play on Much Ado about Nothing. Isolated, the reference may seem extraordinarily far-fetched, but compare number 12 and relate the other references to the nil-factor. ⌐

26. "'Your pound of flesh'" (XIII, 225).

    ⌐The Merchant of Venice, I.iii.150, et passim. ⌐

-27. "'What are you doing in London?'
'Nothing at all, sir,' rejoined Mark.
'How's that?' asked Martin" (XIII, 235).

    ⌐This is another example of the disconcerting "Nothing" answer reminiscent of the love-test in King Lear. It especially reflects the echoing of the response in the Fool's interchange with the King later. ⌐

-28. "'Oh,' said Martin, checking himself, and folding up the letter, 'that's nothing!'. . . .
'Which I shouldn't have said nothing about sir,' added Mark. . . .
'Long to look back upon,' said Mary, echoing his cheerful tone, 'but nothing in their course!'
'Nothing at all!' cried Martin" (XIV, 246).

    ⌐Nil-factor⌐

-29. "Was there nothing jarring and discordant even in his tone of courage...?"

    "'I thank him for that last act,' said Martin, 'and for nothing else'"
                     (XIV, 247).

    ⌐Nil-factor⌐

30. "'He has written some powerful pamphlets, under the signature of 'Suturb,' or Brutus reversed" (XVI, 277).

    ⌐Suturb, "a man of fine moral elements" (XVI, 277) relates to the stoicism of Julius Caesar. Compare "He said so with a stoical indifference" (XVI, 272). ⌐

31. "Mr. Norris the son said nothing, but he made a wry face and dusted his fingers as Hamlet might after getting rid of Yorick's skull" (XVII, 293).

       /Here is an interesting relationship of the nil-factor to Hamlet. /

-32. Chapter XVIII contains an interplay of references to nothing, anything, and something, commencing with the opening lines ("Change begets change. Nothing propagates so fast").

33. "'It only proves, sir, what was so forcibly observed by the lamented theatrical poet--buried at Stratford--that there is good in everything'" (XIX, 320).

       /Indeed he showed that there is good even in nothing--as the reflections of the nil-factor indicate; Dickens is very likely referring to Much Ado about Nothing, II.i.75: "Tell him there is measure in every thing." /

-34. "Mr. Mould emphatically said, 'everything that money could do was done.' 'And what can do more, Mrs. Gamp?' exclaimed the undertaker, as he emptied his glass and smacked his lips.
'Nothing in the world, sir.'
'Nothing in the world,' repeated Mr. Mould" (XIX, 325).

35. "A question of philosophy arises here. . . . Now, there being a special Providence in the fall of a sparrow, it follows (so Mr. Pecksniff would have reasoned), that there must be a special Providence in the alighting of the stone, or stick, or other substance which is aimed at the sparrow" (XX, 334).

       /Though the ultimate source is Jesus's Sermon-on-the-Mount, Dickens takes directly after Shakespeare in Hamlet, V.ii.208-209:
           "there's a special providence in the fall of a sparrow";
the reference to "philosophy" recalls Horatio's stoicism. /

-36. Cherry: "Not she. She had seen nothing but her father until now."

Merry: "She was called and came, all flushed and tumbling from reposing on the sofa; but none the worse for that. No, not at all. Rather the better, if anything" (XX, 339).

       /The nothing-anything balance again recalls Lear. /

-37. "'Have you nothing else to say?' cried Charity. 'Am I to be driven mad, papa?'" (XX, 343).

       /An interesting gloss on Lear again in a chapter entitled "A Chapter of Love." /

-38. "'Do something.'

"'Bless you, <u>that's</u> nothing'" (XXIII, 388).

$\sqrt{}$Compare number 17. $\sqrt{}$

39. "'It is merely an hysterical affection; nothing more'" (XXIV, 390).

$\sqrt{}$This is related to King Lear's "Hysteria passio!"
(II.iv.55). $\sqrt{}$

-40. "It was memorable for nothing but embarrassment and confusion."

'You haven't a right to anything.'

'I've heard something of you. . . .'

'I am not afraid of many things, I hope. . . . and certainly not of
anything that you will do'" (XXIV, 396-397).

$\sqrt{}$Surely once again the <u>nothing-anything-something</u> cluster
is not unintentional and relates obliquely <u>Lear</u>. $\sqrt{}$

-41. "Nothing more passed. . . .

'It's nothing worth mentioning.'

'Oh, bother your <u>nonsense</u> . . . .'

Tom Pinch, in his guilty agitation, shook a bottle of Dutch Drops until
they were nothing but English Froth . . . .

And there was nothing personal in this. . . .

A flat something" (XXIV, 398-401).

$\sqrt{}$Here the nil-factor undergoes an abrupt change at the end
with a reference to "a flat something" (the implication
being that indeed something has to come from all these
nothings). $\sqrt{}$

-42. "'Nothing to the purpose, I suppose?'

'There's nothin' new?'
'Nothin' at all, my dear,' said Mrs. Gamp. 'He's rather wearin' in his
talk from making up a lot of names; elseways you needn't mind him.'
'Oh, I shan't mind him,' Mrs. Prig returned. 'I have somethin' else to
think of'" (XXV, 423).

$\sqrt{}$Here is another <u>nothing-something</u> cluster (modified). $\sqrt{}$

*43. "Wings of Love" (double reference) (XXVI, 429).

> ⌊Hill: "Proverbially swift, a figure of speech that is
> expressed in Shakespeare's unapproachable manner in 'The
> Merry Wives of Windsor,' Act II, Sc. 2: 'I have pursued
> her as love hath pursued me, which hath been on the wing
> of all occasions.'"⌋

44. "Shakespeare's an infernal humbug, Pip! What's the good of Shakespeare,
Pip? I never read him. What the devil is it all about, Pip? There's
a lot of feet in Shakespeare's verse, but there ain't any legs worth
mentioning in Shakespeare's plays, are there, Pip? Juliet, Desdemona,
Lady Macbeth, and all the rest of 'em, whatever their names are, might
as well have no legs at all, for anything the audience know about it,
Pip. Why, in that respect, they're all Miss Biffins to the audience,
Pip. I'll tell you what it is. What the people call dramatic poetry
is a collection of sermons. Do I go to the theatre to be lectured? No,
Pip. If I wanted that, I'd go to church. What's the legitimate object
of the Drama, Pip? Human nature. What are legs? Human nature. Then
let us have plenty of leg pieces, Pip, and I'll stand by you, my buck!"
(XXVIII, 460).

> ⌊This reflection on Shakespeare at least cannot be considered
> bardolatrous in the pejorative sense of that word. It is
> especially interesting as related to Dickens's other Pip in
> Great Expectations, where the very same kind of commentary
> is found after the description of Wopsle's production of
> Hamlet. Also compare the paper entitled "Legs" in Household
> Words, IX (15 April 1854), 209-212, e.g.: "If the heart be
> the stronghold of vitality, the legs are the outposts of
> life. The legs die first. The outposts are captured before
> the citadel is stormed. Mrs. Quickly put her hand upon poor
> dying Sir John Falstaff's legs, and they were 'as cold as
> a ⌊sic⌋ stone'"--p. 212).⌋

-45. "'Get out of my sight!'" (XXVIII, 464).

> ⌊Though such a remark is ordinary enough that it need not be
> traced back to Lear, none the less the King's explosive ex-
> clamations whereby he banishes Kent may well have remained
> in Dickens's memory. This is particularly possible when one
> considers that the allusions to sight (the verbal play similar
> to that related to the nil-factor) are structurally functional
> in the drama and reveal the King's spiritual blindness as
> opposed to Gloucester's physical blindness. Thus the King's
> remarks serve as perhaps the best evidence of irony. Consider
> especially "Hence and avoid my sight!" and "Out of my sight!"
> Lear, I.i.123, 156.⌋

46. " 'A father asking pardon of his child,' said Mr. Pecksniff, 'is, I believe, a spectacle to soften the most rugged nature'" (XXX, 479).

    / Lear's asking forgiveness of Cordelia comes to mind: "You must bear with me. Pray you now, forget and forgive; I am old and foolish" (IV.vii.84); "when thou dost ask me blessing, I'll kneel down / And ask of thee forgiveness" (V.iii.10-11). /

-47. "'One of my birds,' Mr. Pecksniff said, 'has left me for the stranger's breast; the other would take wing to Todgers's! Well, well, what am I? I don't know what I am, exactly. Never mind!'" (XXX, 480).

    / Cf. Lear's "We too alone will sing like birds i' th' cage" (V.iii.9). Many similar references to birds as caged and otherwise are evident in Dickens's writings, here and elsewhere. /

-48. "'But I have ever,' said Mr. Pecksniff, 'sacrificed my children's happiness to my own--I mean my own happiness to my children's--and I will not begin to regulate my life by other rules of conduct now. . . . Do not think of me, my girl! . . . I shall get on pretty well, no doubt'" (XXX, 480).

    / This is an indirect play on Lear's pride. /

-49. "His views upon this subject were at first so very limited that another difference, involving possibly another shaking, threatened to ensue; but by degrees they came to something like an understanding, and the storm blew over" (XXX, 480).

    / This again may be an allusion to Lear's wrath, as reflected finally in Nature itself during the storm scene. /

50. "As he sat down by the old man's side, two tears: not tears like those with which recording angels blot their entries out, but drops so precious that they use them for their ink: stole down his meritorious cheeks" (XXXI, 502).

    / The source of this allusion is very probably _Measure for Measure_, II.ii.121: "Plays such fantastic tricks before high heaven / As make the angels weep"; cf. _King Lear_, IV.iii.30-32: "she shook / The holy water from her heavenly eyes / That clamour moistened." It is possible that Dickens derived this from Milton, _Paradise Lost_, Book I, line 619: "Tears, such as angels weep, burst forth"; however, Milton most likely got the line from Shakespeare. So Dickens's allusion is at least indirectly, most likely directly, to Shakespeare. /

51. "There was the rub!" (XXXII, 517).

    / This is obviously derived from Hamlet's to-be-or-not-to-be soliloquy. /

*52. "It was (as the shrill boy cried out in an ecstasy) quite the Last
Scene from Coriolanus" (XXXIV, 549).

      /Hill: "The last act of the play, but not quite the last
      scene (the assassination). In Act V, Scene III, Coriolanus'
      wife, Virginia, accompanied by his mother, Volumnia,
      introduces into his presence young Marcus and Valeria.
      The whole noble scene should be read for comparison with
      preposterous Mrs. Hominy and Elijah Pogram." _/

53. "And though home is a name, a word, it is a strong one; stronger than
magician ever spoke, or spirit answered to, in strongest conjuration"
(XXXV, 555).

"Vanished awfully, like spectres" (XXXV, 556).

"As if he were a figure in a magic-lantern" (XXXV, 527).

"Oh! what a different town Salisbury was in Tom Pinch's eyes to be sure,
when the substantial Pecksniff of his heart melted away into an idle
dream!" (XXXVI, 562).

"A dreamy haze . . . in which they sometimes showed to magical advantage"
(XXXVI, 564).

      /These are all allusions to the magic of The Tempest; they form
      a kind of cluster. The fourth is, to be sure, most directly
      related to Shakespeare:
              "Yea, all . . . shall dissolve,
            And, like this insubstantial pageant faded,
            Leave not a rack behind. We are such stuff
            As dreams are made on, and our little life
            Is rounded with a sleep" (IV.i.173-177).
      According to the Folger Library General Reader's Shakespeare,
      here "Prospero is saying that life itself is as illusory
      /dream-like_/ as the magic show he has just evoked." _/

-54. "A thousand pleasant nothings" (XXXVI, 584); earlier: "the thousand
useless odds and ends you do" (II, 24).

      /These allusions help to round off the nil-factor in the
      chapter. Cf. "that man naturally . . . would have done
      nothing but grin and stare" (567); "Do begin at something
      or other, Tom" (571); "Nothing particular you'd like" (573);
      "there's everything in 'em!' 'Bless your soul, Tom, nothing
      but' . . . . 'there might be something in it'" (574); "'she
      has anything to do'" (576); "'I have nothing more to say'"
      (581); "said nothing" (582). The final allusion is related
      to the more colloquial "sweet nothings" though here, humorously
      enough, in a more literal sense. _/

-55. "'I say nothing,' said Charity. 'If I had not already known what
shocking things treachery and deceit are in themselves, Mr. Pinch. . . .
But I don't say anything. . . .'
There was something hidden here, which piqued Tom's interest and troubled
his tender heart. When, in a moment's irresolution, he looked at Charity,
he could not but observe a struggle in her face between a sense of triumph
and a sense of shame; nor could he but remark how, meeting even his eyes,
which she cared so little for, she turned away her own, for all the
splenetic defiance in her manner" (XXXVII, 583).

$\underline{/}$An echo is here of the love-test. $\underline{}$

-56. "'The Elements may have me when they please. I'm ready'" (XXXVII, 593).

$\underline{/}$Possibly this suggests Lear "contending with the
fretful elements" (III.i.4); cf. my explication of
the trip to America in terms of a $\underline{Lear}$ influence later
in this chapter. $\underline{}$

*57. "'Your bosom's lord sits lightly on its throne, Mr. Chuzzlewit, as
what's-his-name says in the play. I wish he said it in a play which did
anything like common justice to our profession, by the bye. There is an
apothecary in that drama, sir, which is a low thing; vulgar, sir; out
of nature altogether?" (XLI, 647).

$\underline{/}$Romeo and Juliet, V.i.3. $\underline{}$

58. "The Atlantic Ocean and the Red Sea being, in that respect, all one,
Martin hugged her instantly" (XLIII, 666).

$\underline{/}$The phrase in that respect suggests an oblique allusion
to Macbeth: "making the green, one red" (II.ii.63), one
of the most famous of Shakespearian emendations. Since
Dickens had his hand in emending Shakespeare, he might
well have been cognizant of this one too. (The allusion
in Macbeth is to making the green expanse of oceans
everywhere completely red with blood.) $\underline{}$

-59.   "'There is nothing else?'
'Nothing else,' said Mr. Pecksniff buoyantly. . . .
'You have nothing more to say?' inquired the old man. . . .
Mr. Pecksniff would not say what rose to his lips. For reproaches,
he observed, were useless.
'You have nothing at all to urge? You are sure of that? If you
have, no matter what it is, speak freely. I will oppose nothing that you
ask of me,' said the old man" (XLIII, 678).

$\underline{/}$Nil-factor$\underline{}$

-60. "It is the custom to use as many words as possible, and express nothing whatever.
A caution from Mr. Tapley; a hasty interchange of farewells, and of something else which the proverb says must not be told of afterwards; a white hand held out to Mr. Tapley himself, which he kissed with the devotion of a knight-errant; more farewells, more something else's" (ALIII, 682).

/ Nothing-something cluster /

-61. "'There is nothing the matter?'

'There's nothing the matter with her.'
'There is nothing the matter with her!' cried Mr. Pecksniff" (XLIV, 684).

/ Nil-factor /

-62. "'Suppose we talk about something else, now,' observed Jonas drily" (XLIV, 685).

"A flexible adaptability to anything and everything" (XLIV, 688).

"Nothing was more probable, they all agreed. . . .
    'You said nothing about that, Chuzzlewit.' . . .
    'There is nothing like building our fortunes on the weaknesses of mankind'" (XLIV, 689).

    'I have Something to do,' said Jonas. 'Good-bye!'" (XLIV, 693).

/ The nil-factor cluster here is resolved, through the use of a capitalized "Something." /

63. "The starts with which he left his couch, and looking in the glass, imagined that his deed was broadly written in his face, and lying down and burying himself once more beneath the blankets, heard his own heart beating Murder, Murder, Murder, in the bed; what words can paint tremendous truths like these!" (XLVII, 735).

/ Macbeth, II.ii.36, 42: "Macbeth does murder sleep"; "Macbeth shall sleep no more." /

-64. "And then Tom (as John Westlock had done on his arrival) ran off to the loaf to cut some bread-and-butter for them; and before he had spread a single slice, remembered something else, and came running back again to tell it; and then he shook hands with them again; and then he introduced his sister again; and then he did everything he had done already all over again; and nothing Tom could do, and nothing Tom could say, was half sufficient to express his joy at their safe return" (XLVIII, 739).

/ Something-everything-nothing cluster /

-65. "Jonas heard this with a sinking heart. He knew that they were on his heels, and felt that they were resolute to run him to destruction. Inch by inch the ground beneath him was sliding from his feet; faster and faster the encircling ruin contracted and contracted towards himself, its wicked centre, until it should close in and crush him" (LI, 790).

⌈This is very likely a hidden allusion to the wheel of Fortune, especially as revealed in Lear, e.g., "The wheel is come full circle" (V.iii.173), indicating that the cycle of iniquity has closed upon itself.⌉

66. "Sinning more against himself than others" (LII, 815).

⌈King Lear, III.ii.58-59: "I am a man / More sinned against than sinning"; Dickens modifies the famous line to suit his purposes.⌉

II

A most interesting article in a recent issue of Language by Henry M. Hoenigswald broaches a subject long in need of objective, scientific treatment, one particularly relevant to this discussion of Martin Chuzzlewit.[334] In an attempt to apprehend absence rather than presence (or, if one likes, to note the presence of absence), he relates himself to contemporary endeavors to ascertain the symmetrical properties of the vacuum.[335] His aim is to cope with "contexts which demand introduction of the factor Nothing--or as I shall call it, in order

---

[334] "Some Uses of Nothing," Language, XXXV (1959), 409-420.

[335] Compare Eleanor N. Hutchens's metaphorical use of the vacuum: "The transfer of power from right to wrong is brought about, in a significant number of the plays, by the creation of a power vacuum and the consequent filling of it. When right, either moral or legal, fails to carry out all its proper functions, there occurs a power vacuum into which wrong moves with a force thus generated by the negative behaviour of right itself." "The Transfer of Power in King Lear and The Tempest," A Review of English Literature, IV (1963), 82-93. She refers significantly to Lear's creation of "space."

to avoid Polyphemus' predicament, NIL." "One such context," he discloses, "arises in historical work. No theory of change can do without nil." Some of the concluding remarks are of special pertinence:

> The synchronic properties of nil are in part rather dubious. Nil
> is of course unrecognizable; whether or not it is sometimes physically
> associated with a transitional glide or with an empty morph is beside
> the point as soon as we leave mere phones and morphs behind. Nil is
> therefore arbitrary; it has to be, since our criterion for setting it
> up comes from outside: from another corpus, from history. And yet,
> or rather because of that, nil has one very definite asset: it has
> privileges of occurrence. Nil--in fact, any number of successive nils,
> if needed--may be said to occur between any two segments that cluster,
> and to occur there only.[336]

The implications of Hoenigswald's remarks are rather significant. For one thing, they indicate how what may most objectively be termed the nil-factor depends upon its context and how its qualities, for instance duration, relate directly to those factors qualifying it; in itself, it is altogether arbitrary. So, though Shakespeare hardly intended his title Much Ado about Nothing to be taken too literally, he might have left room for it to be taken linguistically. For Hoenigswald defers the matter of the synchronic consideration of the nil-

---

[336] Hoenigswald, p. 418.

factor to another only because he believes that it can best be treated
diachronically (that is, in terms of historical development rather than as
a contemporaneous phenomenon). Thus he finds the traditional lacuna in the
development of language to be an aspect of his "nil"; gradual deterioration
of language may be explained in such terms (for example, the degeneration of
huswif, Old English for housewife, into the modern English hussy involved the
factor of nil when the second syllable of the older word underwent a change
and thereby the first acquired a diminutive ending). Perhaps the change has
an evolutionary basis (the human mouth-cavity is smaller than it used to be
since man has evolved), but whether the change represents a shift toward the
better or the worse has not been determined. At any rate, the deterioration
of wif in the historical shift from huswif to hussy indicates an omission, if
not deletion, which may be characterized as the nil-factor. The gradual
unrounding of the English vowels through the course of the centuries represents
a similar loss or omission.

But why should this nil-factor not be ascertained synchronically too?
Surely the omission of words, the various forms of syncope and ellipsis which
exist, suggests that the factor of nil operates in the modern construction of
speech patterns also. Every sentence fragment may be thus explained. An
obvious example would be a fragment starting "Not that he . . ." instead of "The
reason is not that he. . . ." In like manner, the great number of fragments in
Dickens's novels should be linguistically understood. The same principle should
hold true for certain isolated expressions, especially when their exact meaning
is blurred. Thus the briefest answer to a question, "yes" or "to be sure,"
for instance, originally represents a telescoped form of a longer, more complete
statement ("yes, that is true" or "to be sure, his reason is sound"). Sometimes,

however, such a brief response deliberately creates multiple meaning, which
the addition of an affirmative or explanatory statement would eliminate,
something the speaker does not desire.

In line with these suggestions, I am inclined to believe that
frequently the use of the word nothing, a verbal sign for an idea which,
strictly speaking, has no denotative reference, represents a form of the nil-
factor. It is an instance of the factor operative on the synchronic rather than
diachronic level. And it is specially intriguing because, though it relates
metalinguistically to absence as such, it also retains a concrete quality that
allows it to be evaluated in a manner Hoenigswald's nil-factor could not be.
The evident difference is that this aspect of nil, the word nothing itself, is
just that: a word, and so has linguistic properties. Thus Shakespeare's
and Dickens's uses of this word may also be meaningful in terms of the nil-
factor, and such a meaningfulness points to an influence, as I shall show in
Part III. Lear, above all, deserves attention here, for there is strong
reason to believe that Dickens was particularly aware of word-repetition or
Wiederholungsfiguren in that tragedy. And, to be sure, the nil-factor is
much more pronounced in Lear than in any other play Shakespeare wrote--
including, indeed, Much Ado.

III

The influence of Lear upon Dickens was undoubtedly pervasive, stemming
as it did from his friendship with William Charles Macready and from the article
he wrote for Forster's "Theatrical Examiner" section of The Examiner.
Philip Collins writes that "it is clear that . . . Dickens was haunted . . .

when writing about fathers and daughters, by King Lear";[337] likewise, Ford
relates the tragedy to The Old Curiosity Shop,[338] and Mrs. Tillotson compares
it to Dombey and Son (the salvation of Mr. Dombey by Florence recalls that
of the King by Cordelia). Isolated allusions attest to the extent of the influence, such as that pointed out by Collins in A Tale of Two Cities.[340] That
Macready's version of the tragedy was highly lauded, even though he depreciated
the Fool,[341] is evident from De Vigny's "effusive . . . praise for Macready's
interpretation of King Lear $\sqrt{}$ 'croire à la vue réelle de Cordelia' $\underline{}$ 7."[342] He
also was esteemed for his production of Much Ado about Nothing; Dickens wrote
that he saw the actor play Benedick (letter to Miss Coutts of 28 February 1843)
and composed a review for Forster on the comedy: "Macready as Benedick."[343] That
the title of Shakespeare's comedy caught his fancy is evident from his reference
to "that Much Ado about Nothing" (letter to W. H. Wills of 15 November 1855) and
to such a reference as the following in a letter to W. H. Wills of 13 August 1857:
"I have altered the names thus: A Journey in Search of Nothing." One can also

---

[337]Dickens and Crime, p. 300.

[338]Dickens and his Readers, pp. 69 and 193.

[339]See Collins, p. 332n.

[340]Collins, p. 332n.

[341]"It was not until 1838," writes Kenneth Muir, "that Macready, with some
misgivings, introduced the Fool." The New Arden Edition, p. xliv. Dickens's
review aforementioned in The Examiner, 4 February 1838, p. 69, has much on the
Fool.

[342]James F. Marshall, "Alfred de Vigny and William Charles Macready,"
Publications of the Modern Language Association, LXXIV (1959), 99. Marshall
writes that "Macready strengthened Vigny's appreciation of Shakespeare" (p. 101).

[343]The Examiner, 4 March 1843, loc. cit.

point to the mock titles that he invented for imaginary volumes at Tavistock
House, such as Drowsy's Recollections of Nothing. Another of these titles,
Heaviside's Conversations with Nobody, relates to the story in Household Words
called "Nobody, Somebody, and Everybody," which John C. Eckel[344] has traced from
Dickens's "Contributor's Book." There are numerous allusions in Chuzzlewit to
the word nobody (for example, the nobody-anybody quibble in II, 23), and Dickens
very likely knew of the Renaissance drama Nobody and Somebody. It is doubtful
whether he read it, however; probably he knew about the existence of the play at
least in part from Shakespeare's allusions to it in King Lear (II.i.83) and
The Tempest (III.ii.131-132). Thus, insofar as Eleanor Hutchens writes that
the nil-factor is operative in the valediction-play in much the same manner,
though by no means to such an extent, as in Lear,[345] the nobody references are
related to those on nothing and thereby constitute another form of the nil-factor.

To understand just how Dickens adapted another form of the nil-factor from
the tragedy by transforming it in Chuzzlewit, one ought to examine the final stage
of the love-test. After the King has asked Cordelia to praise him (using the word
love itself, which may carry its Old English connotation over from lofian, to
praise),[346] the following dialogue takes place:

> Cordelia. Nothing, my lord.
>
> Lear. Nothing?

---

[344] The First Editions of the Writings of Charles Dickens: Their Points and
Values (New York, 1932), p. 185.

[345] Hutchens, p. 91.

[346] This point is elaborated upon in Terry Hawkes's article, "'Love' in King
Lear," Review of English Studies, X (1959), 178-181.

> Cordelia. Nothing.
>
> Lear. Nothing will come of nothing; speak again. (I.i.86-89)[347]

In a most interesting article on Shakespeare and the nil-factor, "Much Ado about Nothing,"[348] Paul A. Jorgensen sums up his position as follows: "Writers who ingeniously shaped Nothing into many significances aid employ the pun $\lfloor$ that on the word noting, as used in Much Ado, as Helge Kökeritz confirms $\rfloor$,[349] but their medium demanded the use of other kinds of manipulation than punning. In attempting a dramatic, rather than expository, elaboration, Shakespeare would give the playwright's equivalent of the poet's imaginative shaping. Out of a trifle, a misunderstanding, a fantasy, a mistaken overhearing, a 'naughtiness,' might come the materials for a drama--as happened, less deliberately perhaps, in King Lear."[350] What Jorgensen is hinting at is that Cordelia's flat response to the King's question, her apparent refusal to commit herself and offer the praise asked of her, amounts to a 'naughtiness.' This is indeed interesting with regard to the origin of the word naughty itself: good-for-nothing. Cordelia's response is, then, a literal application of naughtiness; not only is she stubborn in

---

[347]Lines 87-88 do not occur in the Pied-Bull 1608 Quarto and therefore may in all likelihood represent a later theatrical interpolation. If this is the case, the precisely Shakespearian nature of the influence on Dickens needs very careful consideration, for the novelist may have been influenced rather by what has been presumed to be Shakespeare's but what is really a later addition. At any rate, since the Folio text very likely was sanctioned by the dramatist, one can argue that he did not object to its reading, so that a theatrical influence is still valid to consider. It is doubtful whether Shakespeare himself composed the Folio's elaboration.

[348]Originally in Shakespeare Quarterly, V (1954), 287-295, reprinted with slight alterations in Redeeming Shakespeare's Words (Berkeley and Los Angeles, 1962), pp. 22-42.

[349]The discovery of this pun is credited to Richard Grant White in The Works of William Shakespeare (Boston, 1857), III, 226-227, and has been corroborated by Kökeritz in Shakespeare's Punctuation (New Haven, 1953). See Jorgensen, p. 40.

[350]Jorgensen, pp. 41-42.

offering praise, be her motives sincere and well intended, and thus a "naughty"
child in that respect, but she is naughty precisely by being "naught-y," by her
use of nothings. Jorgensen sees this well enough; he qualifies his statement with
"less deliberately perhaps" because the grand elaboration on the nil-factor following
Cordelia's answer seems too ingenious to have been consciously intended. But
that elaboration is unmistakable. Kenneth Muir, in his recent Arden Edition of the
tragedy, comments in a note on Cordelia's response to the King: "Nothing _/ This
word is echoed throughout the play."[351] G. B. Harrison similarly writes:

> Shakespeare uses "nature," "natural," "naturally," forty-seven times
> in Lear. The words become a sinister echo throughout the play.
> The word "nothing" likewise is terribly significant. Cordelia,
> when her turn comes to praise her father and so justify his favouritism, is
> tongue-tied and can utter only "Nothing, my Lord."
> "Nothing?" echoes Lear.
> "Nothing."
> "Nothing will come of nothing, speak again."
> Lear is wrong, for from this "nothing" comes everything. The word
> echoes in the parallel story of Gloucester, also mistaking the loyalty of
> his children.
> "What paper were you reading?" he asks, as Edmund ostentatiously
> conceals the false letter which is to ruin Edgar.
> He too replies, "Nothing, my Lord," and again from "nothing" follows
> everything.[352]

351
    Muir, p. 9. He writes, "Baldwin, Shakespeare's Small Latine, ii, 543, cites
Germbergius, Carminum Proverbialium, 1583, p. 154 and Persius iii.84: 'de nihilo
nihilum, in nihilum nil posse reverti.'" Kittredge adds, "Marston, What You Will,
IV, i, 248 (ed. Bullen, II, 398): 'Out of nothing, nothing is bred.' See Apperson,
English Proverbs, pp. 454, 455." The basic Latin is ex nihilo nihil fit and is found
in Marcus Aurelius (Meditations, IV, 4), to whom it is ascribed by Diogenes Laertius
in his life of Diogenes of Apollonia. Another source is Lucretius's De Rerum Natura,
I, 206: "Nihil igitur / Fieri de nihilo posse, fatendum est." Lucretius's doctrine
that nothing at all was created is opposed to Christian beliefs of creation ex nihilo.

352Introducing Shakespeare (Baltimore, 1954), p. 139, with Harrison's punctuation.
He deliberately avoids taking the expression literally; instead, he "psychologizes"
it. For the consideration of echoing from a literal standpoint, see Robert F.
Fleissner, "The 'Nothing' Element in King Lear," Shakespeare Quarterly, XIII (1962),
67-70 (the titular quibble relates to Donne's "quintessence /_ quinta essentia: fifth
element_/ even of nothingness" in his "Nocturnall on St. Lucy's Day"). For an extension of this view, see J. P. Dyson, "The Structural Function of the Banquet Scene
in Macbeth," Shakespeare Quarterly, XIV (1963), 369-378.
My earlier study is to be regarded as bibliographical in nature, an analysis
of the text of the 1623 Folio. See note 347 of the present work. (Any resemblance
between my conception and that of any modern existentialist or "absurdist" is
entirely coincidental.)

Thus Eleanor Hutchens writes, "'Nothing will come of nothing,' warns Lear, never more mistaken. The repetition of the word in the parallel scene of Gloucester's deception, and later by the Fool (I.iv), shows its significance."[353] Harbage also parodies the King's dictum by remarking that "everything is related to everything."[354] Sigurd Burckhardt, on the other hand, interprets the King's prophecy as I do, claiming that in a very literal way nothing does come of nothing.[355] Even the poet Edwin Arlington Robinson, in his **lyric** "Ben Jonson Entertains a Man from Stratford," is influenced by the extension of the nil-factor in Shakespeare:

> "No, Ben," he mused, "it's Nothing. It's all Nothing.
> We come, we go; and when we're done, we're done;
> Spiders and flies—we're mostly one or t'other—
> We come, we go; and when we're done, we're done."
> "By God, you sing that song as if you knew it!"
> Said I, by way of cheering him; "What ails ye?"
> "I think I must have come down here to think,"
> Says he to that, and pulls his little beard;
> "Your fly will serve as well as anybody,
> And what's his hour? He flies, and flies, and flies,
> And in his fly's mind has a brave appearance;
> And then your spider gets him in her net,
> And eats him out, and hangs him up to dry.
> That's Nature, the kind mother of us all.
> And then your slattern housemaid swings her broom,
> And where's your spider? And that's Nature also.
> It's Nature, and it's Nothing. It's all Nothing."[356]

---

[353] Hutchens, p. 85.

[354] Harbage, p. 88.

[355] "King Lear: The Quality of Nothing," *Minnesota Review*, II (1961), 33-50. Burckhardt himself italicizes the fulfillment of the prophecy ("does"). We both see some irony involved in the way Lear's statement glosses his own tragedy, but we differ with regard to Cordelia's role.

[356] *The Drama: A Quarterly Review of Dramatic Literature*, V (1915), 551. Robinson's use of "flies" may indicate another *Lear* influence; cf. "As flies to wanton boys are we to th' gods; / They kill us for their sport" (IV.i.36-37). This famous passage in the play is echoed by Dickens in *Our Mutual Friend* when Mr. Boffin remarks, "I see your young man up at this present elevation, chopping at the flies on the windowsill with his penknife" (VIII, 93).

Indeed, John F. Danby finds the references to Nature in Lear so pronounced that
he says that the tragedy "can be regarded as a play dramatizing the meanings of
the single word 'Nature.'"[357] In the same manner, one can justifiably argue that
the play may also be regarded as dramatizing the meanings of the single word
"Nothing." Whereas Danby believes that "the idea of Nature . . . in orthodox
Elizabethan thought, is always something normative for human beings,"[358] so that
its function in the tragedy is to serve as a kind of backdrop for the unnatural
things that finally do happen, the references to the nil-factor likewise represent
Elizabethan conventionality but may here function in an even more structural manner.
For not only is the love-test in effect repeated in the underplot, as I have
mentioned, but the Lear-Cordelia interchange is likewise reflected in the scenes
where the King and his Fool exchange sallies of wit and bitterness. In many ways,
the dialogue between king and jester is more reflected in Dickens's treatment than
the earlier one between king and daughter, which sets the play in motion but does
not serve as the central focus of interest. Number 14 in the list of annotated
references is particularly relevant here. After Tom Pinch answers a question with
"Nothing" (just as Cordelia does), the interlocutor is taken aback (just as Lear is);
but whereas Cordelia tries to explain why she has failed to answer what was expected
of her ("Unhappy that I am, I cannot heave / My heart into my mouth"), Tom apologizes:
"When I say nothing . . . I am wrong, and don't say what I mean." Thus what is
potentially tragic in Shakespeare becomes potentially comic in Dickens. But the
comic influence also comes from Shakespeare when the echoing of the nil-factor
between Fool and King is considered, for example, "Can you make no use of nothing,

---

[357]
Shakespeare's Doctrine of Nature: A Study of "King Lear" (London, 1949), p. 15.

[358]
Danby, p. 21.

nuncle?" "Why, no, boy; nothing can be made out of nothing" (I.iv.131-134);
"thou art an O without a figure. I am better than thou art now; I am a fool,
thou art nothing. Yes, forsooth, I will hold my tongue; so your face bids me,
though you say nothing. Mum, mum" (I.iv.192-197). The striking combination of
"say nothing" with "Mum, mum" suggests that the old story of Mum-chance being
hanged for saying nothing is reflected here[359] and that, even as Regan says
"jesters do oft prove prophets" (V.iii.72), so the Fool is foretelling the death
of Cordelia by hanging as a result of her literal saying of "nothing." Yet
is this not reading into the play far beyond Shakespeare's intent?

Assuredly it is not. The copious structure built upon Cordelia's
"Nothing" has a basis in the very heart of mediaeval thought. As mentioned earlier,
the derivation of naughty from good-for-nothing points to such a moral tradition.
One need but refer to the Renaissance homilies and treatises on the theme of
idleness and sloth, such as A Lyttle Treatyse Called the Image of Idlenesse (1558)
and William Fulwood's The Enimie of Idlenesse (1568). Cordelia's response,
then, was "idle" in effect, if not in intent. The most convincing background
for the relationship between the nil-factor and the deadly sin of sloth is in
the Morality Play Mankind. Here are a few telling excerpts: The Founder of the
universe is described as having "made all thynge of nought, / For the synfull

---

[359]
The precise origin of this expression is unknown, and the OED suggests
that though it relates especially to a game of cards, it could have a mediaeval
or Renaissance basis. At any rate, Jonathan Swift employs the phrase in "A
Compleat Collection of Genteel and Ingenious Conversation": "Methinks you look
like Mum-chance, that was hang'd for saying nothing." See Satires and Personal
Writings by Jonathan Swift (London, 1958), p. 225. The nil-factor is used as
bait throughout the Genteel Conversation, e.g.: "there's nothing in it,"
"naught's never in danger," and "make much of naught." The purpose is to
satirize a do-nothing society.

synner, to hade hym revyude, / And, for hys redempcyon, sett hys own Son at
nought" (6-8); but "the synfull creature" "wyll repent hys neclygence" (23);
"How may yt be excusyde be-for the Iustyce of all, / When for euery ydyll worde
we must yelde a reson?" (167-168). Thus the reference to "ydyll worde"
specifically relates the nil-factor to the concept of idleness. Lines 169-176
in the play contain an appeal for making use of one's talents, for doing
something instead of nothing. Soon the abstraction Nought emerges. Mankind
commands the temptation ("to do nothing") to depart: "Hens I sey, New-gyse, Now-
a-days, and Nowte! / Yt was seyde be-forn all the menys xull $\lceil d \rfloor$ be sought /
To perverte my condycions and brynge me to nought" (377-379). The character
Nought is clearly distinguished from Naughtiness as Mischief, who also appea.s
and claims that he is "wers then nought!" (408). A high comic point in the drama
occurs when Mischief calls out: "Nought, cum forth!" (663). Nought, busy writing,
has nothing to show for himself indeed; he recites his nonsense for the benefit
of everyone: "blottybus in blottis, / Blottorum blottibus istis" (674). Not
only did this serve as a basis for Shakespeare, but it no doubt had an influence
upon the Renaissance drama Nobody and Somebody, to which Shakespeare refers twice
at least. Indeed, the letter Nought composes is written in Anno regni regis nulli:
the regnal year of King Nobody (686).[360] Moreover, it is plausible that Wilmot,
Earl of Rochester, was thinking of the Morality Play Mankind when he wrote his
most famous poetic satire, "On Nothing. A Satire on Mankind." If Wilmot was
not thinking of the earlier play, at least the association he makes is so close

---

[360] All quotations from Mankind are from Joseph Quincy Adams, Chief Pre-
Shakespearean Drama (Cambridge, Mass., 1924), pp. 304-324. Cf. the philosophic
thought of Sir John Davies in Nosce Teipsum as quoted by James E. Phillips,
"The Tempest and the Renaissance Idea of Man," in Shakespeare 400: Essays by
American Scholars on the Anniversary of the Poet's Birth, ed. James G. McManaway
(New York, 1964): "Or as Davies put it, a 'declining pronenesse unto nought, /
Is euen that sinne that we are borne withall'" (p. 149). (The italics are in
the volume without a notation.)

to the other that the universal character of the relationship is manifest.
In this connection, it is worth recalling that Henry Fielding also was interested
in the same theme and composed "An Essay on Nothing."[361] Dickens, however,
was very likely influenced not by Mankind or "A Satire on Mankind" but by
Shakespeare and possibly by Fielding, though there is no evidence that he had
read the essay in question.

It would be idle here perhaps to reconsider the allusions to the nil-
factor in Chuzzlewit. However, the fact that Dickens found the opening scene
in Lear, as reiterated in the Lear-Fool exchange, archetypal is evident, not
only in this novel, but in sundry other places. A punning play on the nil-factor
emerges in "A Journey in Search of Nothing" (an article in which Dickens had a
hand, at least in reworking the title): "Here we have, at last, discovered
nothing. Nothing? Did I say Nothing?" A letter to Forster (6 March 1842)
reflects the same thing: "'Nothing,' says my friend. 'Nothing!' says I." In
Nicholas Nickleby, the nil-factor emerges strongly:

> "What's that, sir?"
> "Nothing, please sir," said the little boy.
> "Nothing, sir!" exclaimed Mr. Squeers.
> "Please sir, I sneezed," rejoined the boy, trembling
> till the little trunk shook under him.
> "Oh! sneezed, did you?" retorted Mr. Squeers. "Then
> what did you say 'nothing' for, sir?" (IV, 30).

One again recalls Tom Pinch's apology: "When I say nothing . . . I am wrong, and
don't say what I mean." Bitterly Squeers retorts a few lines later: "What is it?

361
    The essay is discussed in Henry Knight Miller, Essays on Fielding's
"Miscellanies": A Commentary on Volume One (Princeton, 1961). See Complete
Works, ed. W. E. Henley (London, 1902), XIV, 309. Sister M. Geraldine, C. S. J.,
in "Erasmus and the Tradition of Paradox," Studies in Philology, LXI (1964), 55-
56, writes, "Edward Dyer's Prayse of Nothing in the 'eighties is witty but not
satiric; and so is Cornwallis's essay of the same title some years later. . . .
The paradox is a matter of verbal manipulation."

Nothing; less than nothing" (IV, 31). Then there is the nil-factor in Our

Mutual Friend:

> "All this is nothing," said Lightwood.
> "Nothing?" repeated Riderhood, indignantly and amazedly.
> "Merely nothing. . ." (XI, 154).

Here are a number of instances of the nil-factor in Copperfield:

> "Copperfield," said Traddles, turning to me, "you feel, I
> am sure, that nothing could be more reasonable or considerate."
> "Nothing!" cried I. (XLI, 583)
>
> "Poor Dick, who is simple and knows nothing" (XLV, 636)[362]
>
> "Some unhappy cause of separation. . . . It may have **grown** up
> out of almost nothing" (XLV, 637).
>
> "Even you are nothing here."
> "Nothing!" exclaimed Mrs. Markleham. "Me, nothing! The child
> has taken leave of her senses" (XLV, 641).
>
> "I can remember nothing. . . ."
> "Makes her mother nothing!" exclaimed Mrs. Markleham. (XLV, 643)

A particular striking example is the following from Hard Times:

> Here Sissy fairly sobbed as confessing with extreme contrition
> to her greatest error, "I said it was nothing."
> "Nothing, Sissy?"
> "Nothing, Miss. . . " (IX, 51).

It is not improbable that Dickens was reflecting in these very lines his awareness

of Cordelia's culpability, of her tragic fault of hybris which leads to her demise.

---

[362]There may be an allusion to the "poor fool" here which relates to the
discussion following on "And my poor fool is hanged!"

It is also possible that Dickens is purposely transforming something
Shakespearian for his own purposes, that he is pretending that Sissy might
have erred just as Cordelia might have. And it is further possible that
Cordelia does not even have a tragic fault to begin with, though this
interpretation (Professor Duthie's) has been taken severely to task.[363]
To come to a reasonable conclusion, one should compare the following reference
from David Copperfield as also an implicit allusion to Cordelia:

> "And when you had made sure of the poor little fool," said my aunt--
> "God forgive me that I should call her so, and she gone where you
> won't go in a hurry--because you had not done wrong enough to her
> and hers, you must begin to train her, must you? begin to break her,
> like a poor caged bird, and wear her deluded life away, in teaching
> her to sing your notes?"
> "This is either insanity or intoxication," said Miss Murdstone. (XIV, 207)

Here again (as with "Poor Dick" cited earlier) there appears to be a reference
to King Lear: the first line, "And . . . poor little fool," reflects the
much-discussed opening of Lear's last speech, "And my poor fool is hanged" (V.
iii.305). Elsewhere I have argued that though Shakespeare probably meant "poor
fool" here to refer quite literally to the Fool in the play, Dickens very
likely accepted the standard nineteenth-century interpretation, namely that the
term was an expression of endearment referring to the daughter. Macready, since
he played down the Fool's role, probably had much to do with perpetrating

---

[363]Thus J. Blakemore Evans writes in his review of the New Cambridge Edition
of the tragedy for the Journal of English and Germanic Philology, LX (1961), 323:
"Professor Duthie's general introduction is a careful, sound synthesis and
analysis of Lear criticism for the past hundred years, though for my own taste too
much emphasis is placed on the so-called Christian interpretation. This is not
to deny that, as J. C. Maxwell has said, Lear is 'a Christian play set in a
pagan world,' but when the Christian interpretation leads Professor Duthie to
assert that 'In Cordelia there is nowhere any fault' (p. xxv), I feel the grounds
of Shakespearian tragedy begin to shake beneath me." My essay on Lear
aforementioned reconsiders Cordelia's flaw by comparing it with Antigone's.

this interpretation. Dickens could have accepted the theory that the King was mad at this point in the drama and was confusing, at least verbally, his daughter with his Fool; if so, he would have anticipated twentieth-century views such as William Empson's and Josephine Waters Bennett's. But what is most likely, in my judgment, is that he accepted the conventional view that "poor fool" referred to Cordelia and related to that the notion that the Fool was being referred to connotatively (apparently a reversal of the dramatist's intentions). Evidence for this is in the quotation from Copperfield. After the opening line, where the identification of "poor little fool" and a female is made, the apologetic qualification ("God forgive me that I should call her so") reflects Dickens's own atttitude toward Cordelia as a tragic heroine. As such, it relates to the aforementioned quotation from Hard Times ("sobbed as confessing with extreme contrition to her greatest error"). That such an implication is clearly possible may be seen from the subsequent allusions to "a poor caged bird" (relating to Lear's "We two alone will sing like birds i' th' cage" earlier in the same scene-- compare number 47) and "insanity."

Thus Dickens's overall references to the nil-factor bear upon the Lear influence; those in Chuzzlewit do in particular. Should such a stress on vacuity, even as based upon the Morality Play tradition behind Shakespeare's writings, seem difficult to understand in terms of the Victorian age, one has only to refer to John Henry Cardinal Newman on the subject. His words serve as a fitting tribute and final moral gloss upon Dickens's use of the word nothing:

> There is nothing irrational in submitting to undeniable incompatibilities, which we call apparent, only because, if they were not apparent but real, they could not co-exist. Such, for instance, is the contemplation of Space; the existence of which we cannot deny, though its idea is capable, in no sort of posture, of seating itself (if I may so speak) in our minds;--

for we find it incomprehensible to say that it runs out infinitely; and it seems to be unmeaning if we say that it does
not exist till bodies come into it, and thus is enlarged according
to an accident.[364]

In effect, then, Dickens in writing on the nil-factor, is by no means writing
about nothing as such. By combining references to anything, something, and
everything, he is suggesting dramatic contrasts and thus providing, sometimes
in a purely comic manner, a means of escape from the frustration of a nihilistic
Weltanschauung.

IV

Aside from the nil-factor, the Lear influence in Chuzzlewit is
pervasive enough to be considered in terms of major character relationships.
Various characters throughout the novel are reminiscent of the Shakespearian
Fool: Tom Pinch (who is like "Poor Tom" as well as the "Poor Fool"), old
Chuffey, Chevy Slyme, and other minor figures. Jack Lindsay, in commenting
on Barnaby Rudge, makes a remark that can also be applied to Chuzzlewit here:
"He was trying to return to the Shakespearian Fool, but couldn't assume a
folk tradition."[365] Lear himself is reflected in Old Chuzzlewit, especially
as revealed in numbers 6-7 in the list of annotated references. Just as the
King considers himself obliged to judge others, the worth of his daughters,
so Old Chuzzlewit finds it necessary to weigh the honesty of his relatives
and friends. Item 7 relates the Old Chuzzlewit-Lear parallel to young Martin

---

[364] The Idea of a University, ed. Martin J. Svaglic (New York, 1960),
p. 348.

[365] "Barnaby Rudge" in Dickens and the Twentieth Century, p. 94.

Chuzzlewit. The reference to "universal self!" and what follows clearly anticipates
the patronizing attitude of Martin in the early part of the novel: a form of the
old Grecian wine of hybris in the new Victorian bottles of smugness or self-
complacency. Martin, fortunately, regains his sense of moral equilibrium from his
trip to America. Pecksniff, though described as too much of a hypocrite to represent
another Victorian Lear, none the less has a relationship to his daughters which
recalls that of the King. The following passage is especially pertinent:

> And first of Mr. Pecksniff, it may be observed, that having provided for
> his youngest daughter that choicest of blessings, a tender and indulgent
> husband; and having gratified the dearest wish of his parental heart by
> establishing her in life so happily; he renewed his youth, and spreading
> the plumage of his own bright conscience, felt himself equal to all kinds
> of flights. It is customary with fathers in stage-plays, after giving
> their daughters to the men of their hearts, to congratulate themselves
> on having no other business on their hands but to die immediately: though
> it is rarely found that they are in a hurry to do it. Mr. Pecksniff,
> being a father of a more sage and practical class, appeared to think that
> his immediate business was to live; and having deprived himself of one
> comfort, to surround himself with others.   (XXX, 476-477)

The reference to "fathers in stage-plays" who, after giving their daughters to
suitors, plan on retiring but, in fact, do not, recalls the beginning of Shakespeare's
tragedy. Lear announces that "'tis our fast intent / To shake all cares and business
from our age, / Conferring them on younger strengths while we / Unburdened crawl
toward death" (I.i.37-40). And yet he is not "in a hurry" to do such crawling,
as Dickens suggests: he lives with his older daughters, first Goneril and then
Regan, and they find him making a nuisance of himself especially because of the
disorderly knights who accompany him (so they say). Lear, of course, is in his
splenetic old age and cannot be altogether blamed; his daughters, by revealing
ingratitude and thereby shirking the Commandment that one should honor one's father

(an implicit Christian motif in a predominantly pagan play), reveal their ugly
natures. In the same chapter in which Dickens commences with a reference to
"fathers in stage-plays," he describes a situation immediately thereafter
reminiscent of the Lear-Cordelia dialogue prompting the tragedy:

> "Cherry," cried Mr. Pecksniff, "what is amiss between us?
> My child, why are we disunited?"
> Miss Pecksniff's answer was scarcely a response to this gush
> of affection, for it was simply, "Bother, pa!"
> "Bother!" repeated Mr. Pecksniff in a tone of anguish.
> "Oh! 'tis too late, pa," said his daughter, calmly, "to
> talk to me like this. . . ."
> "This is hard!" cried Mr. Pecksniff. . . . "This is very
> hard! She is my child. I carried her in my arms. . ." (XXX, 477).

The most obvious similarity is that between the repetition of the word Bother
and that of Nothing (in the drama). The attitude of father toward child is also
similar (the reference to the father carrying his daughter in his arms perhaps
recalls the end of the tragedy where Lear emerges with Cordelia in his arms); the
implications of ingratitude are present in both works; finally, even the name
Cherry ("fond" for Charity) recalls the love-test where Cordelia, Lear's favorite,
answers in a manner other than to his liking. Lest the relationship seem too
far-fetched even now, one would do well to refer to items 21 and especially 55
in the list of annotated references, places where the Charity-Cordelia reminiscence
is repeated.

In fact, Chapter Thirty is a seminal one in the novel with regard to
the influence of the tragedy. Pecksniff reflects on human nature in much the same
way that Lear does: "Ah, human nature, human nature! Poor human nature!" (477).
Charity, in remarking that she is "not quite a fool, and . . . not blind" (479),

recalls the relationship between Cordelia and the Fool, one which almost makes
of Lear's youngest daughter a "poor fool" in the end; the allusion to blindness
likewise reflects on the motif of references to sight in the play as mentioned
earlier. "A father asking pardon of his child," says Pecksniff, "is, I believe,
a spectacle to soften the most rugged nature" (479), and one thinks of the King
asking forgiveness of his daughter toward the end of the tragedy (see item 46).
Charity persists in reminding her father "over and over again, that she wasn't
quite a fool, and wasn't blind, and wouldn't submit to it" (479). The implications
are that Pecksniff himself may be rather blind morally. It is true, he does turn
out somewhat tragically toward the end of the novel, but the parallel with the
Shakespearian tragedy does not extend any further than that. Dickens's transformation of the Shakespearian situation is clearly, as it should be, much more
Dickens than Shakespeare. Jonas Chuzzlewit may remind one slightly of the
ambitious Edmund and his murderous activities in the context of other allusions
to Lear, but aside from such a passing similarity the comparison falls short.

One cardinal point of similarity remains to be considered, however. Just
when Martin and his friend are bound for America, the description of the ocean
waves is remarkably like the description of Lear in the storm, if only through
verbal influence:

A dark and dreary night; people nestling in their beds or circling late
about the fire; Want, colder than Charity, shivering at the street-corners;
church-towers humming with the faint vibration of their own tongues, but
newly resting from the ghostly preachment 'One!' The earth covered with
a sable pall as for the burial of yesterday; the clumps of dark trees, its
giant plumes of funeral feathers, waving sadly to and fro; all hushed, all
noiseless, and in deep repose, save the swift clouds that skim across the
moon, and the cautious wind, as, creeping after them upon the ground, it
stops to listen, and goes rustling on, and stops again, and follows, like
a savage on the trail.

Whither go the clouds and wind, so eagerly? If, like guilty spirits, they repair to some dread conference with powers like themselves, in what wild regions do the elements hold council, or where unbend in terrible disport?

Here! Free from that cramped prison called the earth, and out upon the waste of waters. Here, roaring, raging, shrieking, howling, all night long. Hither come the sounding voices from the caverns on the coast of that small island, sleeping, a thousand miles away, so quietly in the midst of angry waves; and hither, to meet them, rush the blasts from unknown desert places of the world. Here, in the fury of their unchecked liberty, they storm and buffet with each other, until the sea, lashed into passion like their own, leaps up, in ravings mightier than theirs, and the whole scene is madness.

On, on, on, over the countless miles of angry space roll the long heaving billows. Mountains and caves are here, and yet are not; for what is now the one, is now the other; then all is but a boiling heap of rushing water. Pursuit, and flight, and mad return of wave on wave, and savage struggle, ending in a spouting-up of foam that whitens the black night; incessant change of place, and form, and darker grows the night, and louder howls the wind, and more clamorous and fierce become the million voices in the sea, when the wild cry goes forth upon the storm 'A ship!'

Onward she comes, in gallant combat with the elements, her tall masts trembling, and her timbers starting on the strain; onward she comes, now high upon the curling billows, now low down in the hollows of the sea, as hiding for the moment from its fury; and every storm-voice in the air and water, cries more loudly yet, 'A ship!'

Still she comes striving on: and at her boldness and the spreading cry, the angry waves rise up above each other's hoary heads to look; and round about the vessel, far as the mariners on the decks can pierce into the gloom, they press upon her, forcing each other down, and starting up, and rushing forward from afar, in dreadful curiosity. High over her they break; and round her surge and roar; and giving place to others, moaningly depart, and dash themselves to fragments in their baffled anger.

(XV, 250-251)

Of these, paragraphs two and three relate strikingly to the description of the storm:

Kent.   Where's the King?

Gentleman. Contending with the fretful elements;
            Bids the wind blow the earth into the sea,
            Or swell the curled waters 'bove the main,
            That things might change or cease; tears his white hair,
            Which the impetuous blasts with eyeless rage
            Catch in their fury and make nothing of;
            Strives in this little world of man to out-storm
            The to-and-fro conflicting wind and rain. (III.i.3-11)

Lear. Blow, winds, and crack your cheeks! rage! blow!
——— You cataracts and hurricanoes, spout
Till you have drenched our steeples, drowned the cocks!
You sulph'rous and thought-executing fires,
Vaunt-couriers of oak-cleaving thunderbolts,
Singe my white head! And thou, all-shaking thunder,
Strike flat the thick rotundity o' th' world,
Crack Nature's moulds, all germens spill at once
That make ingrateful man!

Rumble thy bellyful! Spit, fire! spout, rain!
Nor rain, wind, thunder, fire are my daughters.
I tax not you, you elements, with unkindness . . . .
Your high-engendered battles 'gainst a head
So old and white as this. O, ho! 'tis foul! (III.ii.1-9,
14-24)

Note the following correspondences in particular: (1) The allusion to "contending
with the fretful elements" connects with "in what wild regions do the elements
hold council, or where unbend in terrible disport"; (2) the next line, "Bids
the wind blow the earth into the sea," relates to the next line in Dickens,
"Here! Free from that cramped prison called the earth, and out upon the waste
of waters"; (3) the concept of "fretful elements" is again established with
reference to "roaring, raging, shrieking, howling, all night long" and to "angry
waves"; (4) the phrase "impetuous blasts with eyeless rage / Catch in their
fury and make nothing of" surely influenced Dickens when he wrote: "rush the
blasts from unknown desert places of the world. Here, in the fury of their
unchecked liberty, they storm and buffet with each other." For, indeed, the
combination of "blasts," "rage," "in their fury," and "make nothing of" relates
very strongly to the similar combination in Dickens: "blasts," ⎣"raging,"
"angry"--two sentences before⎦, "in the fury of their" and "unchecked liberty."
When the novelist then concludes the paragraph with the final comment that
"the whole scene is madness," the reader sensitive at all to Shakespearian
influences in the book, and to Lear in particular, is apt to say that the

"scene" referred to is an allusion to the very scene of the drama where the

King is out in the storm and finally goes mad.[366]   The combination of "blasts"

and "fury" is also too close to be mere coincidence. And, if we wish to

check the influence in the second and third paragraphs by referring to neighboring

allusions, we can do this, also, with profit. Thus Kent's opening speech ("Who's

there besides foul weather?"--III.i.1) relates to Dickens's opening comment: "A

dark and dreary night." Reference to "the to-and-fro conflicting wind and rain"

relates to "waving sadly to and fro . . . the cautious wind" in the first

paragraph. And in paragraph number four, "spouting-up" and "constancy in nothing"

very possibly relate to "spout" (III.ii.14) and "make nothing of" (III.i.9), even

though the two references are not clustered together in the drama as they are

in the novel. The repetition of "the elements" (in paragraphs two and five)

points especially to the word-play on "elements" here in the tragedy, occurring

also in two places: "fretful elements" (III.i.4) and "you elements" (III.ii.16).

The last allusion is not only to the weather but to the traditional four elements:

so earth, air, fire, and water are represented with "Nature's moulds" (III.ii.8),

"fire," "rain," and "wind" (III.ii.14-15). Two of the four are then repeated

immediately thereafter. Dickens, we may assume, did not have anything quite so

metaphysical in mind when writing Chuzzlewit. He does refer to a single "deadly

element" toward the end of the sixth paragraph but does not elaborate. Yet, another

influence is that of "curled waters" in the play (III.i.6) upon "curling billows"

in the fifth paragraph. And, though no ship is mentioned in the play, Lear's

---

366
    That he is mad long before the specific stage direction Enter Lear Mad
is the argument of Josephine Waters Bennett in "The Storm Within: the Madness
of Lear," Shakespeare Quarterly, XIII (1962), 137-155. It is possible that she
takes Shakespeare too literally. Certainly neither Martin nor Mark is mad,
even though Dickens does not hesitate to say that "the whole scene is madness."

"head / So old and white" (III.ii.23-24) in all probability was echoed in Dickens's allusion to "hoary heads" in the sixth paragraph. In the spirit of comedy, the resulting sea-sickness of Martin and Mark might be contrasted with Lear's spiritual suffering as a Dickensian playfulness upon the borrowed theme. In brief, we can legitimately speculate that if the novelist did not actually have Shakespeare's tragedy at his elbow when he composed his description, he at least had read it not long before. In utilizing it for his own purposes, he was doing much the same thing as Thomas Hardy, whose work has been compared with Shakespeare's,[367] did in his famous opening chapter about Egdon Heath.[368]

TABLE OF CORRESPONDENCES

King Lear	Martin Chuzzlewit
"contending with the fretful elements"	"combat with the elements"
"Bids the wind blow"	"louder howls the wind"
"blow the earth into the sea"	"Free from . . . the earth, and out upon the . . . waters"
"white hair," "white head," "a head / So old and white"	"whitens the black night," "hoary heads"
"blasts with eyeless rage / Catch in their fury"	"angry . . . blasts," "the fury of their unchecked liberty"
"make nothing of"	"constancy in nothing"
"Strives in"	"striving on"
"out-scorn"	"roaring, raging, shrieking, howling," "angry," "ravings"
"to-and-fro"	"to and fro"
"rage"	"raging"
"spout" (used twice)	"spouting-up"
"elements"	"elements" (used twice)
"horrible pleasure"	"terrible disport"

---

[367] See F. L. Gwynn, "Hamlet and Hardy," Shakespeare Quarterly, IV (1953), 207-208.

[368] This will be the subject of a separate study of mine.

CHAPTER SIX:

THE LEAR-CORDELIA MOTIF IN THE OLD CURIOSITY SHOP

Perhaps the best-known instance of a major Shakespearian influence
on Dickens is that of Lear on The Old Curiosity Shop. The existence of this
influence has been promulgated largely by George Harry Ford in Dickens and
his Readers; although he is cautious about asserting that a deliberate
parallel was intended, he does make the strong statement that "the author
was making a bid to write another Lear." Here is his full pronouncement:

> The death scene which Dickens most admired in all literature was that
> of King Lear, as acted by Macready. In The Old Curiosity Shop, a reader
> senses again and again that the author was making a bid to write another
> Lear—which incidentally may account for some of the intensity of
> Macready's own emotions in reading the novel. The parallel is especially
> marked in the scenes describing the old grandfather's grief after
> Nell's death, and a comparison therefore seems eminently fair. The end
> of King Lear has remained profoundly moving and the other has become
> profoundly embarrassing. One difference may be that of situation. In
> Lear, the strong are defeated; in The Old Curiosity Shop, it is the weak
> who suffer. One situation is potentially tragic and the other potentially
> pathetic. More important are differences of style. Dickens' preliminary
> description of the snowstorm is effective and vivid, but as our attention
> is directed from the background towards the child's bed, the false notes
> begin; the author steps forward to comment in his own person.[369]

More recently Philip Collins, editor of the Pilgrim Edition of Dickens's letters
(not yet completed at the time of this writing), has commented obliquely on the
same influence:

---

[369] Ford, p. 69. This was the point of departure used in "The Lear-Cordelia
Motif in Dickens's The Old Curiosity Shop."

In the scene $\lfloor$ in A Tale of Two Cities $\rfloor$ when Manette is "restored to life" by his daughter Lucie (who is to be the one "golden thread tying him to the present and to reality"), Dickens might well have used King Lear's words, "You do me wrong to take me out of the grave." He nearly does. At the end of that chapter, which is also the end of Book One, Mr. Lorry asks Manette, "I hope you care to be recalled to life?" and "the old answer" comes: "I can't say." The use of the reunion between father and daughter as a symbol of rebirth or resurrection, or of the relation between body and soul, is of course not peculiar to Shakespeare and Dickens: it reflects an universal emotional pattern. But it recurs particularly often in the later plays of Shakespeare, and throughout Dickens's work; one thinks of Little Nell and her grandfather, and of Florence Dombey, Louisa Gradgrind, and Little Dorrit, and their fathers.[370]

He concludes: "The Dickensian treatment, especially in TTC, even more resembles Pericles--but I would not assert that Dickens was 'influenced' by either play; if he was Lear is much more likely."[371] Now, evidently what Collins means by "I would not assert that Dickens was 'influenced'" is that he does not wish to commit himself. But here he gets involved, whether he likes it or not, in a simple problem of definition. For he does concede that Dickens was "haunted . . . when writing about fathers and daughters, by King Lear."[372] If he was "haunted," he was indeed "influenced."

A considerable amount of labor has been expended to show over and over again that the major influence upon Dickens in depicting the death of Little Nell was the death of Mary Hogarth. The novelist had indeed written Forster: "Dear Mary died yesterday, when I think of this sad story" (7 January 1841). On the surface, then, it seems that the story, after it was fully composed, recalled a biographical incident. But this does not mean that he was under her influence in

---

[370]
Dickens and Crime, p. 133.

[371]
Ibid., p. 332n.

[372]
Ibid., p. 300.

the act of composition. The whole Mary Hogarth parallel seems to relate more
to retention than to intention: it enforces the relationship between the novelist
and his life, plays up to the theory of "total recall," and ignores what may
be more interesting with regard to the novel qua novel, that is, as a craftsman-
like work of art. Besides, if one is to trace biographical influence to its
roots, where should one stop? Does not the name Nell conceivably come from Maria
Beadnell too? And what about Forster's remarks? He writes, "I was responsible
for the tragic ending. He had not thought of killing her. . . . I asked him to
consider whether it did not necessarily belong even to his own conception, after
taking so mere a child through such a tragedy of sorrow, to lift her also out of
the commonplace of ordinary happy endings, so that the gentle, pure, little figure
and form should never change to the fancy. All that I meant he seized at once
and never turned aside from it again."[373] Dickens had written Forster of the
latter's "valued suggestion."[374] Amid all the scrambling for pinpointing biographical influences, the novelist's letter to Joseph S. Smith (12 February 1842)
needs special attention. Dickens states once and for all that he did not have
anything biographical in mind: "Let me say, in answer to your letter, that the
wanderings, history, and death of Nell, are quite imaginary, and wholly fictitious."
Following up this suggestion, Paul C. Kitchen writes that "Dickens admits a

---

[373]
    Quoted from Forster's biography of Dickens by T. W. Hill in "Notes on
The Old Curiosity Shop," The Dickensian, XLIX (1955), 86.

[374]Letter of 17 January 1841 with Dickens's underscoring. Sister M. Audrianne
Welch, in "The Old Curiosity Shop: A Structural Analysis," unpubl. master's thesis
(Catholic University, 1950), notes Dickens's letter to Latimer on 13 March 1841
"some five weeks after the last issue (carrying the Curiosity Shop) had been published" (p. 46): "I never had the design and purpose of a story so distinctly marked
in my mind, from its commencement. All its quietness arose out of a deliberative
purpose; the notion being to stamp upon it from the first the shadow of that early
death."

connexion [between Nell and Mary Hogarth], but he implies, as he clearly indicates elsewhere, that the people of fiction pursue an existence of their own, forever independent of those who live in the so-called real world."[375] He rightly deplores the extent to which biographical analysis had gone in actually departing from the novelist's own conscious intent. Nell is, first and foremost, a persona.

But, if Dickens is to be strictly believed, how then can there be a true influence of the tragedy upon him in the novel? There is a slight problem here but by no means as grave a one as that confronting the biographical critic. There appears to be some lee-way in Dickens's statement, forthright as it is. He speaks of his work as "quite imaginary, and wholly fictitious," but this does not necessarily preclude that he was influenced by another literary work which is also "quite imaginary, and wholly fictitious." His principal point is simply to assert that, by describing Nell, he was not laying bare his soul in the market place; he does not absolutely deny that the very "imaginary" or "fictitious" part of his achievement may have, in part, a literary source. We recall, too, that the story of King Lear and his daughters is entirely legendary. So all I claim is that if Dickens was influenced at all in writing the novel, a literary source is by far the least apt to be far-fetched. If so, the Shakespearian influence would represent probably the most significant influence.[376]

375
   TLS, 4 Sept. 1937, p. 640.

376
   Apparently no one has yet considered the possibility that "The Dream of the Dying Girl," which Dickens mentions in a letter to T. G. Ouseley (14 March 1839), may also have been influential. Dickens refers to it as "that beautiful little poem" and recommends it for publication. Earlier, I have suggested that the death of Falstaff might also have been influential.

It is worthwhile recalling the actual genesis of the novel, the so-called "little St. James-square story." Forster has commented on it as follows: "It was at a celebration of his birthday in the first of his Bath lodgings, 35 St. James's-square, that the fancy which took the form of little Nell in the Curiosity Shop first dawned on the genius of its creator. No character in prose fiction was a greater favourite with Landor. He thought that, upon her, Juliet might for a moment have turned her eyes from Romeo, and that Desdemona might have taken her hair-breadth escapes to heart, so interesting and pathetic did she seem to him."[377] Thus, from the very start, Shakespeare has been associated with Nell, perhaps, one might add, not so much because of Juliet or Desdemona, but because of Nell, wife of Pistol and female friend of Falstaff. Yet one is more apt to remember Cordelia, because of Lord Jeffrey's famous comment: "nothing so good as Nell since Cordelia."

There certainly is a fairy-tale element in the novel, as Edgar Johnson has appropriately indicated in terming the work "a sad Hans Christian Andersen fairy tale, a summer transformation of some sort of a snow princess slowly melting away. Indeed, for all the vivid solidity with which it renders sordid realities like Quilp's wharf and Sampson Brass's house in Bevis Marks and the rapacious figures around Nell and her grandfather, the entire tale has about it something fabulous."[378] In a previous paper, I discovered separately this very "sad Hans Christian Andersen" touch as "the fancy which took the form of Little Nell."[379] It is noteworthy that Professor Johnson and I arrived at these judgments independently.

---

[377] I, 177. Sara Coleridge wrote Aubrey de Vere (Memoirs and Letters): "I admire Nell in The Old Curiosity Shop exceedingly. The whole thing is a good deal borrowed from Wilhelm Meister"; Forster interposes: "I may state it as within my knowledge that the book referred to was not then known to Dickens" (Ley ed., p. 723n).

[378] Johnson, I, 325.

[379] Cf. its title: "'Fancy's Knell.'"

In connection with this fancifulness, Walter Donald Head writes that
Dickens "always sought to blend accurate observation with imaginative interpretation. As an editor, his constant plea was for 'fancy' /Letters to Wills,
p. 73, p. 113ff_7. To his fancy, he gave full reign in composing his plots. It
affects his characters, aside from the playful style of presenting them, chiefly
in his method of blending character, mood, and story."[380] One recalls, not just
the elfin Nell, but the Puckish figure of Quilp, "a second Richard Crookback," as
his wife takes him to be.[381] Is it possible, then, that Dickens was influenced
here by Renaissance folk-lore, by tales of Puck utilized also in A Midsummer Night's
Dream? The possibility should not be overlooked. In The Monthly Magazine, a three-
volume work on The Frolics of Puck was summarized in a manner that probably did
not escape Dickens's attention and may also have inspired him to make a purchase:

> The volumes in question are founded upon the adventures of a frolicksome
> sprite, whose existence was formerly believed by most of the nations of
> Europe--known by different appellations, but recognized as the same by
> its peculiar characteristics. In England it has been domesticated for
> ages as Robin Goodfellow, and was conspicuous in all sorts of mishievous
> /ˉsic_7 conspiracies against old and young--the aged crone in her chimney
> corner, or the maiden at her churn. . . .
>
> This facetious little gentleman, having been re-christened by Shakespeare,
> Puck, is the hero of the work, and is introduced to us by the author, con-
> triving and executing a manoeuvre against the Queen of Fairyland. . . .
> Puck sojourns for some time upon the earth, and makes use of his elfin
> power to play a few pranks. . . .[382]

Here is a basis for the dwarf Quilp, who is bent upon leading Nell astray. Yet in
terms of the overall Lear influence, he surely represents a Dickensian Edmund.

---

[380]Head, p. 16.

[381]
    Spilka, in referring to Quilp as "a second Richard Crookback" (namely,
Shakespeare's Richard III), considers him to be Dickens's "greatest comic villain."
Papers of the Michigan Academy of Science, Arts, and Letters, XLV (1960), 429.

[382]From an anonymous review in the Monthly Magazine, XVII (1834), 337.

This is by no means **odd** even though he is called a "second Richard Crookback" in the novel and another "Richard Gloster" by Thomas Hood in his review (a critical paper which Dickens commends in his Preface); for both Edmund and Richard are "of Gloucester," the former being an earl and the latter a duke, and both have similar soliloquies, and the relationship between the two has become a commonplace in literary scholarship.[383] Thus much of what has been said regarding Quilp as another Richard is applicable to Quilp as another Edmund; for example, Ernest E. Polack writes, "It is much the same with him /Richard III_7. Although 'determined to prove a villain,' he conceals his villainy under a mask of such irresistible humour, that even when he has cogitated or performed some absolutely remorseless deed, we feel, like Juliet's nurse, that we 'cannot choose but laugh.' . . . His wooing of Queen Anne has become one of the great things in literature. He must have possessed something of that personal attraction which is said to have characterised Cataline. Quilp also must have had some such charm as this, or why would pretty little Mrs. Quilp have married him?"[384] Even so, Edmund is grotesquely humorous: not crippled like Richard, he is a misfit of Nature, a bastard. As such he commands his own ruthless smirk.

After Nell and Quilp, the most important Shakespearian characters in the novel are the grandfather, Kit Nubbles, and Dick Swiveller. In some ways, particularly in the final scenes, Nell's grandfather does resemble Cordelia's father, but this parallel should not be carried too far: basically the Grandfather is a pathetic figure and Lear is tragic. Still a few cardinal points of

---

[383] Thus W. Perrett writes, "The affinity of Edmund, 'earl of Gloucester,' with Richard III has been noticed." The Story of King Lear from Geoffrey of Monmouth to Shakespeare, Palaestra Books, XXXV (Berlin, 1904), p. 26n.

[384] "Humorous Villains: A Comparison between Daniel Quilp and Shakespeare's Richard the Third," The Dickensian, VI (1910), 183.

comparison should not be bypassed. When the Grandfather falls upon his knees and asks forgiveness of Nell (XII), the association with Lear is indeed revealing. One recalls the King's plea to Cordelia, "I'll kneel down / And ask of thee forgiveness" (V.iii.10-11) as well as "Pray you now, forget and forgive; I am old and foolish" (IV.vii.84-85). The use of the nil-factor in the tragedy, which I have considered in the previous chapter on Chuzzlewit, seems to re-echo in some of the Grandfather's words, for example, "I can do nothing for myself. . . ; I don't know how it is, I could once, but the time's gone" (XV, 111); "Nothing to fear! . . . Nothing to fear if they took me from thee! Nothing to fear if they parted us! Nobody is true to me. No, not one. Not even Nell!" (XXIV, 170). Particularly striking is his feeling of self-pity and helplessness: "You keep me poor, and plunder me, and make a sport and jest of me besides. . . . Ye'll drive me mad among ye" (XLII, 295); this surely recalls Lear's exclamations before the heath scenes, for example, "O, let me not be mad, not mad, sweet heaven! Keep me in temper; I would not be mad!" (I.v.45-46); "Our basest beggars / Are in the poorest things superfluous. / Allow not nature more than nature needs, / Man's life is cheap as beast's. . . . You see me here, you gods, a poor old man, / As full of grief as age, wretched in both. . . . O Fool, I shall go mad!" (II.iv.260-263, 268-269, 282). When the Grandfather is beside dying Nell, he recognizes certain signs of life which recall a similar recognition of Lear's:

> "She is still asleep," he whispered. "You were right. She did not call--
> unless she did so in her slumber. She has called to me in her sleep
> before now, sir; as I have sat by, watching, I have seen her lips move,
> and have known, though no sound came from them, that she spoke of me.
> I feared the light might dazzle her eyes and wake her, so I brought it
> here" (LXXI, 501).

> He came back, whispering that she was still asleep, but that he thought
> she had moved. It was her hand, he said--a little--a very, very little--
> but he was pretty sure she had moved it--perhaps in seeking his. He had
> known her do that, before now, though in the deepest sleep the while.
> (LXXI, 503)

The parallel lines by King Lear are the following: "She's dead as earth. / Lend me a looking-glass; If that her breath will mist or stain the stone, / Why, then she lives" (V.iii.261-263); "Do you see this? Look on her! Look--her lips! / Look there, look there!" (V.iii.310-311). That the Grandfather, like Lear, thinks that his beloved girl is alive when she is, in fact, deceased is evident enough from his decision to sit by her grave, murmuring, "she will come tomorrow!" He does this daily until, when spring finally arrives, he is found dead upon her tombstone. Yet one should also remember that whereas the Grandfather bursts into tears several times in the novel, Lear restrains himself. This proves that the King is naturally nobler and thus more stoic than the Grandfather, but it does not disprove influence: there is considerable talk about weeping in the tragedy, enough so to have had an effect upon the sentiment in the novel. Thus the latter has such descriptions as these: "The child thought, more than once, that he was moved: and had forborne to speak. But, now, he shed tears--tears that it lightened her aching heart to see--and making as though he would fall upon his knees, besought her to forgive him. 'Forgive you--what?' said Nell, interposing to prevent his purpose. 'Oh grandfather, what should I forgive?' 'All that is past, all that has come upon thee, Nell . . .'" (XII, 89); "Then, pointing to the bed, he burst into tears for the first time" (LXXII, 508). Compare Lear: "And let not women's weapons, water drops, / Stain my man's cheeks. . . . You think I'll weep; / No, I'll not weep: / I have full cause of weeping, but this heart / Shall break into a hundred thousand flaws / Or ere I'll weep" (II.iv.273-274, 278-282); "The good-years shall devour them, flesh and fell, / Ere they shall make us weep!" (V.iii.23-25). Finally, the descriptions of Nature in the novel, especially the rainfall-windstorm-snowfall sequence which adumbrates the approaching deaths, has certainly some parallel with the storm scenes in Lear, wherein the King "Strives in this little world of man to out-storm / The to-and-fro conflicting wind and rain" (III.i.10-11).

Moreover, Lear's Fool is represented in The Old Curiosity Shop--in a double capacity; at times he is captured in the character of Kit Nubbles, and at other times he is more akin to Richard Swiveller. That such a parallel would be by no means far-fetched has been argued by a number of Dickensians. Thus Earle Davis writes, "There is, of course, the general influence of Shakespeare upon his most serious dramatic efforts in plot and character. . . . Mr. Van Amerongen sees some similarities of treatment which may have been suggested by Shakespeare's fools."[385]

In the first chapter Kit Nubbles introduces himself to the reader: he is Nell's friend much as the Fool in Lear is Cordelia's. "'Foolish Nell!' said the old man fondling with her hair. 'She always laughs at poor Kit'" (I, 7). Nubbles then is described as having "an uncommonly wide mouth, very red cheeks, a turned-up nose, and certainly the most comical expression of face" (I, 7), thus looking something like the stage jester. Consider the following interchange between Kit and the Grandfather as also reminiscent of the Fool's conversation with Lear during the storm scenes:

> "A long way, wasn't it, Kit?" said the old man.
> "Why then, it was a goodish stretch, master," returned Kit.
> "Did you find the house easily?"
> "Why then, not over and above easy, master," said Kit.
> "Of course you have come back hungry?"
> "Why then, I do consider myself rather so, master," was the answer.
> (I, 7)

---

[385] "Literary Influences upon the Early Art of Charles Dickens," pp. 161-162 (the reference is to Van Amerongen, p. 222). See also Jack Lindsay, "Barnaby Rudge," in Dickens and the Twentieth Century, p. 94.

This kind of diffident parleying is not unlike the comic interplay between the King and his jester, albeit the obviousness of the riddles does support a more serious undercurrent of meaning whereby Lear and the Fool momentarily change places; that is, the Fool becomes wise to the King's foolishness. Compare the following:

> Fool. Canst tell how an oyster makes his shell?
>
> Lear. No.
>
> Fool. Nor I neither; but I can tell why a snail has a house.
>
> Lear. Why?
>
> Fool. Why, to put's head in; not to give it away to his daughters, and leave his horns without a case.
>
>
> Fool. The reason why the seven stars are no moe than seven is a pretty reason.
>
> Lear. Because they are not eight.
>
> Fool. Yes, indeed; thou would'st make a good fool. (I.v.26-32, 35-38)

There is an acute difference in style between the two kinds of repartee. Though Shakespeare bases more on the jest and is therefore in a sense "wittier," Dickens is more successful in having the reader laugh with rather than simply at his characters. Thus although Kit's remarks cause Nell to laugh after he is finished, like a good Dickensian character he himself joins in the merriment: "It was a great point too, that Kit himself was flattered by the sensation he created, and after several efforts to preserve his gravity, burst into a loud roar, and so stood with his mouth wide open and his eyes nearly shut, laughing violently" (I, 8). When the Grandfather asks Nell if she knows that he loves her, the child responds, "Kit knows you do," and her friend characteristically echoes her thoughts, even as the Fool echoes Cordelia's: "Kit, who in despatching his bread and meat had been swallowing two-thirds of his knife at every mouthful with the coolness of a juggler, stopped short in his operations on being thus appealed to, and bawled 'Nobody isn't such a fool as to say he doosn't,' after which he incapacitated himself for further conversation by taking a most prodigious sandwich at one bite" (I, 8-9). Kit's response, in the light of Shakespeare's tragedy, is somewhat ironic; that the King failed to live up to his true love for his youngest daughter underscores the tragic circumstances, so that in effect he has become the very kind of fool who, Kit says, does not exist.

The other character based in part on the Fool in Lear makes his entrance in the second chapter: Richard Swiveller. Taking upon himself some of the "sophistication" of Shakespeare's jester--a limited worldliness but a kind that Kit Nubbles lacks--Swiveller comments upon life from the extrovert's point of view without bashfulness. Eventually he is to be seen more in Dickensian terms than as an analogue to a Shakespearian Fool, since even his nickname is derivable from the surname of his creator.[386]

Finally, a basic similarity between Lear and Curiosity Shop, one which serves to round out the other correspondences and furnishes a central thematic core for considering both works, is the theme of the apparent and the real. In the drama, the world of the apparent is strongly established by the

---

[386] Jack Lindsay writes that "we often find Dickens signing letters as 'Dick.' . . . He put Dick into the Lant Street where he had stayed during the happier half of his blacking-work days." Charles Dickens (London, 1950), p. 196. See van Amerongen, p. 222. Cf. Mr. Dick of David Copperfield. Charles Dickens's initials are, as is well-known, present in that title of his so-called most autobiographical novel in reverse order.

It is thus significant that Dickens wanted to make a great deal out of Swiveller.

characteristic metaphor of sight,[387] one which significantly relates the main
plot to the sub-plot. When Goneril tells the King that she loves him "dearer
than eyesight" (I.i.56), she introduces the image, and there is a hint of Lear's
"blindness of reason" to follow. Metaphorically, her "love" is such that it will
cost him his "eyes." When he rejects the daughter who loves him most, his
blindness begins: "Hence, and avoid my sight!" (I.i.124). Kent, banished as
well, advises him to "see better" (I.i.154). His spiritual blindness reaches a
climax in his "eyeless rage" (III.i.9) during the storm scene of the third act.
The Fool is able "to see" (and not only the points of his jokes) whereas the King
cannot. Act Three ends when Gloucester, having been misled by Edmund even as Lear
was by his daughters, is blinded by Cornwall for his efforts to reconcile the
King with Cordelia. Projecting his madness into Gloucester, as earlier he had
projected his own inconstancy into Cordelia by calling her "my sometime daughter"
(I.i.119), Lear ridicules the Earl's physical blindness. At the end of the fourth
act, when he becomes reconciled to Cordelia, Lear begins to recognize "fair
daylight" (IV.vii.53) again, but the consequences of his original incapacity to
see what was going on have become so overwhelming that tragedy is seemingly
inevitable. In the last act, however, he has recovered enough sight to face his
end stoically with Cordelia: "Wipe thine eyes; / The good years shall devour them,
flesh and fell, / Ere they shall make us weep" (V.iii.23-24). Thus the references
to sight and blindness function as a symbol of the world of the apparent in the
play. Even so do some of the references to clothes.[388] The King tears off his

---

[387]
    Cf. Paul J. Alpers, "King Lear and the Theory of the 'Sight Pattern,'" in
Reuben A. Brower and Richard Poirier, eds., In Defense of Reading: A Reader's
Approach to Literary Criticism (New York, 1962), pp. 133-152.

[388]Robert B. Heilman, who suggested the idea of a "sight pattern" in his
controversial volume on Lear, This Great Stage (Baton Rouge, 1948), also refers
to the "clothes pattern" in the tragedy.

clothes in Act Three as a wild gesture prompted by his madness and his desire to return to the simplicity of the state of Nature. In fine, Edgar's remark to Gloucester, "You're much deceiv'd. In nothing am I chang'd / But in my garments" (IV.vi.9-10), is indicative of the reign of the apparent throughout much of the play.

This same theme of the apparent and (by contrasting implication) the real is evident in the opening chapters of the novel. Much of The Old Curiosity Shop relates to the dream-world, a modification of the world of the apparent. Thus Warrington Winters has written on "Dickens and the Psychology of Dreams"[389] and George Harry Ford concludes that "the unifying device of The Old Curiosity Shop is the dream."[390] The very title suggests this world, one which is then described in terms of "an air-built castle" and "strange furniture that might have been designed in dreams" (I, 1, 5). Master Humphrey tells the Grandfather that he should not "attach too great weight to a remark founded on first appearances" (I, 8). The Grandfather bids Nell to sleep soundly, and she refers to the pleasant dreams she anticipates after her prayers.[391] "The bell wakes me," she says when they part, "even in the middle of a dream" (I, 11). In leaving the shop, the narrator steps aside, as it were, to comment on his own: "We are so much in the habit of allowing impressions to be made upon us by external objects, which should be produced by reflection alone, but which without visible aids, often escape us,

---

[389] Publications of the Modern Language Association, LXIII (1948), 984-1006.

[390] Dickens and his Readers, p. 64n.

[391] These lines are reminiscent of Hamlet (V.ii.348): "Good night, sweet prince, / And flights of angels sing thee to thy rest!" Thus the Grandfather says, "Sleep soundly, Nell, . . . and angels guard thy bed! Do not forget thy prayers my sweet" (I, 11). Notice the repetition of sweet, angels, and thy as well as the parallel structure (e.g., "Good night, sweet prince" and "Sleep soundly, Nell"). Thus there may be an intimation of Hamlet here just as there is one of Falstaff at the end.

that I am not sure I should have been so thoroughly possessed by this one
subject, but for the heaps of fantastic things I had seen huddled together
in the curiosity-dealer's warehouse" (I, 13). He finds that Nell seems "to
exist in a kind of allegory" (I, 13) and imagines her "in her future life,
holding her solitary way among a crowd of wild grotesque companions; the only
pure, fresh, youthful object in the throng" (I, 13). As he lies in bed
thereafter, the dream-image recurs as he imagines "alone in the midst of all
this lumber and decay and ugly age, the beautiful child in her gentle slumber,
smiling through her light and sunny dreams" (I, 14).

These dream-references emerge again later in the novel when the "crowd
of wild grotesque companions" really comes to life. They serve there, I suspect,
as presentiments of ensuing death. Consider, for example, the description of
Codlin's Punch and Judy performance (XVI). The old man and his granddaughter
have, in the course of their wanderings, entered a cemetery where a group of
actors is rehearsing: a typical Dickensian reference to the theater. The son
of the leading performer notices that the Grandfather's eyes are arrested by the
figure of Punch who "seemed to be pointing with the tip of his cap to a most
flourishing epitaph, and to be chuckling over it with all his heart" (XVI, 116).
The Fool in Lear again comes to mind. Codlin finally "twitched Punch off the
tombstone" (XVI, 117), but the point has been made: the foreboding of death is
grotesquely present.[392] A few pages later Nell comes upon a feeble old woman
who asks her to read a tombstone for her, explains how often she comes to the

---

[392]
By itself, without the ensuing presentiments, such a reflection would not
be significant enough to represent an adumbration of the death of Nell and her
grandfather. For Dickens simply enjoys writing about graveyards. In Edwin
Drood, graveyard references may be symbolic in a minor way, but surely the opening
scene in Great Expectations would not be.

tomb of her dead husband and mourns (XVII). Nell thoughtfully retraces
her steps back to her grandfather as if soberly contemplating the reality
of her approaching demise. Whereas the Grandfather, former proprietor of a
curiosity shop, takes special delight in the puppet display, with Punch on
the gravestone, Nell in her feminine way finds greater delight in the flowers
adorning the cemetery. Then, shortly after meeting Codlin, they come upon
Vuffin, "the proprietor of a giant," and a little lady without legs or arms
(XIX, 134) as well as "a silent gentleman who earned his living by showing
tricks upon the cards," one whose very name relates him to William Shakespeare
in the guise of Prospero the Magician: Sweet William.[393] Indeed, Vuffin remarks
that "if you was to advertise Shakespeare played entirely by wooden legs, it's
my belief you wouldn't draw a sixpence" (XIX, 135), a comment pointing to the
influence of the dramatist. These extraordinary figures may also serve as
a prelude to the death scenes. But the most obvious such adumbration occurs
when Grandfather and Nell encounter the old schoolmaster who shows a "great
deal of concern for a little child, Harry," described as having "curls about
his face, and . . . eyes . . . very bright," yet "their light was of Heaven, not
earth" (XXV, 180). Without a doubt, the death of Harry anticipates that of Nell.
So Dickens writes: "The poor schoolmaster sat in the same place, holding the
small cold hand in his, and chafing it. It was but the hand of a dead child.
He felt that; and yet he chafed it still, and could not lay it down" (XXV, 181).
Surely we have here once again a reminder of Lear's belief that his Cordelia may
still be alive, the peaceful thought with which he himself succumbs.

Finis

---

[393]Dickens considered the title Sweet William to be "a pleasant satire upon
his ugliness" (XIX, 134), but very possibly the sweetness of Shakespeare, as
in his "sugar'd" sonnets, is echoed here as well. Interestingly enough, in
1960 the Catholic University Speech and Drama Department produced a musical
comedy on the life of Shakespeare with the same title.

BIBLIOGRAPHY

I. Books

Adams, Joseph Quincy, ed. <u>Chief</u> <u>Pre-Shakespearean</u> <u>Drama</u>. Cambridge, Massachusetts, 1924.

Allott, Kenneth, ed. <u>Matthew</u> <u>Arnold</u>: <u>A</u> <u>Selection</u> <u>of</u> his <u>Poems</u>. London, 1954.

Altick, Richard D., and Matthews, William R. <u>Guide</u> <u>to</u> <u>Doctoral</u> <u>Dissertations</u> <u>in</u> <u>Victorian</u> <u>Literature</u>: <u>1886-1958</u>. Urbana, 1960.

Amerongen, J. B. van. <u>The</u> <u>Actor</u> <u>in</u> <u>Dickens</u>: <u>A</u> <u>Study</u> <u>of</u> the <u>Histrionic</u> and <u>Dramatic</u> <u>Elements</u> <u>in</u> <u>the</u> <u>Novelist's</u> <u>Life</u> <u>and</u> <u>Works</u>. New York, 1927.

Aylmer, Felix. <u>Dickens</u> <u>Incognito</u>. London, 1959.

Baker, Ernest A. <u>The</u> <u>History</u> <u>of</u> the <u>English</u> <u>Novel</u>. Vol. VII. London, 1936.

Baldwin, Thomas Whitfield. <u>William</u> <u>Shakspere's</u> <u>Five-act</u> <u>Structure</u>: <u>Shakspere's</u> <u>Early</u> <u>Plays</u> <u>on</u> <u>the</u> <u>Background</u> <u>of</u> <u>Renaissance</u> <u>Theories</u> <u>of</u> <u>Five-act</u> <u>Structure</u> <u>from</u> <u>1470</u>.

Ball, Adolf. <u>Dickens</u> <u>und</u> <u>seine</u> <u>Hauptwerke</u>: <u>Eine</u> <u>Kritische</u> <u>Studie</u>. Braunschweig, 1885.

Baugh, Albert C., et al. <u>A</u> <u>Literary</u> <u>History</u> <u>of</u> <u>England</u>. New York, 1948.

Brower, Reuben A., and Poirier, Richard, eds. <u>In</u> <u>Defense</u> <u>of</u> <u>Reading</u>: <u>A</u> <u>Reader's</u> <u>Approach</u> <u>to</u> <u>Literary</u> <u>Criticism</u>. New York, 1962.

Butt, John Everett, and Tillotson, Kathleen Mary. <u>Dickens</u> <u>at</u> <u>Work.</u> London, 1957.

Canning, Albert Stratford George. <u>The</u> <u>Philosophy</u> <u>of</u> <u>Charles</u> <u>Dickens</u>. London, 1880.

Chesterton, Gilbert Keith. <u>Criticisms</u> <u>and</u> <u>Appreciations</u> <u>of</u> <u>the</u> <u>Works</u> <u>of</u> Charles <u>Dickens</u>. London, 1933.

Cockshut, A. O. J. <u>The</u> <u>Imagination</u> <u>of</u> <u>Charles</u> <u>Dickens</u>. New York, 1962.

Collins, Philip. <u>Dickens</u> <u>and</u> <u>Crime</u>, Cambridge Studies in Criminology, XVII. London, 1962.

Crotch, W. Walter. <u>The</u> <u>Pageant</u> <u>of</u> <u>Dickens</u>. Rev. ed. London, 1916.

——————————. <u>The</u> <u>Soul</u> <u>of</u> <u>Dickens</u>. London, 1916.

Danby, John F. Shakespeare's Doctrine of Nature: A Study of "King Lear." London, 1949.

Davis, Earle. The Flint and the Flame: The Artistry of Charles Dickens. Columbia, 1963.

Dexter, Walter, ed. The Letters of Charles Dickens. 3 vols. London, 1938.

Dibelius, Wilhelm. Charles Dickens. Leipzig, 1916.

Dickens, Charles. Works. 20 vols. New York, n.d.

Eckel, John C. The First Editions of the Writings of Charles Dickens: Their Points and Values. Rev. ed. New York, 1932.

Eliot, Thomas Stearns. Selected Essays: 1917-1932. 2nd ed. New York, 1950.

Engel, Monroe. The Maturity of Dickens. Cambridge, Massachusetts, 1959.

Faulkner, William. Light in August. New York, 1950.

Fawcett, Frank Dubrez. Dickens the Dramatist, on Stage, Screen and Radio. London, 1952.

Fielding, K. J. Charles Dickens: A Critical Introduction. London, 1958.

_____. The Speeches of Charles Dickens. Oxford, 1960.

Fitz-Gerald, Shafto Justin Adair. Dickens and the Drama. London, 1910.

Ford, George Harry. Dickens and his Readers: Aspects of Novel Criticism since 1836. Princeton, 1955.

Ford, George Harry, and Lane, Jr., Lauriat, eds. The Dickens Critics. Ithaca, 1961.

Forster, John, et al. Dramatic Essays: John Forster, G. H. Lewes. London, 1896.

_____. The Life of Charles Dickens. 2 vols. London, 1872-1874.

_____. The Life of Charles Dickens, ed. J. W. T. Ley. London, 1928.

Furness, Horace Howard, ed. The New Variorum Edition of "Hamlet." 2 vols. London, 1877.

Gissing, George Robert. Critical Studies of the Works of Charles Dickens. New York, 1924.

Gross, John J., and Pearson, Gabriel, eds. Dickens and the Twentieth Century. London, 1962.

Harbage, Alfred Bennett. William Shakespeare: A Reader's Guide. New York, 1963.

Harrison, George Bagshawe. Introducing Shakespeare. Baltimore, 1954.

Harrison, Michael. Charles Dickens: A Sentimental Journey in Search of an Unvarnished Portrait. London, 1953.

Heilman, Robert Bechtold. Magic in the Web: Action and Language in "Othello." Lexington, 1956.

——————————————. This Great Stage: Image and Structure in "King Lear." Baton Rouge, 1948.

House, Humphry. The Dickens World. London, 1941.

Jerrold, Blanchard, ed. The Best of All Good Company: A Day with Charles Dickens. London, 1871.

Johnson, Edgar. Charles Dickens: His Tragedy and Triumph. 2 vols. New York, 1952.

Johnson, Edgar, and Johnson, Eleanor. The Dickens Theatrical Reader. Boston, 1964.

Johnson, Edgar. The Heart of Charles Dickens, as Revealed in his Letters to Angela Burdett-Coutts; Selected and Edited from the Collection in the Pierpont Morgan Library. Boston, 1952.

Kitton, Frederic George. Dickensiana: A Bibliography of the Literature Relating to Charles Dickens and his Writings. London, 1886.

Leacock, Stephen. Charles Dickens: His Life and Work. New York, 1936.

Leary, Lewis, ed. Contemporary Literary Scholarship: A Critical Review. New York, 1958.

Lettis, Richard, and Morris, William E., eds. Assessing Great Expectations. San Francisco, 1960.

Lindsay, Jack. Charles Dickens: A Biographical and Critical Study. London, 1950.

Lubbock, Percy. The Craft of Fiction. New York, 1921.

Matz, Bertram Waldrom, ed. Miscellaneous Papers. London, 1908.

McLuhan, H. M., ed. Alfred Lord Tennyson: Selected Poetry. New York, 1956.

Miller, Henry Knight. Essays on Fielding's "Miscellanies": A Commentary on Volume One. Princeton, 1961.

Miller, John Hillis. Charles Dickens: The World of his Novels. Cambridge, Massachusetts, 1958.

Monod, Sylvère. Dickens Romancier: Etude sur la Création Littéraire dans les Romans de Charles Dickens. Paris, 1953.

Muir, Kenneth, ed. King Lear. Based on the ed. of W. J. Craig, 8th ed., rev. The Arden Edition. London, 1955.

Orwell, George. Dickens, Dali & Others: Studies in Popular Culture. New York, 1946.

Pearson, Hesketh. Dickens: His Character, Comedy, and Career. New York, 1949.

Pemberton, Thomas Edgar. Charles Dickens and the Stage: A Record of his Connection with the Drama as Playwright, Actor and Critic. London, 1888.

Perrett, Wilfrid. The Story of King Lear from Geoffrey of Monmouth to Shakespeare, Palaestra Books, XXXV. Berlin, 1904.

Pitt, Valerie. Tennyson Laureate. London, 1962.

Pollock, Sir Frederick, ed. Reminiscences of William Charles Macready. 4 vols. London, 1875.

Praz, Mario. The Hero in Eclipse in Victorian Fiction, trans. Angus Davidson. New York, 1956.

Priestley, John Boynton. Charles Dickens: A Pictorial Biography. New York, 1962.

_____. The English Comic Characters. New York, 1925.

Robinson, Edwin Arlington. Collected Poems. New York, 1937.

Rolfe, William J., ed. Hamlet. New York, 1878.

Ruskin, John. Works, ed. E. T. Cook and Alexander Wedderburn, Vol. VII. London, 1905.

Sacks, Claire, and Whan, Edgar, eds. Hamlet: Enter Critic. New York, 1960.

Sampson, George. The Concise Cambridge History of English Literature. Cambridge, 1959.

Santayana, George. Soliloquies in England and Later Soliloquies. New York, 1922.

Shore, William Teignmouth. Charles Dickens and his Friends. London, 1909.

_____. Shakespeare's Self. London, 1920.

Smith, David Nichol, ed. Shakespeare Criticism: A Selection. London, 1953.

Stonehouse, John Harrison, ed. Catalogue of the Library of Charles Dickens, Reprinted from Sotheran's "Price Current of Literature," numbers CLXXIV and CLXXV. London, 1925.

Suter, Henry Charles. _Dramatic Episodes from Dickens_. London, n.d.

Svaglic, Martin J., ed. _The Idea of a University_ by John Henry Newman. New York, 1960.

Swift, Jonathan. _Satires and Personal Writings_. London, 1958.

Tilley, Morris Palmer. _A Dictionary of the Proverbs in England in the Sixteenth and Seventeenth Centuries_. Ann Arbor, 1950.

Tillotson, Kathleen Mary. _Novels of the Eighteen-Forties_. Oxford, 1954.

Toynbee, William, ed. _The Diaries of William Charles Macready, 1833-1851_. 2 vols. London, 1912.

Trewin, John Courtenay. _Mr Macready_. London, 1955.

Unger, Leonard. _T. S. Eliot_. Minneapolis, 1961.

Van Ghent, Dorothy (Bendon). _The English Novel: Form and Function_. New York, 1953.

Wagenknecht, Edward. _Cavalcade of the English Novel_. New York, 1943.

——————————. _The Man Charles Dickens_. New York, 1929.

Webster, Margaret. _Shakespeare Without Tears_. Rev. ed. Cleveland, 1955.

Wilson, Edmund. _The Wound and the Bow: Seven Studies in Literature_. Boston, 1941.

Wilson, John Dover. _What Happens in "Hamlet."_ Cambridge, 1951.

Winterich, John T. _An American Friend of Dickens_. New York, 1933.

Wright, Aldus, and Clark. The Globe Edition of Shakespeare's Plays. Rev. Cambridge, 1861.

Woollcott, Alexander. _Mr. Dickens Goes to the Play_. London, 1922.

II. Articles

Altick, Richard D. "Hamlet and the Odor of Mortality," _Shakespeare Quarterly_, V (1954), 167-176.

Anonymous. "A Californian Conjuring Trick," <u>All the Year Round</u>, XXXIX, n. s., XIX (1877), 253-261.

_____. "Dickens, the Great Magician," <u>The Dickensian</u>, IV (1908), 145-147.

_____. "Legs," <u>Household Words</u>. IX (1854), 209-212.

_____. "The Magic Crystal," <u>Household Words</u>, II (1850), 284-288.

_____. "The Monomaniac," <u>The Monthly Magazine</u>, XVIII (1834), 200-210.

_____. "Out-conjuring Conjurors," <u>Household Words</u>, XIX (1859), 433-439.

_____. "Re-touching the Lord Hamlet," <u>Household Words</u>, XVI (1857), 545-548.

_____. Review of <u>The Frolics of Puck</u>, 3 vols., in <u>The Monthly Magazine</u>, XVII (1834), 337-338.

_____. Review of <u>Great Expectations</u> in <u>The Atlantic Monthly</u>, VIII (1861), 380-382.

_____. "The Sensational Williams," <u>All the Year Round</u>, XI (1864), 14-17.

_____. "Shakespeare and Dickens," <u>The Dickensian</u>, I (1905), 146-147.

_____. "Something that Shakespeare Wrote," <u>Household Words</u>, XV (1857), 49-52.

_____. "Speculation on Ghosts!: With the Singular Circumstance of a Dream," <u>The Monthly Magazine</u>, XVII (1834), 423-432.

_____. "Touching the Lord Hamlet," <u>Household Words</u>, XVI (1857), 372-376.

Bennett, Josephine Waters. "The Storm Within: the Madness of Lear," <u>Shakespeare Quarterly</u>, XIII (1962), 137-155.

Boege, Fred W. "Point of View in Dickens," <u>Publications of the Modern Language Association</u>, LXV (1950), 90-105.

Bowen, H. E. "'I'll Break my Staff . . . I'll Drown my Book'" in <u>Renaissance Papers 1961</u>. Durham, 1961. Pp. 47-56.

Brown, E. K. "David Copperfield," <u>The Yale Review</u>, XXXVII (1948), 650-666.

Burckhardt, Sigurd. "King Lear: The Quality of Nothing," <u>Minnesota Review</u>, II (1961), 33-50.

Bush, Douglas. "Tennyson's 'Ulysses' and <u>Hamlet</u>," <u>Modern Language Review</u>, XXXVIII (1943), 38.

Calhoun, Jean S. "'Hamlet' and the Circumference of Action," <u>Renaissance News</u>, XV (1962), 281-298.

Calhoun, P., and Heaney, Howell J. "Dickensiana in the Rough," Papers of the Bibliographical Society of America, XLI (1947), 293-320.

Carlisle, Carol Jones. "William Macready as a Shakespearean Critic" in Renaissance Papers 1954. Durham, 1954. Pp. 31-39.

Carter, John Archer. "The World of Squeers and the World of Crummles," The Dickensian, LVIII (1962), 50-53.

Castieau, John B. "The Fictions of Forster," The Dickensian, XII (1916), 264-269.

Chevalier, W. A. C. "Shakespeare and Dickens as Men of Affairs," The Dickensian, III (1907), 44-47, 66-69.

Chew, Samuel C. Review of John Dover Wilson's What Happens in "Hamlet" in The New York Herald Tribune Books, 9 February 1936, p. 5.

Christian, Eleanor E. "Recollections of Charles Dickens. His Family and Friends," Temple Bar, LXXXII (1888), 481-506.

Churchill, R. C. "Dickens, Drama and Tradition," Scrutiny, X (1942), 358-375.

Clark, Cumberland. "Shakespeare and Dickens." A lecture delivered to the Dickens Fellowship, Shakespeare Reading Society, London, and the Shakespeare Club, Stratford-on-Avon. London, 1918.

Clinton-Baddeley, V. C. "Wopsle," The Dickensian, LVII (1961), 150-159.

Collins, Philip. "Dickens on Ghosts: An Uncollected Article," The Dickensian, LIX (1963), 5-14.

Connell, J. M. "The Religion of Charles Dickens," Hibbert Journal, XXXVI (1938), 225-235.

Connolly, Thomas E. "Technique in Great Expectations," Philological Quarterly, XXXIV (1955), 48-55.

Curtoys, W. F. D. "Tobias Smollett's Influence on Dickens," The Dickensian, XXXII (1936), 249-254.

Davies, Edith M. "The Cock Lane Ghost," The Dickensian, XXXV (1938 / 1939), 10-13.

Dibble, R. F. "Charles Dickens: His Reading," Modern Language Notes, XXXV (1920), 334-339.

Dibelius, Wilhelm. "Dickens und Shakespeare," Jahrbuch der Deutschen Shakespeare-Gesellschaft (Berlin, 1916), pp. 76-83.

Dickens, Charles. "The Ghost of the Cock Lane Ghost Wrong Again," Household Words, VI (1853), 420.

Dickens, Charles. "Macready as Benedick," The Examiner, 4 March 1843, p. 132.

_____. "On Mr. Fechter's Acting," The Atlantic Monthly, XXIV (1869), 242-244.

_____. "The Restoration of Shakespeare's Lear to the Stage," The Examiner, 4 February 1838, p. 69.

_____. "Stray Chapters: No. I. The Pantomime of Life," Bentley's Miscellany, I (1837), 291-297.

_____. "Stray Chapters: No. II. Some Particulars Concerning a Lion," Bentley's Miscellany, I (1837), 515-518.

Dickens, Charles, and Horne, R. H. "Shakespeare and Newgate," Household Words, IV (1851), 25-27.

Dickens, Charles, et al. "A Haunted House," Household Words, VII (1853), 481-483.

Doran, Madeleine. "That Undiscovered Country," Philological Quarterly, XX (1941), 413-427.

Draper, John W. "The Prince-Philosopher and Shakespeare's Hamlet," West Virginia University Studies, III (1937), 39-43.

Duffield, H. "The Macbeth Motif in Dickens's Edwin Drood," The Dickensian, XXX (1934), 263-271.

Dunn, Ellen Catherine. "The Storm in King Lear," Shakespeare Quarterly, III (1952), 329-333.

Evans, J. Blakemore. Review of the New Cambridge Edition of King Lear, in The Journal of English and Germanic Philology, LX (1961), 323-329.

F. "Shakespeare and Mrs. Gamp," The Dickensian, V (1909), 164.

Fielding, K. J. Review of Dickens and the Twentieth Century, in The Dickensian, LIX (1963), 45-47.

Fleissner, Robert F. "Falstaff's Green Sickness Unto Death," Shakespeare Quarterly, XII (1961), 47-55.

_____. "'Fancy's Knell,'" The Dickensian, LVIII (1962), 125-127.

_____. "Lear's 'Poor Fool' as the Poor Fool," Essays in Criticism, XIII (1963), 425-427.

_____. "The Misused Sacrament in King John," The Shakespeare Newsletter, X (1960), 28.

_____. "The 'Nothing' Element in King Lear," Shakespeare Quarterly, XIII (1962), 67-70.

Fleissner, Robert F. "Shylock and Fagin," Nexus /Catholic University student-faculty publication_7, III (1957), 17-20.

Forker, Charles R. "Shakespeare's Theatrical Symbolism and its Function in Hamlet," Shakespeare Quarterly, XIV (1963), 215-229.

Fraser, J. A. Lovat. "Gashford and his Prototype," The Dickensian, II (1906), 39-41.

Fraser, Russell. "A Charles Dickens Original," Nineteenth Century Fiction, IX (1955), 301-307.

Furmiss, Harry. "A Shakespeare Birthday: A Reminiscence of Charles Dickens," The Pall Mall Magazine, XXXVII (1906), 423-428.

Geraldine, C. S. J., Sister M. "Erasmus and the Tradition of Paradox," Studies in Philology, LXI (1964), 41-63.

Germer, Rudolf. "Die Bedeutung Shakespeares für T. S. Eliot," Jahrbuch der Deutschen Shakespeare-Gesellschaft, XCV (1959), 112-132.

Gordon, Elizabeth Hope. "The Naming of Characters in the Works of Charles Dickens" in University of Nebraska Studies in Language, Literature, and Criticism, 1. Lincoln, 1917.

Griskin, Ingleberry. "Merrie England in the Olden Time: Her Gambols, Songs, and Flashes of Merriment, with the Humours of her Ancient Court-Fools, Will Summers, Dick Tarlton, and Archibald Armstrong," Bentley's Miscellany, V (1839), 98-108.

Gwynn, Frederick L. "Hamlet and Hardy," Shakespeare Quarterly, IV (1953), 207-208.

Hagan, Jr., John H. "The Poor Labyrinth: The Theme of Social Injustice in Dickens's 'Great Expectations,'" Nineteenth Century Fiction, IX (1954), 169-178.

——————————. "Structural Patterns in Dickens's Great Expectations," English Literary History /ELH_7, XXI (1954), 54-66.

Hammerle, Karl. "Transpositionen aus Shakespeares King Lear in Thomas Hardys Return of the Native," Wiener Beiträge zur Englischen Philologie, LXV (1957), 58-73.

Hardy, Barbara. "The Change of Heart in Dickens' Novels," Victorian Studies, V (1961), 61-67.

Hawkes, Terry. "'Love' in King Lear," Review of English Studies, X (1959), 178-181.

Heilman, Robert Bechtold. "The New World in Charles Dickens's Writings, Part I," The Trollopian /later: Nineteenth Century Fiction_7, I, 3 (1946 / 1947), 25-43.

Heilman, Robert Bechtold. "The New World in Charles Dickens's Writings, Part II," The Trollopian, I, 4 (1946 / 1947), 11-26.

Hill, T. W. "Books that Dickens Read," The Dickensian, XLV (1949), 81-90.

_____. "A Dickensian's View of Shakespeare," The Dickensian, XII (1916), 93-97.

_____. "Notes on Martin Chuzzlewit," The Dickensian, XLII (1946), 141-148, 196-203; XLIII (1947), 28-35.

_____. "Notes on The Old Curiosity Shop," The Dickensian, XLIX (1953), 86-93, 137-142, 183-191.

_____. "Notes to David Copperfield," The Dickensian, XXXIX (1943), 79-88, 123-131, 197-201; XL (1943), 11-14.

_____. "Notes to Great Expectations," The Dickensian, LIII (1957), 119-126, 184-186; LIV (1958), 53-60, 123-125, 185; LV (1959), 57-59.

Hill, T. W., and Miller, William. "Charles Dickens's Manuscripts," The Dickensian, XIII (1917), 181-185.

Hoenigswald, Henry M. "Some Uses of Nothing," Language, XXXV (1959), 409-420.

Hookham, Paul. "Samuel Johnson and Samuel Pickwick: A New Point of View," The Dickensian, VII (1911), 126-128.

Houghton, R. E. C. "Hardy and Shakespeare," Notes and Queries, n.s., VIII (1961), 98.

Howells, William Dean. "Dickens's Later Heroines," Harper's Bazaar, XXXIII (1900), 1415-1421.

Hutchens, Eleanor N. "The Transfer of Power in King Lear and The Tempest," A Review of English Literature, IV (1963), 82-93.

Jackson, Frederick G. "Dickens the Actor," The Dickensian, III (1907), 173-178.

Jerdan, William. "Nonsense! A Miscellany about Love," Bentley's Miscellany, IV (1838), 167-172.

Johnson, Samuel. "Preface to Shakespeare" (1765), in Johnson on Shakespeare: Essays and Notes Selected and Set Forth with an Introduction by Walter Raleigh. London, 1908.

Jones, C. Sheridan. "Charles Dickens and the Occult," The Occult Review, XXIV (1916), 276-283.

Jones, Howard Mumford. "On Rereading Great Expectations," The Southwest Review, XXXIX (1954), 328-335.

Jorgensen, Paul A. "Much Ado about Nothing," Shakespeare Quarterly, V (1954), 287-295.

Keast, W. R. "Imagery and Meaning in the Interpretation of King Lear," Modern Philology, XLVII (1950), 45-64.

Langley-Levy, Doris. "The Fascination of Steerforth," The Dickensian, XVIII (1922), 191-193.

Law, Marie Hamilton. "The Indebtedness of Oliver Twist to Defoe's History of the Devil," Publications of the Modern Language Association, XL (1925), 892-897.

Lindberg, John. "Individual Conscience and Social Injustice in Great Expectations," College English, XXIII (1961), 118-122.

Maginn, W. "Shakspeare Papers.--No. I. Sir John Falstaff," Bentley's Miscellany, I (1837), 494-508.

Marshall, James F. "Alfred de Vigny and William Charles Macready," Publications of the Modern Language Association, LXXIV (1959), 98-101.

Marshall, William H. "The Image of Steerforth and the Structure of David Copperfield," Tennessee Studies in Literature, V (1960), 57-65.

Matz, Bertram Waldrom. "La Belle Sauvage Inn," The Dickensian, XII (1916), 121-126.

Mayhew, Edward. "The Good-for-nothing," Bentley's Miscellany, IV (1838), 94-104.

Maynard, Theodore. "The Catholicism of Dickens," Thought, V (1930), 87-105.

McNulty, J. H. "Bleak House and Macbeth," The Dickensian, XL (1944), 188-191.

——————. "An Imaginary Conversation between Dickens and Shakespeare," The Dickensian, XXXIII (1937), 122-125.

——————. "A Most Ingenious Debate," The Dickensian, XXXI (1935), 201.

Meissner, R. "Der Name Hamlet," Indogermanische Forschungen, XLV (1927), 370-394.

Miller, William. "Dickens Reading at the British Museum," The Dickensian, XLIII (1947), 83-84.

Minck, J. Murray. "Daniel Quilp," The Dickensian, XIII (1917), 73-75.

Morley, Malcolm. "More about Crummles," The Dickensian, LIX (1963), 51-56.

——————. "Private Theatres and Boz," The Dickensian, LIX (1963), 119-123.

Moynahan, Julian. "The Hero's Guilt: The Case of Great Expectations," Essays in Criticism, X (1960), 60-79.

Needham, Gwendolyn B. "The Undisciplined Heart of David Copperfield," Nineteenth Century Fiction, IX (1954), 81-107.

Nisbet, Ada. "The Autobiographical Matrix of Great Expectations," The Victorian Newsletter, 15 (1959), pp. 10-13.

Norris, E. Ashby. "Mr. Peggotty, Gentleman," The Dickensian, V (1909), 241-244.

Partlow, Jr., Robert B. "The Moving I: A Study of the Point of View in Great Expectations," College English, XXIII (1961), 122-131.

Pendered, M. "Soul Drama," The Dickensian, XXXV (1939), 243-249.

Phillips, James E. "The Tempest and the Renaissance Idea of Man," in Shakespeare 400: Essays by American Scholars on the Anniversary of the Poet's Birth, ed. James G. McManaway. New York, 1964. Pp. 147-159.

Phillips, T. M. "Dickens and the Comic Spirit," The Dickensian, XII (1916), 100-103, 130-132.

Polack, Ernest E. "Humorous Villains: A Comparison between Daniel Quilp and Shakespeare's Richard the Third," The Dickensian, VI (1910), 182-184.

Rauh, Sister Miriam Joseph. "Discerning the Ghost in Hamlet," Publications of the Modern Language Association, LXXVI (1961), 493-502.

_____. "Hamlet, a Christian Tragedy," Studies in Philology, LIX (1962), 119-140.

Reed, J. "The Fulfilment of Pip's Expectations," The Dickensian, LV (1959), 12-18; LVI (1960), 121-126.

Reiss, Edmund. "Whitman's Debt to Animal Magnetism," Publications of the Modern Language Association, LXXVIII (1963), 80-88.

Rice, Charles. "Notes concerning Edmund Kean and his Family and the Death of Charles Dickens." A portfolio in the Folger Shakespeare Library. London, 1868

Roberts, Helen. "The Idea of Friendship as Revealed in the Works of Dickens," The Dickensian, IV (1908), 38-40.

Rosenberg, Marvin. "The Dramatist in Dickens," Journal of English and Germanic Philology, LIX (1960), 1-12.

Siegel, Paul N. "Discerning the Ghost in Hamlet," Publications of the Modern Language Association, LXXVIII (1963), 148-149.

Simmonds, C. H. "Peter Parley and Dickens," The Dickensian, XVIII (1922), 129-132.

Simpson, Evelyn. "Jonson and Dickens," in Essays and Studies of the English Associatic XXIX (1944), 82-92.

Soellner, Rolf. "'Hang up Philosophy!': Shakespeare and the Limits of Knowledge," Modern Language Quarterly, XXIII (1962), 135-149.

Spilka, Mark. "Little Nell Revisited," Papers of the Michigan Academy of Science, Arts, and Letters, XLV (1960), 427-437.

Sprinchorn, Evert. "The Handkerchief Trick in Othello," Columbia University Forum, VII (1964), 25-30.

Stabler, Arthur P. "King Hamlet's Ghost in Belleforest?," Publications of the Modern Language Association, LXXVII (1962), 18-20.

Staff, Frank. "Dickens the Conjuror, and a Mystery Solved," The Dickensian, XXXIX (1943), 61-63.

Stange, G. Robert. "Expectations Well Lost: Dickens' Fable for his Time," College English, XVI (1954), 9-17.

Staples, Leslie. "Dickens and Macready's Lear," The Dickensian, XLIV (1948), 78-80.

_____. "The Ghost of a French Hamlet," The Dickensian, LII (1956), 70-76.

Stoll, Elmer Edgar. "Heroes and Villains: Shakespeare, Middleton, Byron, Dickens," Review of English Studies, XVIII (1942), 257-269.

_____. "Not Fat or Thirty," Shakespeare Quarterly, II (1951), 295-301.

Stone, Harry. "Dark Corners of the Mind: Dickens' Childhood Reading," The Horn Book Magazine. June 1963.

_____. "Dickens's Artistry and The Haunted Man," The South Atlantic Quarterly, LXI (1962), 492-505.

Suddaby, John. "'What the Dickens' Dates from Shakespeare-Falstaff Days," The Dickensian, XII (1916), 298-300.

Van de Kieft, Ruth M. "Patterns of Communication in Great Expectations," Essays in Criticism, XV (1961), 325-334.

Vandiver, Edward P. "Dickens' Knowledge of Shakspere," The Shakespeare Association Bulletin, XXI (1946), 124-128.

Voss-Moeton, J. F. G. Heerma van. "Tears in Literature: Particularly in Dickens," The Dickensian, LVIII (1962), 182-187.

Wagenknecht, Edward. "Immortal Memory," The Dickensian, LVIII (1962), 133-141.

Walters, J. Cuming. "Dickens and the Shakespeare Mystery," The Dickensian, XII (1916), 89-91.

Walters, J. Cuming, and Ley, J. W. T. "The Fictions of Forster: Two Views," The Dickensian, XII (1916), 285-289.

Walzel, Oskar. "Shakespeares Dramatische Baukunst," Jahrbuch der Deutschen Shakespeare-Gesellschaft (Berlin, 1916), pp. 1-35.

Ward, E. T. "Gamps," The Dickensian, XXIV (1927), 41-43.

Watson, George. "The Meaning of 'Kubla Khan,'" A Review of English Literature, II (1961), 21-29.

Whipple, Edwin P. "Dickens's Great Expectations," The Atlantic Monthly, XL (1877), 327-333.

Wilson, Angus. "Charles Dickens: A Haunting," The Critical Quarterly, II (1960), 101-108.

Winters, Warrington. "Dickens and the Psychology of Dreams," Publications of the Modern Language Association, LXIII (1948), 984-1006.

Ziegler, Albert F. "The Haunted Man: Sermon," The Dickensian, LVIII (1962), 145-148.

III. Theses

Carr, C. D. P., Sister Mary Callista. "Catalogue of the Dickens Collection at the University of Texas." Unpubl. doctoral diss. Austin, 1961.

Clark, Jr., Harold Frank. "Household Words: A Bibliographical Study of Mid-Nineteenth Century Reading Taste." Unpubl. doctoral diss. Stanford, 1958.

Cotter, Mary A. "The Writings of Charles Dickens to the Year 1837." Unpubl. master's thesis. Cornell, 1935.

Davis, Earle. "Literary Influences upon the Early Art of Charles Dickens." Unpubl. doctoral diss. Princeton, 1935.

Fleissner, Robert F. "The Lear-Cordelia Motif in Dickens's The Old Curiosity Shop." Unpubl. Master's thesis. Catholic University, 1958.

Garis, Robert Erwin. "Moral Attitudes and the Theatrical Mode: A Study of Characterization in 'Bleak House.'" Unpubl. doctoral diss. Harvard, 1956.

Head, Walter Donald. "An Analysis of the Methods Used by Dickens in Presenting his Characters." Unpubl. doctoral diss. Vanderbilt, 1958.

Keresztes, Ethel. "Dickens and the New York Stage." Unpubl. Master's thesis. New York University, 1946.

Welch, Sister M. Audrianne. "The Old Curiosity Shop: A Structural Analysis."
Unpubl. master's thesis. Catholic University, 1950.

Wilson, Frank. Dickens in seinen Beziehungen zu den Humoristen Fielding und Smollett.
Leipzig, 1899.

IV. Letters not in Collections

Gathorne-Hardy, Robert. Letter to the Editor of the London Times Literary Supplement,
6 February 1964, p. 107.

Kitchen, Paul C. Letter to the Editor of the London Times Literary Supplement,
4 September 1937, p. 640.

Rendall, Vernon. "Dickens and Shakespeare": Letter to the Editor of The Dickensian,
XII (1916), 75-76.

****

Additional material added to the revised edition of this dissertation is not included
in the Bibliography.

THE TRUE TEXT OF DICKENS'S REVIEW OF MACREADY'S PRODUCTION OF KING LEAR
HITHERTO UNPUBLISHED

Haymarket Theatre*

Mr Macready appeared on Wednesday Evening in King Lear. The House was crowded in every part, before the rising of the curtain, and he was received with deafening enthusiasm. The emotions awakened in the audience by his magnificent performance, and often demonstrated during its progress, did not exhaust their spirits. At the close of the Tragedy, they rose in a mass to greet him with a burst of applause that made the building ring.

Of the many great impersonations with which Mr Macready is associated, and which he is now, unhappily for dramatic art in England, presenting for the last time, perhaps his Lear is the finest. The deep and subtle consideration he has given to the whole play, is visible in all he says and does. From 'his rash denunciation of the gentle daughter who can only love him and be silent, to his falling dead beside her, unbound from the rack of this tough world, a more affecting, truthful, and tremendous picture never surely was presented on the stage.

---

* A transcription from the original manuscript in the Victoria and Albert Museum in London with the gracious permission of the Keeper of the Library. Its catalogue number is F. MS. 169. It has been authenticated by Mr. Leslie C. Staples, Editor of The Dickensián. The manuscript was published, but with inaccuracies, first in The Examiner, 27 Oct. 1849, and then in The Dickensian, XLIV (1948), 80. See the table of variant readings at the end of this appendix.

"The greatness of Lear," writes Charles Lamb "is not in corporal dimension, but in intellectual: the explosions of his passion are terrible as a volcano: they are storms, turning up and disclosing to the bottom that sea, his mind, with all its vast riches. It is his mind which is laid bare. This case of flesh and blood seems too insignificant to be thought on; even as he himself neglects it. On the stage we see nothing but corporal infirmities and weakness, the impotence of rage."

Not so in the performance of Wednesday night. It was the mind of Lear on which we looked. The heart and soul and brain of the ruin'd piece of nature, in all the stages of its ruining, were bare before us. What Lamb writes of the character, might have been written of this representation of it, and been a faithful description.

To say of such a performance that this or that point is most observable in it for its excellence, is hardly to do justice to a piece of art so complete and beautiful. The tenderness, the rage, the madness, the remorse and sorrow, all come of one another, and are linked together in a chain. Only of such tenderness, could come such rage; of both combined, such madness; of such a strife of passions and affections, the pathetic cry

> Do not laugh at me;
> For, as I am a man, I think this lady
> To be my child Cordelia.

Only of such a recognition and its sequel, such a broken heart.

Some years have elapsed since I first noticed Miss Horton's acting of the Fool, restored to the play, as one of its most affecting and necessary features, under Mr Macready's management at Covent Garden. It has lost nothing in the interval. It would be difficult to praise so exquisite and delicate an assumption, too highly.

Miss Reynolds appeared as Cordelia for the first time, and was not (except in her appearance) very effective. Mr Stuart played Kent, and but for fully justifying his banishment by his uproarious demeanour towards his sovereign, played it well. Mr Wallack was a highly meritorious Edgar. We have never seen the part so well played. His manner of delivering the description of Dover cliff--watching his blind father the while, and not looking as if he saw the scene he describes, as it is the manner of most Edgars to do--was particularly sensible and good. Mr Howe played with great spirit and Mrs Warner was most wickedly beautiful in Goneril.

The play was carefully and well presented and its effect upon the audience hardly to be conceived.

****

Table of Variant Readings   (Excluding Discrepancies in Punctuation)

Key: E The Examiner

     D The Dickensian

Paragraph 2   affecting, truthful, and tremendous| affecting, truthful, and awful E D

Paragraph 4   the heart and soul and brain | the heart, soul, and brain E D

292

Paragraph 5   all come . . . in a chain ⌉ all come . . . in one chain E :

                            all came . . . in a chain D ;

        Cordelia. Only of ⌉ Cordelia; of such E : Cordelia; only of

                       such D

Paragraph 8   conceived ⌉ conceived from this brief description E

Nota Bene

After this book was printed and just before it was bound, an article by William J.
Carlton entitled "Dickens or Forster? Some King Lear Criticisms Re-examined" appeared
in The Dickensian, LXI (1965), 133-140. Although previous scholarship had supported
the contention that Dickens was the author of "The Restoration of Shakespeare's Lear
to the Stage" (notably the comment on Dickens's letter to Forster of ?23 January 1838
in the Pilgrim Edition of the Letters, I, 357), Mr. Carlton has produced considerable
new evidence to show that John Forster wrote the review. I anticipated the possibility
of this being done in my note "Lear's 'Poor Fool' and Dickens," which appeared in
Essays in Criticism, XIV (1964), 425 (see n. 146 of the present volume), but the real
credit goes to Leslie C. Staples, Editor of The Dickensian, who presented the problem
in his article (listed in my bibliography) and corroborated my own doubts by telephone.